D1058962

Til Far og Vicki.

K. N.

To Maureen.

K. S.

Preface

The objective of this book is to present a comprehensive methodology for the design and implementation of large real-time systems in Ada. The reader is expected to have a good basic understanding of the Ada programming language.

Programming languages and design methodologies have typically been treated independently of each other. Many texts that describe the Ada programming language have recently been published. Other texts describe design methodologies for real-time systems without emphasis on a particular implementation language.

Ada is the first widely used programming language that is particularly amenable to the design of real-time systems. It incorporates real-time features such as tasking, interrupt handling, and representation clauses. It also has excellent design features such as packages, context clauses, and separate compilation. Ada is not "just another programming language"; it is also a design tool.

This book treats the design of large real-time systems in the context of the Ada real-time and design features. The design methodology presented anticipates that Ada will be the implementation language. This methodology could be adapted to real-time systems where other programming languages (e.g., C, Pascal, Fortran, Jovial, or CMS-2) would be used for the implementation by using

Ada for the top-level design; the detailed design would be language dependent.

The emphasis of this book is on a practical step-by-step methodology without "handwaving." It uses numerous graphical illustrations and design and coding examples. Although it necessarily uses small examples for illustration, the methodology presented will scale up to large real-time systems. This book collects Ada design and programming principles into a single volume.

This book can be used as an advanced upper level undergraduate or graduate text in Software Engineering. The emphasis is on *design*, not on programming. The goal of this book is to prepare advanced students to take the very important step from programming ("in the small") to designing real-time systems using Ada. It is also intended for practicing software engineers who are familiar with Ada and who want to expand their expertise to include an Ada real-time design methodology.

The prerequisites for using this book include a good understanding of Ada syntax and semantics (especially the tasking features), an appreciation for real-time systems (i.e., a non-Von Neumann mind set), and a working knowledge of traditional structured design.

Part 1 of the book contains refresher material on the primary features of real-time systems, with an emphasis on concurrency. Part 2 describes the language-independent general principles and tools required in designing large real-time systems. A heavy emphasis is placed on graphical tools and the use of a program design language (PDL). Part 3 includes general Ada design principles, including the use of packages, generics, tasking paradigms, and sequential design with Ada. Part 4 presents a complete, consistent design methodology for real-time systems designed and implemented in Ada. Part 5 describes how an Ada real-time design can be evaluated. This is especially important during the first system implementation by new Ada designers and programmers. An extensive bibliography on real-time systems, Ada, and design principles is included. The Appendixes include a series of case studies. Each case study represents a complete design of a problem described in a requirement specification, and illustrates specific design principles described in the text.

Parts 1 through 5 are suitable course material for teaching a semester-long course on Ada real-time design methodology. The case studies can be integrated as part of the classroom instruction, with student exercises created by changing the requirement specifications. Suggested requirements changes and alternate designs are listed at the end of each case study. Shorter courses (e.g., seminars) can be conducted by using the case studies to demonstrate various aspects of the design principles. A trimester course can be conducted by covering Parts 1 through 4, and incorporating the case studies as described for the semester-long course. Part 5 can then be covered as a seminar in a subsequent trimester.

The reader who is not following a formal course of instruction, and whose goal it is to become proficient in designing with Ada, is urged to study carefully the case studies and to perform the suggested exercises. It is vital to attempt your own solution to the problem stated in the requirement specification before looking at the design presented in the appendixes. Parts 1 through 5 would be required reading for a thorough understanding of the subject matter. The casual reader who only requires an overview of the design methodology can read the chapters in Part 4, but he or she should be aware that "a little knowledge can be a dangerous thing" because the complexities of Ada can only be learned from hands-on experience.

Kjell Nielsen
Ken Shumate

San Diego, California
October 1987

Acknowledgements

We wish to thank several individuals for their contributions during the preparation of this manuscript. Bryce Bardin provided input to the formalization of the LVM/OOD approach. Kathy McCann and Tom Burger participated in discussions on concurrency issues and reviewed parts of the manuscript. Steve Opie reviewed and commented on some of the case studies.

We also wish to acknowledge helpful criticism from the many students who participated in our Ada courses at Hughes Aircraft Company, Sanders, and Unisys.

We are especially grateful to Corinne Finney and Pat Deets for producing the graphics on the Macintosh.

The material in Chapter 22, and the case study in Appendix A have been adapted (with ACM's kind permission) from the authors' article "Designing Large Real-Time Systems with Ada," *Communications of the ACM*, Number 8, August 1987 (pp. 695–715), Copyright 1987, Association for Computing Machinery, Inc.

On Our Inability To Do Much

"Summarizing: As a slow-witted human being I have a very small head and I had better learn to live with it and to respect my limitations and give them full credit, rather than to try to ignore them, for the latter vain effort will be punished by failure."

> Edsger Dijkstra
> *Structured Programming*
> Academic Press 1972, page 3

On Understanding Programs

"Eventually, one of our aims is to make such well-structured programs that the intellectual effort (measured in some loose sense) needed to understand them is proportional to program length (measured in some equally loose sense)."

> Edsger Dijkstra
> ibid, page 20

Contents

List of Figures

List of Tables

Real-Time Systems

This part introduces the concepts of a real-time system. It is not adequate to give a simple definition of such a system, and Chapter 1 describes the major characteristics of a real-time system. The systems usually include hardware devices that need to be controlled by the software we are designing, and Chapter 2 describes typical hardware interfaces and the kind of design considerations we need to be concerned with. Most real-time systems include two or more hardware devices that operate asynchronously at widely differing speeds, leading to the concept of concurrent operations for these devices. Concurrent operations are also used in decomposing a large system into a set of parallel processes. Chapter 3 describes the concept of concurrency and how we model various forms of asynchronous behavior in terms of processes, communication between processes, synchronization points required for process communication, and how processes communicate via the rendezvous *mechanism in Ada.*

Characteristics

A real-time system can be defined as a controlled (by software or firmware) system that performs all its process functions within specified time constraints. Although this is a brief and concise definition, it is inadequate in fully describing the primary features of real-time systems. We can supply such a description by discussing the characteristics of real-time systems.

A real-time system usually includes a set of independent hardware devices that operate at widely differing speeds, e.g., a magnetic disk and a line printer. These devices must be controlled such that the system as a whole is not dependent upon the speed of the slowest device, i.e., the faster devices must not be forced to wait and operate in synchronization with the slower devices. This would be a waste of resources, and stringent performance requirements may not be satisfied. Our aim is to design real-time systems that optimize the capabilities of the hardware devices involved, and that satisfy the stated performance requirements. Examples of the real-time systems we need to control include airline reservations, process automation, air traffic control, and robotics.

The context diagram shown in Figure 1-1 depicts a remote data acquisition system for a Remote Temperature Sensor (RTS) system. The hardware devices consist of the input and output channels of

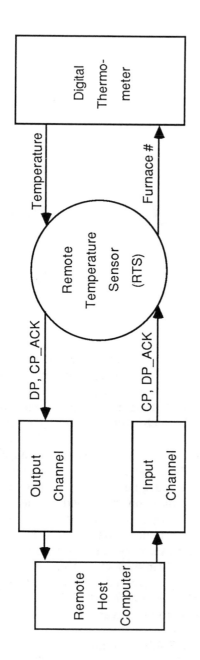

CP -- Control Packet (Host -> RTS)
DP -- Data Packet (RTS -> Host)
_ACK -- ACK or NAK

Figure 1-1. RTS Context Diagram

the host computer, and the digital thermometer. The host computer sends control data to the RTS (this is the system we need to design and implement), including the furnace number whose temperature must be read by the digital thermometer and the frequency with which the temperature should be read. Our control system (RTS) determines when the furnace number should be sent to the digital thermometer, receives a corresponding temperature value from the digital thermometer, and prepares data messages that are sent to the host computer via the output channel. In designing the RTS we will have to consider (see the case study in Appendix A) the required interfaces to the hardware devices and their speed of operation, which leads us to an important aspect of real-time design: the construction of device drivers and interrupt handlers. We must also decompose the functionality of the RTS into a set of suitable software modules that can be implemented as a set of Ada packages, subprograms, and tasks.

A different way of characterizing a real-time system is to realize that it is much more difficult to design and implement than a non-real-time system. Some of these difficulties include:

1. Control of hardware devices such as communication lines, terminals, and computer resources

2. Processing of messages that arrive at irregular intervals, with fluctuating input rates, and with different priorities

3. Control of fault conditions with facilities for various degrees of recovery

4. Handling of queues and buffers for storage of messages and data items

5. Modeling of concurrent conditions into a proper set of concurrent processes

6. Allocation and control of concurrent processes to processors (if more than one processor is available)

7. Handling of communication and synchronization between concurrent processes

8. Protection of data shared between concurrent processes

9. Scheduling and dispatching (including priority handling) of concurrent processes

10. Handling of stringent time requirements and performance specifications

11. Interfacing with a real-time clock, and avoiding (or at least minimizing) "drift" problems (see Chapter 15)

12. Testing and debugging of multiprocess systems

13. Design of (software) simulators for the hardware devices that are not available for the test phase

14. Reduction of complexity into manageable units that can be designed and implemented by teams of designers and programmers

We can also characterize real-time systems by the way they typically operate. A real-time system is expected to run continuously in an automated fashion with extremely high reliability. This is important from both performance and cost points of view. A processing plant with frequent shutdowns is not very cost effective, and an air traffic control system with a high failure rate would not make the skies very safe for flying. The requirement for high reliability is implemented with extensive error detection and recovery features. Some systems are designed with duplicate (stand-by) hardware components, and a switch-over is performed to the stand-by component when an error condition is detected. Other systems are designed with a "fail-soft" capability where the control program performs a "graceful degradation" by first saving as much of the current program states and data as possible, and then attempts to stage a recovery. Another aspect of the operation is the rapid processing required to satisfy the performance requirements of some real-time systems. Consider, for example, the on-board calculations of the trajectory of a heat-seeking missile. The hit/miss performance is directly related to how fast the processor can calculate required changes in the trajectory based on the data supplied by the missile's sensors.

Our primary design goals for real-time systems are to build them with a high degree of correspondence [ALL81], and to strive for simplicity. Correspondence in this context means how closely the software solution matches the problem specification. Examples of correspondence include the degree to which a system is inherently concurrent and the corresponding concurrency modeled in the solution, the data structures created and their corresponding operations, and the degree of non-determinism (e.g., traditional cyclic scheduling specified with major and minor time frames versus the non-deterministic scheduling mechanism in Ada) present in the problem and its corresponding solution. A high degree of correspondence ensures that the problem solution closely matches the stated requirements and aids the designer in determining correctness. A simple design contributes to making the solution easy to understand

and maintain, and enhances reliability. Some of the tools we utilize to satisfy these design goals include guidelines for dealing with hardware interfaces, and for modeling the system into a set of concurrent processes. This is discussed in Chapters 2 to 4.

Hardware Interfaces

In the context diagram shown in Figure 1-1 we noted three pieces of hardware that our system (RTS) needed to interface with: the input and output channels of the host computer and the digital thermometer. As part of the design process we must create the necessary software components that accept inputs from these devices, and that transmit messages and signals to the devices. Control data arriving from the host computer must be accepted by RTS and checked for valid formats. At the appropriate time, RTS sends a furnace number to the digital thermometer and waits to receive the corresponding temperature value. RTS creates a data message containing the furnace number and its temperature value and transmits the message to the host computer via the output channel. The design elements used to control the interfaces to hardware devices are loosely classified as device drivers and interrupt handlers. These elements are described in the following paragraphs.

2.1 Device Drivers

Device drivers are required for both input and output devices, and the design considerations depend upon whether we have an input or an output device:

1. *Input devices.* Design considerations for input device drivers include:

    a. Scheduled or irregular arrival of messages

    b. Continuous or burst transmission

    c. Message formats

    d. Transmission protocol

    e. Polling mode (by the device driver) or interrupt mode (by the transmitter)

    f. Rate of incoming messages versus processing required and whether or not they must be handed off to a buffer process for intermediate storage

    g. Error detection and handling of invalid messages and transmission protocol

    h. Handling of incoming messages when hand-off buffer is full (e.g., incoming messages can be ignored, or oldest message can be overwritten)

    i. Failure of the input device

2. *Output devices.* The design considerations for output device drivers are considerably less complex than for input devices and include:

    a. Transmission protocol (e.g., the whole message can be transmitted as a unit, or character by character with the output device sending an interrupt after each character which means "I'm ready to receive the next character")

    b. Error detection and handling of improper protocol by the output device

    c. Failure of the output device

2.2 Interrupt Handlers

The traditional concept of an interrupt handler is that it is a part of a real-time executive or a supervisor program, and written in assembly language or a suitable high-order language (HOL). Ada has neither an executive nor a supervisor program; real-time facilities such as task scheduling and dispatching are part of the run time support, and interrupt handling is available with Ada language constructs. Interrupt handling in Ada is usually written as part of a device driver, and not as a separate unit, and the traditional concept

```
task Tx_Host_Msg is
  entry Output_Channel;
  for Output_Channel use at Output_Channel_Adr;

  entry Transmit_DP (D : in DP_Format);
end Tx_Host_Msg;


task body Tx_Host_Msg is
  Output_Buffer : Character;
  for Output_Buffer use at Output_Buffer_Adr;
begin
  loop
    accept Transmit_DP (D : in DP_Format) do
      for I in D'Range loop
        Output_Buffer := D(I);
        accept Output_Channel;  -- interrupt from output channel
      end loop;
    end Transmit_DP;
  end loop;
end Tx_Host_Msg;
```

Figure 2-1. Interrupt Handling in a Device Driver

of an "interrupt handler" may not be appropriate. An example of interrupt handling within a device driver is shown in Figure 2-1. The task specification for the device driver Tx_Host_Msg contains the entry declaration for Output_Channel which is associated with the interrupt location Output_Channel_Adr, and the entry declaration Transmit_DP. The task body contains a local declaration Output_Buffer which is associated with the buffer location of the output channel. The executable statements of the task body accept a request to transmit a message to the host (via the output channel). The transmission is performed inside the for-loop one character at a time. After a character has been placed in the output buffer, the task waits for an interrupt from the output channel signaling that it is ready for the next character. The interrupt is handled with the single statement "accept Output_Channel;", and a separate interrupt handler is not required.

As we design the device drivers to control the hardware interfaces, we are also concerned with how these drivers must interface with the rest of the system. The general approach is to design the device drivers as part of a set of concurrent processes. These processes need to communicate and sometimes share data. This leads us to the concepts of "cooperating sequential processes" [DIJ68], and "communicating sequential processes" [HOA78]. To fully appreciate the design principles described in the later chapters, we need to understand the general concepts of process synchronization and communication, and mutual exclusion and protection of shared data, and the details of how processes communicate in Ada. This is discussed in Chapter 3.

3

Concurrency

In this chapter we review the concepts used in describing concurrent programs. Even though we assume the reader has some previous knowledge of these concepts, we present a set of definitions that are used consistently throughout the remainder of the book. We start the chapter by distinguishing between primitive and nonprimitive processes, and by defining true and apparent concurrency. We next establish the need for concurrent processes to communicate and describe the interactions between communicating processes. We describe the synchronization required between communicating processes, and two of the models proposed for implementing synchronization mechanisms. We complete the chapter by describing the synchronization and communication mechanisms used in the Ada rendezvous.

3.1 Processes

We think of processes as functional or logical elements in a decomposition of a real-time system. They are independent processing entities that can execute simultaneously on separate processors, or that can share a single processor. A process can be further decomposed into subprocesses. If a process can be decomposed into one or more subprocesses, we refer to it as "non-primitive." "Primitive" processes cannot be further decomposed into subprocesses. An example of a process (at the logical level) is shown in Figure 3-1. The process we have called Robot Axis accepts "Stop" and "Resume" signals to determine whether or not to continue to process motion data for axis positioning of a robot controller. For each set of motion data this process receives and manipulates, an acknowledgement is sent to another process (not shown in this figure), and the axis data is updated appropriately. We make no assumptions about the processing speed of Robot Axis; we only know that it has to operate independently of and simultaneously with other processes.

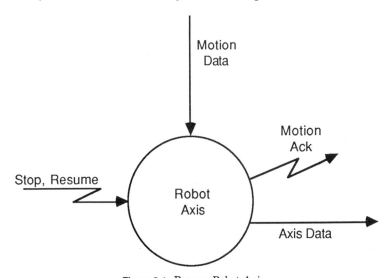

Figure 3-1. Process Robot Axis.

So far we have only considered a process at a logical level. We will now translate logical processes into their equivalent physical software components using Ada constructs. An example of a non-primitive process is illustrated in Figure 3-2 as an Ada package. The package specification of Axis contains the three *entrance procedures* Stop, Resume, and Take_Block. (These entrance procedures are used to control access to the task entries.) The specification does not tell us whether the process is primitive or not, but in the package body we see the declaration of the two Ada tasks Axis_Controller and Axis_Manager. Axis is thus a non-primitive process since it contains other processes (Ada tasks) within it. The details of the two task bodies have been deferred using the *separate* clause, and we cannot determine at this level whether or not the two tasks represent primitive processes. A task body can have task declarations

```
with Definitions;  use Definitions;

package Axis is
  procedure Stop;
  procedure Resume;
  procedure Take_Block (B : in Motion_Block);
end Axis;


package body Axis is
  task Axis_Controller is
    entry Take_Block (B : in Axis_Block);
    entry Axis_Interrupt;
  end Axis_Controller;

  task Axis_Manager is
    entry Stop;
    entry Resume;
    entry Take_Block (B : in Motion_Block);
  end Axis_Manager;

  task body Axis_Controller is separate;
  task body Axis_Manager    is separate;

  procedure Stop is
  begin
    Axis_Manager.Stop;
  end Stop;

  procedure Resume is
  begin
    Axis_Manager.Resume;
  end Resume;

  procedure Take_Block (B : in Motion_Block) is
  begin
    Axis_Manager.Take_Block (B);
  end Take_Block;

end Axis;
```

Figure 3-2. Nonprimitive process (package Axis).

within it, which will make that task a non-primitive process. In general, it is not recommended that tasks contain nested task declarations because of the inherent debugging problems, but there may be cases where this is justified. An example of a primitive process is shown in Figure 3-3 for the subunit Axis_Manager. The declarative part only contains local objects, there are no task declarations. The executable part is implemented within a *select* statement and represents a single thread of control. Packages and subprograms can be declared within an Ada task and would not invalidate the single thread of control of a primitive process.

The concept of two or more processes operating simultaneously leads us to the notion of *concurrency*. Processes can operate with *true* concurrency if their executions overlap in time on separate processors. If the processes share a processor, they operate with *apparent* concurrency. We are not concerned here with the distinction between true and apparent concurrency, and our task is to design a set of concurrent processes that can execute on one or more processors. In the sharing of a processor, the execution of the processes is somehow interleaved in a non-deterministic manner that we (the software engineers) do not control. The mechanism for the interleaving is provided for us by an executive or a run time support package.

The processes in a concurrent program may operate entirely independent of each other in an asynchronous manner, or they may be coupled through the use of shared data or message passing between them. The requirement for a coupling between concurrent processes necessitates the provision for a communication mechanism between them.

3.2 Communication

We can describe communicating processes as a set of concurrent processes that access common variables, or that respond to signals or parameters received from other processes. An example of two communicating processes is shown in Figure 3-4a, where the Producer creates data and sends it to a Consumer. The requirements for this type of interaction are that the data items cannot be received faster than they are sent, and that the consumption of the data items must be completed within a finite (but unspecified) time period.

If two or more concurrent processes access shared data, as shown in Figure 3-4b, the data must be protected with a monitor or a critical section, i.e., we must guarantee *mutual exclusion*. If this is not guaranteed, we have the potential for an *erroneous* program where timing problems may occur, but cannot necessarily be reproduced.

```
with Motion;
separate (Axis)

task body Axis_Manager is
  Stop_Flag    : Boolean := False;
  Axis_Motion : Motion_Block;
  Axis_Output : Axis_Block;
begin
  loop
    select
      accept Stop;
        Stop_Flag := True;
    or
      accept Take_Block (B : in Motion_Block) do
        Axis_Motion := B;
      end Take_Block;

      Prepare_Axis_Block (Axis_Motion, Axis_Output);

      if Stop_Flag then
        accept Resume;
      end if;

      Axis_Controller.Take_Block (Axis_Output);
      -- Task waits here for block completion
        Motion.Take_Motion_Ack;
    or
      terminate;
    end select;
  end loop;
end Axis_Manager;
```

Figure 3-3. Primitive process (task body Axis_Manager).

The requirement of mutual exclusion for shared data (or resources) is considered [BEN82, p. 19] to be one of the most important problems in concurrent programming because it represents an abstraction of the interactions between two or more communicating processes.

Figure 3-4c illustrates an example of a communication between two processes where a signal is sent by one process and received by another. Data elements are not consumed or manipulated in this type of communication.

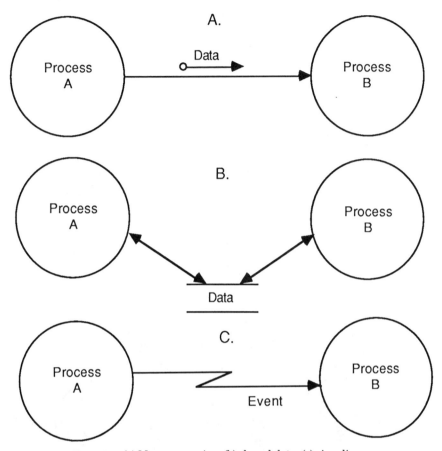

Figure 3-4. (a) Message passing; (b) shared data; (c) signaling.

A complete design for a large real-time system will consist of a set of communicating sequential processes, as shown in Figure 3-5. We are here illustrating a typical combination of process communication with shared data, message passing, and signaling. (The symbols used in this chart will be explained in detail in Chapter 7.)

3.3 Synchronization

The mechanism used to satisfy the timing constraints of two communicating processes and the protection of access to shared data is called *synchronization*. Mutual exclusion is an abstraction of the synchronization problem: we cannot have two concurrent processes access the same data at the same time. If this was allowed, the interleaving of operations could corrupt one or more of the data

18

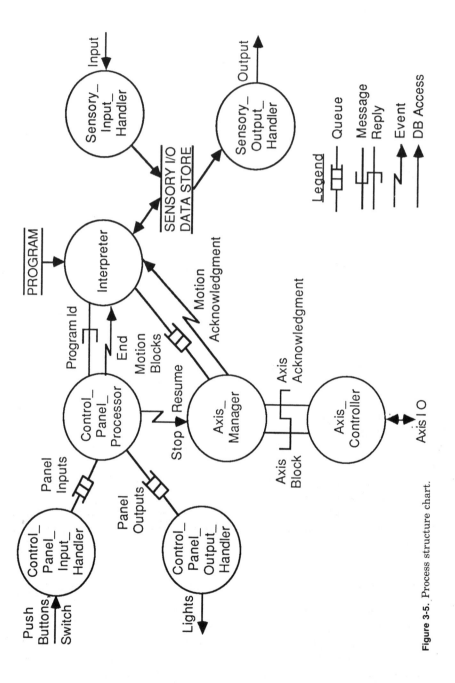

Figure 3-5. Process structure chart.

items accessed, and the result would be an erroneous program. Mutual exclusion will allow only one process to access the shared data within its *critical section*, i.e., the set of instructions for which indivisible operations are guaranteed.

The timing of communicating processes must also be carefully controlled and synchronized. When process A is ready to communicate with process B, but B is not yet ready, process A must be forced to wait until B is ready. We must thus provide *synchronization points* for communicating processes, since we can never make any assumptions about their relative or absolute processing speeds. On a single processor this will involve executive services or run time support for context switching, and for task scheduling, dispatching, and prioritization.

The mechanisms used in solving concurrent programming problems have traditionally been based on a set of primitives including fork/join, parbegin/parend, and cobegin/coend instructions [BRI73, DIJ68], semaphores [DIJ68, BEN82], critical regions [BRI73], monitors [HOA74, BEN82], and coroutines [BEN82, FOR85, KNU69]. It was incumbent on the programmers to use and implement these primitives (usually) at the assembly language level. In modern software engineering the emphasis is on the use of high-level language constructs, and to avoid the use of assembly language. Two important system models (programming languages were not implemented for these systems) describe high level programming primitives for use in implementing a set of communicating concurrent processes. They are important to us because many of their concepts have been included in Ada. These model systems are:

1. *Communicating sequential processes* (CSP) [HOA78]. A program can be described as a set of independent processes that will start simultaneously; execution of the program will complete when all the processes have completed their set of sequential instructions.

   Inter-process communication is expressed by matching input and output commands in which each process names the other, i.e., the communication is symmetric. Values to be output are copied from the caller to the callee. No automatic buffering is provided. Data can only be passed in one direction from the caller to the callee. The processes are delayed until copying can take place. Processes are only allowed to communicate via the specified input and output commands—shared data is not permitted. Input commands in the called process may appear within a conditional (boolean) guard, and will only accept input from the caller when this condition is satisfied. Several guards can be used with a set of alternative input statements, but only one alternative can be selected in an arbitrary fashion if more than one condition is satisfied.

Processes can be created dynamically as the program is running, but the process topology (i.e., process connections) must be specified statically. CSP does not provide for separate compilation, real-time features, or exception handling.

The suggested implementation of this model is for programs that will execute on a single processor, or a fixed network of processors that are connected by I/O channels.

2. *Distributed Processes* (DP) [BRI78]. A program can be specified in terms of a fixed number of concurrent processes that start execution simultaneously and exist "forever."

A process can call common procedures defined within other processes. These procedures are executed when the other processes are waiting for a certain condition to become true. This is the only form for process communication allowed in DP. Processes are synchronized by means of non-deterministic statements called "guarded regions." The caller/called relation between processes is not symmetric, and the called process does not know which process is calling it, unlike CSP. Parameter passing between processes is implemented by:

a. Copying within a common memory

b. Using input/output statements between processors that do not share memory

Shared data between processes is not permitted.

When a process is waiting for a certain condition to become true (e.g., an external procedure call to one of its procedures), the processor is idle. This is not to be considered as a wasted resource, but rather, as a temporary condition of lack of useful work.

The processes are used as program modules in a multiprocessor system with common or distributed memory. Each processor is dedicated to a single process.

DP processes are created statically, and the process topology must be specified (statically) at compile time. There are no facilities for separate compilation or exception handling, but real-time features exist where a process can be associated with a hardware device.

Many of the concepts included in CSP and DP have been incorporated in the general Ada tasking model, and, specifically, in the synchronization mechanism used for the communication between Ada tasks. A comparison of the high-level concurrent programming constructs suggested by CSP and DP and implemented in Ada can be found in References WEL81 and STO82.

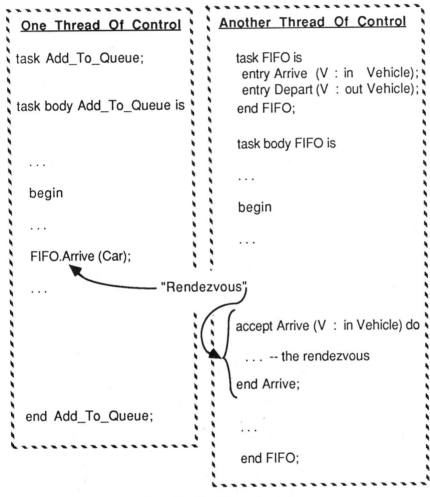

Figure 3-6. The Ada rendezvous.

3.4 Rendezvous in Ada

The synchronization mechanism employed in Ada is called a *rendezvous* between two tasks. An example of a rendezvous is shown in Figure 3-6, where the task Add_To_Queue is calling the task entry Arrive in the second task FIFO. The two tasks execute independently as separate threads of control until the rendezvous takes place. Synchronization between these two tasks is established with a blocking scheme. When Add_To_Queue has executed the statement "FIFO.Arrive (Car);", this task is blocked (at least) until the rendezvous is completed. The rendezvous (statements within the accept body) is executed when the task FIFO reaches the accept statement. If FIFO reaches the accept statement before any calls are made to this entry, the task is blocked and waits for arriving calls. If several calls are made to the same entry, they are placed in a queue for that entry and selected in a first-in–first-out order.

Messages can be passed between tasks in Ada by using parameters exactly as for procedure calls. The three parameter modes *in*, *out*, and *in out* are supported, and messages can thus be passed with or without a reply. Signaling is implemented by parameterless entry calls.

The Ada rendezvous joins together, into a single synchronized thread of control, what had been two separate threads of control. Information may be transmitted while the tasks are executing as a single thread of control. Hence the rendezvous is the Ada mechanism both for task coordination and for sharing of information. The Ada rendezvous is asymmetric in the following ways:

1. The calling task must know the name of the called, or accepting, task as well as the specification of the entry point. The called task does not know the name of its caller. The task providing the entries and accepts is a server. It is essentially passive: it provides a service to any task that knows its name.

2. A task calling an entry point may be on only one queue at a time. It may choose between calls to alternate task entries, but is not allowed to wait for two or more entries in order to be served by the first one ready for a rendezvous. On the other hand, a task providing entries may have a number of tasks queued up waiting for service at a number of different entry points.

3. A calling task may issue an entry call in a procedure nested within the task. The called task may *not* similarly accept a call in a nested procedure. This has implications for modularity as is discussed in later chapters.

The asymmetry described here allows us to distinguish between active (caller) and passive (called or server) tasks. Passive tasks are those that provide services through entries and accepts. Such tasks are general in purpose (sometimes generic), able to cope with the non-determinism of when they are called, and able to administer the queues of tasks waiting for service. Active tasks use the services provided, by issuing entry calls. We sometimes have hybrids of passive and active tasks, where tasks that contain accept bodies make calls to entries in other tasks.

Shared data is allowed in Ada, but mutual exclusion is not guaranteed with any high-order language construct. We highly recommend that the rendezvous mechanism be used in real-time designs to protect shared data as shown in Figure 3-7. The data (Shared) declared in the declarative part of the task body is protected by the two accept bodies for Enqueue and Dequeue. Mutually exclusive access to Shared is guaranteed by placing the two rendezvous within a select statement, since only one rendezvous can be executing at any one time.

```
task Buffer is
   entry Enqueue (S : in  Shared_Type);
   entry Dequeue (S : out Shared_Type);
end Buffer;

task body Buffer is
   Shared : Shared_Type := Initial_Value;
begin
   loop
     select
       accept Enqueue (S : in Shared_Type) do
         Shared := S;
       end Enqueue;
     or
       accept Dequeue (S : out Shared_Type) do
         S := Shared;
       end Dequeue;
     or
       terminate;
     end select;
   end loop;
end Buffer;
```

Figure 3-7. Protected shared data.

In using the Ada rendezvous we encounter non-determinism at two levels. There is an implicit non-determinism present in the blocking mechanism used to synchronize two or more communicating tasks. When one of the tasks that share a processor loses control of that processor, we can make no predictions about when that task will regain control. We can also make no predictions about the order in which a set of tasks with equal priorities will execute on a single processor. There is an explicit non-determinism associated with the selective wait statement that we program within a task body. For example, in the task Buffer shown in Figure 3-7, we can make no predictions about the order in which the two accept bodies will be executed when there are multiple callers waiting on both queues. We will point out the significance of the non-determinism for design decisions at the appropriate places in later chapters.

We have only provided a brief description of the Ada rendezvous here. Detailed accounts can be found in References SHU88, BUR85, PYL85, and BAR84.

Summary

In Chapter 1 we described the major characteristics of real-time systems. These systems typically consist of a set of hardware devices that operate at widely differing speeds, and that are controlled by the software we design. The systems operate in a continuous mode, with stringent performance requirements and with facilities for error detection and recovery. Our primary design goal is to build real-time systems with a high degree of correspondence and simplicity.

We described the requirements for interfacing with various hardware devices in Chapter 2, and how we design device drivers and interrupt handlers. It is relatively simpler to design an output device driver than an input device driver. In general, device drivers should be made as simple as possible. Interrupt handlers in Ada may be incorporated in device drivers rather than designed as separate tasks.

We distinguished between primitive and non-primitive processes in Chapter 3. If a process can be further decomposed into one or more subprocesses, it is non-primitive. Primitive processes cannot be further decomposed; they represent a single thread of control through the concurrent program.

Processes operate with true concurrency if their execution overlaps in time on separate processors. If the processes share a processor, they operate with apparent concurrency, and their execution is interleaved.

Concurrent processes need to communicate. This can be implemented with message passing, signaling, or shared data. Access to shared data (or shared resources) must be protected with mutual exclusion to prevent erroneous programs. A large real-time system will consist of a set of concurrent processes that will communicate via a combination of message passing, signaling, and shared data.

We can make no predictions about the absolute or relative execution speeds of concurrent processes, and they must be carefully controlled with a synchronization mechanism to allow communication between them. Two important models for process communication and synchronization are the classical Communicating Sequential Processes (CSP) and Distributed Processes (DP). Many of the concepts suggested by these two models have been incorporated in the Ada tasking model.

We construct concurrent processes in Ada by using high-level language constructs. There is no executive provided with the language (none is required), only a run time support package. The Ada rendezvous represents the communication and synchronization mechanisms employed in the Ada tasking model. Message passing is implemented similarly to procedure calls with *in*, *out*, and *in out* parameter modes. Signaling is implemented with parameterless task entry calls. Shared data is permitted, but mutual exclusion is not guaranteed and must be carefully designed using Ada programming constructs. Task synchronization is implemented with a task blocking scheme. Necessary mechanisms for context switching, task scheduling, etc., are provided by the run time support package. There is an implicit non-determinism present in the blocking mechanism used to synchronize two or more communicating tasks. An explicit non-determinism is associated with the selective wait statement that we program within a task body.

Designing Large Real-Time Systems

We are primarily interested in developing large *real-time systems that contain from, say, about 30,000 up to millions of lines of code. The development involves teams of designers and programmers that require careful management, including close reviews of the progress of the various development phases. These phases include the traditional requirements analysis, top-level design, detailed design, unit testing, integration testing, and formal acceptance testing. After such a system has been delivered to the customer ("customer" here may include the users within the software developers' own organization), the maintenance phase begins. This phase includes detecting and correcting the "bugs" that were not found during the various test phases, and making enhancements and extensions to the system.*

An important part of the development process for such a large system is the kind and quality of the documentation produced. There is a significant difference between "programming-in-the-small" and "programming-in-the-large." The former requires little or no documentation, whereas the latter requires extensive documentation, sometimes (e.g., for government projects) with a standard set of documents before the system is formally accepted. Chapter 5 describes the characteristics of these two programming approaches. The remainder of the book focuses on approaches used for large programming projects.

The kind of real-time systems we are primarily concerned with are inherently concurrent and usually quite complex. Chapter 6 describes how we manage this complexity with the concept of process abstraction.

In the decomposition and construction of large systems we use several analysis and design tools. Chapter 7 contains a description of the tools we use to manage the complexity of large systems, and how we document the major design decisions we have made.

CHAPTER 5

Programming In The Large

Large programming projects are distinctly different from small programming projects; the difference is not only quantitative, it is qualitative. This chapter addresses the needs of large programming projects, of programming in the large. After an overview of the needs of large projects, we introduce a software design methodology to meet those needs. The description begins with a survey of the software engineering principles leading to the methodology.

5.1 Introduction

For a programming project that can be classified as programming-in-the-small, the whole program is typically produced by a single programmer. Minimal design is performed before the actual coding and testing phases begin, and documentation consists of the code listings and, perhaps, a user's manual. The interfacing with other individuals is minimal, and typically involves learning the system requirements from an analyst or user and reporting progress to a supervisor. The design and programming tools consist of an editor for entering and revising code, a compiler, and a debugger. The complete program for a small programming project consists of one or more software modules that are easily comprehended by a single programmer. Progress (or lack thereof) is easily discernible, since it depends only on the efforts of a single person, and correcting schedule slips is relatively simple. The creation of the individual software modules is not difficult, assuming we are dealing with an experienced programmer, and their interfaces are straightforward since they are implemented by the person who designed them.

Programming abstractions used to support programming-in-the-small include sequencing, decision, looping, function, and procedure constructs. These constructs are used within a single module and do not represent abstractions that relate to the program as a whole. The emphasis of the programming effort is on algorithms rather than on modeling a large system. There is little or no concern for life-cycle support, and reusability is restricted to the availability of special-purpose algorithms such as graphics or mathematical routines.

We are primarily concerned with developing a consistent methodology for the design and implementation of *large* real-time systems. Such systems are usually quite complex, and the development requires a staff of managers, designers, and programmers. The complexity is managed by decomposing the system into smaller and smaller pieces using the process of stepwise refinement [WIR71], or layered virtual machines [DIJ68, DIJ71, and DIJ72]. A large staff of software engineers must also be effectively managed. The primary aspects of programming-in-the-large as compared with programming-in-the-small include the following:

1. *Life-cycle approach.* The development process is based on a software engineering discipline for a complete life cycle. The approach can be the traditional waterfall model [WEG84, page 24] with a step-by-step development and manual tracking of requirements and design decisions; the operational model with automated problem-oriented specifications; or the knowledge-based model with expert-system oriented data bases used to automate the complete life cycle. Reusability is important not only for algorithms, but also for development methodologies and tools.

2. *Extensive planning.* It is essential for a successful completion of a large software project that an extensive planning effort take place, even long before the start of the analysis phase. This planning should include the size, composition, and manpower loading of the software engineering staff; schedules for completion of all the development phases; a list of documents to be produced; the specific design methodology and programming standards to be followed; the set of management tools to be used in

tracking and reporting progress; and a set of test plans for the various test phases.

3. *Design methodology.* A design methodology is required to manage the complexity of the system we are designing, and to ensure a uniform approach and documentation by the various development teams. An appropriate design methodology is introduced in this chapter and described in detail in Part 4.

4. *Team coordination.* It is vitally important that the development teams do not design their individual parts in isolation, and that effective communication be maintained throughout the various development phases. This is accomplished with formal and informal design reviews, and with periodic coordination meetings with members of the various development teams.

5. *Documentation.* It is required that appropriate documentation be produced and maintained as a part of the design process. This is used as an aid during the design, for design reviews and presentations, and to be delivered to the customer for the maintenance phase. The documentation may also be used as input to metrics tools in evaluating a given design, or in choosing the best of alternate designs.

6. *Module interfacing.* Since different teams are producing software modules that will eventually be integrated as a complete program, the interfaces must be carefully designed and maintained during the design phase.

7. *Formal test procedures.* A set of formal test procedures must be developed before the testing can start. These procedures will describe exactly how the various tests will be performed, the required input data, expected output data, and the recording of the actual output data observed. These procedures will be used uniformly by all the teams for the various test phases.

Design abstractions used for programming-in-the-large include data, function, and process abstractions (abstractions are further discussed in Chapter 6). These abstractions can be used to represent major parts of the system (consisting of several modules) and not simply a single module, as was the case for the constructs listed above for programming-in-the-small. We will see in later chapters that Ada supports abstractions for programming-in-the-large as well as for programming-in-the-small.

5.2   Virtual Machines And Objects

The basic idea behind a successful design effort for large software systems is a parallel concern with algorithms and data structures; it is useful to view this process as the construction of virtual machines and objects. The creation of the machines is performed in stages: We first create a set of processes, i.e., process abstraction, that represents the concurrent elements of the system (see Figure 3-5). This set can be viewed as a network of processes, with each node a high-level virtual machine. We next decompose each of the nodes that represents a single thread of control into a hierarchy of lower level machines and objects. We describe the creation of the lower level virtual machines and objects in this chapter. Process abstraction is discussed in Chapter 6.

To construct complex computer programs through the parallel concern with algorithms and data structures, it is advantageous to envision the availability of "virtual machines" that simplify the algorithm (the steps of the program) and to encapsulate the data structures in such a way that only the operations on a data structure are available, i.e., the details of the actual data structure are hidden. Such encapsulated data structures are called *objects*. Both the virtual machines and the objects are layered in the sense that they each depend upon lower level virtual machines and objects.

Virtual machines describe algorithms, the steps taken to solve a problem. The machines consist of both process and procedural abstractions, lower level machines, and the operations exported by objects. They provide the functionality of the program that is commonly referred to as the *application*.

One sort of object encapsulates a data structure. It exports (makes available to users) only operations on the data structure. The operations characterize the behavior of the object. It is useful to think of the operations as "managing" the data structure. Such an encapsulation of a data structure is called an *object manager*.

A different sort of object encapsulates a *definition* of a data structure (a type). It exports an abstract type definition, including operations on instances of the type. The specific instances of the type (variables) are created by the users of this sort of object. The operations "manage" the encapsulated data structure definition. This sort of encapsulation of a data structure is called a *type manager*.

The virtual machines and objects should hide the information contained within them, describing their interface with other software components through abstract interfaces—providing only the minimum information needed to use the machine or object. The ideas of design with virtual machines and objects are equally applicable to sequential and concurrent systems. In concurrent systems, the virtual machines operate in parallel, and the objects often must provide for mutual exclusion.

There should be graphical tools to support a large software design. The tools should provide for pictures that illustrate both virtual machines and objects. To the maximum extent possible, such tools should be automated, with the emphasis on *design* and not on draftsmanship.

The remainder of this chapter integrates the notions described above into a design methodology (for sequential processing) that combines a strong orientation toward the objects of the system, with a parallel concern for the construction of virtual machines. Both the virtual machines and objects may be layered. The sections below first establish the historical foundation for the methodology and then present the design method.

5.3   Foundations Of Layered Virtual Machine/Object-Oriented Design

The foundation of our general design methodology for large real-time systems is based on the concepts of layered virtual machines (LVM) and object-oriented design (OOD). We combine these concepts into a consistent real-time design methodology. The concept of LVM is used to create a top layer as a set of communicating sequential processes. Each process is a virtual machine that executes in parallel with the other processes (virtual machines). We combine the concepts of LVM and OOD (LVM/OOD) to decompose each process into a hierarchy of virtual machines (Ada subprograms) and objects (Ada packages, types, and operations on objects of the type).

The concern for programming-in-the-large has been shared by many prominent software engineers for a long time, and numerous important design concepts have contributed to our methodology. One-half of these concepts is applicable to design in general:

1. Information Hiding

2. Data Abstraction

3. Object-Oriented Design

4. Structured Design

5. Stepwise Refinement (algorithms + data structures)

6. Structured Programming

7. Abstract Specifications

The other half is applicable only to software systems that involve concurrency:

1. Co-Operating Sequential Processes

2. Hierarchical Sequential Processes

3. Communicating Sequential Processes

4. Distributed Processes

5. Structured Design/Real-Time Systems

6. Task rendezvous mechanism

7. Process Abstraction

The following paragraphs describe these concepts. The selection of paper, date, and original contributor is somewhat subjective, but we have tried to follow conventional wisdom in giving credit for the concepts, while restricting ourselves to a single primary literature reference in each case where a single author is considered a significant contributor.

5.3.1 General Concepts

We first discuss the general software design concepts that are important for programming in the large.

5.3.1.1 Information Hiding. This was first described by Parnas [PAR72] and encompasses the idea that we should decompose a system into modules such that each is "characterized by its knowledge of a design decision which it hides from all others." The design decision might relate to either an algorithm or a data structure. The fundamental ideas are summarized as follows:

1. Modules hide design decisions.

2. A module is a responsibility assignment, not a subprogram.

3. Interfaces are simple and do not reveal inner workings.

Some of the benefits of this concept include:

1. The design is easy to understand.

2. The design effort can be partitioned into teams early (no need to agree on a data structure as interface), hence independent development.

3. The design is easy to change.

5.3.1.2 Data Abstraction. The idea of abstract data types has been discussed in the literature for many years. Liskov and Guttag [LIS86] have recently integrated and clarified the construction and use of abstract data types. They define a data abstraction as consisting of " ... a set of objects and a set of operations characterizing the behavior of the objects." Their book is largely concerned with concepts of design, with "... how to do program decomposition based on abstraction." The fundamental ideas include:

1. Abstraction: Simplify analysis by focus only on relevant attributes, "forgetting" things that are different (for some purposes, humans and apes are the same—primates).

2. Abstraction by parameterization and specification.

3. Procedural and iteration abstraction.

4. Data abstraction is focus—"... most often provides the primary organizational tool in the programming process."

5. "A *data abstraction* (or *data type*) consists of a set of objects and a set of operations characterizing the behavior of the objects" (e.g., stack, multi-set).

5.3.1.3 Object-Oriented Design. Object-oriented design has been popularized by Booch [BOO83], drawing on much earlier design literature, specifically including work of Liskov, Guttag, and Parnas. The method involves designing software around abstractions of "objects in the real world problem. It "... lets us map solutions directly to our view of the problem. It seeks a balanced treatment of both objects and operations, but has a strong focus on software objects as "actors," both providing operations as services and using the operations provided by other objects. This concept is strikingly different from the strictly functional decomposition employed by structured design. Booch also introduced an important graphic aid to visualizing program components and their interactions, the object-oriented design (OOD) diagram. We will see examples of OOD diagrams in the case studies. The fundamental ideas of OOD include:

1. An object is described as follows:

    a. An object relates to objects in the real world (problem space).

    b. An object is characterized by operations on and by the object.

    c. An object is an instance of a type.

d. An object may be composed of other, lower-level, objects.

2. The method is based on a short narrative solution approach, identifying objects as nouns and operations as verbs.

3. The main graphics tool is the OOD diagram.

5.3.1.4 Structured Design. Structured design, popularized by Yourdon and Constantine [YOU79], places an emphasis on designing a system of small, independent, "black boxes" that are related to the application. Its focus is on functional abstraction, "what" is being accomplished. The decomposition principle is based on keeping highly related parts of the system together, highly related being measured in terms of "functional relatedness" (cohesion).

An important graphic tool for structured design is the structure chart, showing the partitioning of the software into a hierarchy of modules. The decomposition is shown in terms of the steps in the processing, with each step further decomposed (in layers) into lower level steps. The data flow between modules is an important feature of the structure chart. We will see examples of structure charts in the case studies. The fundamental ideas of structured design include:

1. The art of designing components and their interactions in the best possible way

2. The use of data flow diagrams

3. The use of structure charts

4. The concept of "black boxes"

5. The use of coupling and cohesion for design evaluation

6. A largely functional decomposition (arguable), based on steps in the processing

5.3.1.5 Stepwise Refinement (Algorithms + Data Structures). Wirth [WIR71] considers programming, what we are discussing as design, to be "... a sequence of design decisions concerning the decomposition of tasks into subtasks and of data into data structures." The process proceeds as "stepwise refinement" until the subtasks and data structures are expressible in some programming language. Wirth has also expressed this idea as "algorithms + data structures = programs." (Note that "algorithm" does not imply concern with detailed processing, but rather is an abstract statement of the steps to solve a problem using subprograms.)

The important point that Wirth makes is, "Refinement of the description of program and data structures should proceed in parallel." The fundamental ideas of stepwise refinement include:

1. Programs are developed in a sequence of refinement steps.

2. In each step we decompose an instruction into more detailed instructions (tasks into subtasks).

3. As tasks are refined, data is also refined, decomposed, and structured.

4. "... *refine program and data specifications in parallel.*"

5. Each refinement implies a design decision.

"Algorithms" here *do not* imply great detail, as we may think of a set of instructions inside a subprogram or task body. In Ada parlance, this is decomposition into tasks and subprograms.

5.3.1.6 Structured Programming. A *truly* seminal and fundamentally important work as a contribution to the concepts employed for programming in the large is Dijkstra's "Notes on Structured Programming" [DIJ72]. In this treatise Dijkstra views a program as being executed by its own (virtual) machine, one that has just the necessary instructions and variables to allow the problem to be easily solved. After the problem is "solved" using the virtual machine, the remaining (simpler) problem is to implement each of the instructions of the virtual machine. The new problem is solved by the invention of lower level virtual machines. He emphasizes that "as little as possible" should be accomplished at each step, and that decisions should be postponed for as long as possible. This is especially true in the case of data; the style is to operate as long as possible on "abstract" notions of data.

Dijkstra uses the term "stepwise program composition" to describe the process. He also uses the phrases, "layered hierarchy of machines" and "virtual machines." He is explicit about dealing with stepwise decomposition of both algorithms and data.

About algorithms: "I want my program text to reflect somewhere the fact that the computation has been decomposed into a time-succession of the [three] actions ..." He continues, "... the further refinements of these [three] actions will be given 'somewhere else', perhaps separately, but certainly without relative ordering."

About data: "... we treat the structural refinement of a data type on a footing very similar to the algorithmic refinements ..."

About both algorithms and data Dijkstra goes on to say that the decomposition relative to actions is "only half of what we are trying to do, as we are trying to apply a similar technique to data structures as well." He also points out that at various steps in the design process we must choose to next refine an algorithm or next refine a data structure. (In this book we use the phrase "construction of a virtual machine" for algorithm refinement, and "construction of an object" for data refinement.)

About design in general he comments, "The point is that we try to associate with each level a separate design decision. ..." The fundamental ideas of structured programming include:

1. The emphasis of structuring should be on design, not on coding.

2. Only a minimal commitment should be made at each stage of the design.

3. Design decisions should be postponed as long as possible, especially data structures.

4. We maintain separate design concerns: algorithms and data structures.

5. The design is created with a set of layered virtual machines.

5.3.1.7 Abstract Specifications. The primary contributors to the concept of abstract specifications include Parnas, Liskov, Guttag, and Shaw. The fundamental ideas encompass:

1. The specification for a piece of software that will allow other pieces of software to interact with it (use it) without any additional information.

2. The specification to provide the user of the software *all* necessary information, *and nothing more.*

3. The specification to provide the implementor of the software *all* necessary information, *and nothing more.*

4. The specification is sufficiently formal that it can conceivably be machine tested for consistency, completeness, and so on (this is vital to formal use of the methods).

5. The specification must use terms consistent with the language of a potential user or implementor.

5.3.1.8 Summary of General Concepts. Many important concepts in software engineering deal with data abstraction: how data should be used in the design of large programs. This is the major domain of discourse for Liskov and Guttag, and generally for Parnas as well.

Booch largely builds on their notions, formalizing them to the point of object-oriented design.

The Yourdon and Constantine approach of structured design deals with functional abstraction: emphasizing the abstract algorithms, the steps in the processing. The method is quite well defined and has become a popular approach for software design.

Wirth, although writing earlier than the others, provides for an integration of the two approaches, data abstraction and functional abstraction. He emphasizes stepwise refinement on both abstract algorithms and data. Interestingly enough, he references an early version (1969) of the Dijkstra paper, "Notes on Structured Programming."

Dijkstra's concepts of structured programming started the process of widespread disciplined thought about how to construct programs. His work provided the foundation for much of what came after, and still serves to capture the essential characteristics of how a programmer should think about designing software.

Parnas's notions of abstract specifications has also been important to the development of the design methodology. Although we do not implement the concept of *testable* specifications, it is important that either a virtual machine or an object be used in accordance with its specification rather than its implementation.

Dijkstra's layered virtual machine design builds on, integrates, and attempts to make more intuitive, the other concepts discussed. Its primary source of inspiration is "Notes on Structured Programming."

5.3.2 Strictly for Concurrency

The important concepts applicable only to the design of concurrent software systems are discussed in the following paragraphs.

5.3.2.1 Co-Operating Sequential Processes.
The originator of this concept is Dijkstra [DIJ68a]. His fundamental ideas include:

1. A set of loosely connected processes that need to communicate

2. The mutual exclusion problem for access to common resources

3. The use of semaphores as primitives to implement mutual exclusion

4. The possibility of deadly embrace between two processes

5. The requirement for process synchronization in the implementation of process communication

6.   The concept of "busy wait"

7.   Dekker's Algorithm; Sleeping Barber; Bounded Buffer; and Banker's Algorithm

5.3.2.2 Hierarchical Ordering of Sequential Processes. Dijkstra has described [DIJ71] an orderly design procedure for concurrent systems. The fundamental ideas of this procedure include the following concepts:

1.   Using hierarchical layers to build operating systems will remove non-deterministic features [cycle stealing and interleaving (resulting from hardware interrupts)] and create a deterministic automaton. The hardware initiates the cycle stealing; the software handles interrupts.

2.   A bottom layer is created with a virtual machine (VM) that is able to execute a number of sequential programs in parallel, as if each sequential program had its own private processor.

3.   Higher layers are constructed to operate as a set of harmoniously cooperating sequential processes.

4.   Synchronization primitives are implemented with semaphore operations. Busy wait is not tolerated.

5.   The "Dining Philosophers" problem is used to illustrate the concepts.

6.   An alternate design approach includes Directors/Secretary, where a Secretary is similar to a monitor. Common variables now belong to the secretary. Message passing would take place from the directors to the secretary.

5.3.2.3 Communicating Sequential Processes (CSP). Hoare created a model for a concurrent programming language [HOA78]. Such a programming language has not been implemented, but several of the concepts have been incorporated into the design of the Ada programming language. The fundamental ideas include the following:

1.   Communication between processes takes place via I/O commands.

2.   Symmetric caller/called relations are implemented for process communication.

3.   Boolean guards are available in the called process.

4.   Shared data is not allowed.

5. Synchronization points are provided to delay processes until parameters have been copied. There is no automatic buffering.

6. A set of alternative input statements is available.

7. The model has dynamic process creation, but static determination of the upper bound for the number of processes operating concurrently.

8. Separate compilation, real-time features, or exception handling is not included.

9. The model is specified for multiple processes residing in a single processor, or a network of processors connected by I/O channels.

5.3.2.4 Distributed Processes: A Concurrent Programming Concept. A different model for a concurrent programming language was proposed by Brinch Hansen [BRI78]. Similar to CSP, this model has also not been implemented as a programming language, but several of the ideas have been incorporated into Ada. The fundamental ideas of this model include the following:

1. The model is intended for distributed processor systems, with each processor dedicated to a single process.

2. Each process can access "own" variables only; no shared data is allowed between processes.

3. Process communication is implemented by calling common procedures defined within other processes. Caller/called relations are asymmetric.

4. Process synchronization is by means of non-deterministic statements called *guarded regions.*

5. Parameter passing is implemented by (a) copying within common memory shared between processors; (b) I/O between processors that do not share memory.

6. Only static process creation is allowed.

7. Separate compilation or exception handling is not included.

8. Some real-time features are included.

5.3.2.5 Structured Design/Real-Time Systems. Yourdon and Constantine's structured design concepts have been extended to include real-time features [MEL86]. The fundamental ideas include the following:

1. *Creating the Essential Model.* The use of context diagrams, data flow diagrams (DFDs), state-transition tables and diagrams, and heuristics to create a model of the requirement specifications.

2. *Creating the Implementation Model.* The use of a set of heuristics to transform the essential model into a design representation that can be implemented with a close correspondence to the essential model. The set of heuristics include guidelines for:

   a. *Processor modeling.* Allocating functions to processors.

   b. *Task modeling.* Allocating tasks within a processor.

   c. *Interface modeling.* Determining the proper design for interprocessor interfaces, and for inter-task communication. The latter includes the introduction of intermediary tasks, and caller/called relations.

5.3.2.6 Rendezvous. The *rendezvous* is the basic model for process communication in Ada [ICH79]. The fundamental ideas include the following:

1. Tasks are viewed as independent, asynchronous agents.

2. Synchronization and communication are integrated in the model.

3. Synchronized communication implies extra processes for buffering.

4. Considerable control is exercised with regard to the calling and accepting (called) protocols.

5. Caller/called relations are asymmetric.

6. Interaction with hardware uses the same abstract mechanism as software task interaction.

5.3.2.7 Process Abstraction. Process abstraction is used as a means of reducing the complexity of concurrent systems. Similar to the way modules have been used for procedural abstraction of sequential systems, processes are introduced as abstractions for the elements that will operate in parallel in a concurrent systems. This concept was described in 1980 in connection with processes, channels, and pools in MASCOT (Modular Approach to Software Construction Operation and Test) [ALL81]. More recent references include BUH84, WEG84, CHE85, and FOR85. The fundamental ideas include the following:

1. Process abstraction is similar to procedural abstraction, but a process is an autonomous processing element that executes in parallel with other processing elements. A process has life throughout the execution of a program, as opposed to subprograms which are only executed when they are called.

2. Process abstraction is the major mechanism for decomposition of concurrent programs.

3. The use of this concept is a highly structured approach and contains guidelines for its creation.

4. The emphasis is on creating an abstraction of a network of parallel processes, rather than a hierarchy as is the case for subprograms using structured design.

5.4 Overview of Layered Virtual Machine/Object-Oriented Design

This section presents an overview of the design approach, followed by a detailed discussion of virtual machines, objects, machine/object interaction, and the use of graphics. There are five steps to the process of layered virtual machine design:

1. Invent a machine that will solve the problem. Always think of data abstractly. This is the top-level virtual machine, and for a real-time system this is composed of a set of communicating sequential processes. Each process is a virtual machine that requires further decomposition for the single-thread functionality of that process.

2. Decide on which "instruction" of the virtual machine to consider next. The instruction will be either a lower level virtual machine or an operation of an object:

    a. If the instruction is a virtual machine, refine the instruction by starting at the first step.

    b. If the instruction is an operation of an object, do not refine the instruction at this time. Instead, write the description of the rest of the object, i.e., the rest of the operations on the data structure. This is not easy. Notions of information hiding, object-oriented design, and abstract data types are all important in this effort. It is likely that you will not immediately identify *all* needed operations, but that as you refine the virtual machines, you will find a need for additional operations associated with the object.

3. Repeat the second step for all instructions.

4. Implement the objects. For complex algorithms, it will be necessary to accomplish the implementation by starting at the first step and following the LVM/OOD process. This may involve lower level objects that are hidden from higher levels. This aspect of the design process illustrates that levels of abstraction are important for objects, as well as for virtual machines.

5. Document the design graphically, as well as in some textual manner, and have someone else review and comment, i.e., evaluate the quality of the design. Traditional structured design actually goes beyond consideration of steps in the processing; it offers significant guidelines for design evaluation based on an emphasis of strong locality of function within modules, and low coupling between modules. The interfaces between modules should be as narrow as possible, often consisting of nothing but parameterless subprogram calls.

The process need not be accomplished in exactly the order given. For example, it may be necessary to implement an object completely in order to appreciate timing characteristics. Reuse of existing software modules may provide for some of the needed virtual machines, and will alter the sequence of events. In addition, particularly for a large programming project, many steps will be proceeding in parallel after the initial partitioning. This is a major advantage of the design approach. One of the reasons for the ability to initiate parallel development early in the design process is that the decisions about data structures are buried *inside modules* rather than in the *module interfaces*.

Why do we emphasize documentation of the design? Documenting and explaining the design is an intrinsic part of the design process for programming in the large. The use of graphics is important because people more quickly grasp overall structure and relationship from pictures than they do from text. If we can't evaluate the quality of the design from the graphics, including determining *how the problem is being solved*, we don't have enough graphics.

In accomplishing the five steps outlined above, always remember that there are two viewpoints of design, one corresponding to virtual machines (functional abstraction or design of algorithms), the other corresponding to objects (data abstraction, hiding and design of data structures and their associated operations).

Design by parallel consideration of the two viewpoints emphasizes separation of concerns, layering of abstraction, stepwise refinement and deferring of detail, and an object orientation to the design. It preserves the importance of functional decomposition through use of the virtual machines and incorporates concepts of data abstraction and information hiding. The important relationship between the two viewpoints is that designing a virtual machine *makes use of* the abstractions of the data structures—objects. In turn, the internal design of the object involves a sequence of steps to manipulate the data elements. This is a virtual machine in which the problem to be solved is the method of manipulating the data structure.

The concept of layered virtual machines is treated in detail in Chapter 12 as an Ada design principle for the sequential processing part of a real-time system (i.e., the sequential processing within each Ada task). The complete Ada real-time design methodology is described in Part 4. The primary design concept used to create the parallel elements (processes) of the concurrent system is a form of process abstraction based on the fundamental ideas listed above. The processes we create as abstractions of the concurrent processing elements represent top-level virtual machines in our model solution of the real-time system we are designing. We use the process abstraction concepts further in Chapters 6, 7, and 22. The other design concepts discussed above have been incorporated into our methodology and are illustrated throughout Parts 3 and 4 and in the case studies in the Appendixes.

Process Abstraction

The primary mechanism we use to manage complexity is *abstraction*. By abstracting the major parts of a system we are not unduly concerned with details at an early stage and can concentrate on understanding smaller parts rather than the whole system. In software design and programming we use abstractions at various levels. In structured design [YOU79, PAG80, and MYE78], for example, we partition a system into functional *modules*. A module is an abstraction that represents a certain, well-defined functionality within the system we are designing. At the programming level we transform the functional abstraction of a module into the corresponding program abstraction of a subroutine, procedure, or function, depending upon the specific syntax of the programming language we are using. A module has now been transformed into a collection of program statements that represent a certain algorithm. The representation of the algorithm makes use of other abstractions such as data types and sequence and control statements. We use *integer* and *real* types in our program statements, but we are not concerned with how these types are implemented in binary form on the machine we are using. We are only concerned with the values our data can have, and the operations allowed on the data. When we first identified the module, we were not concerned with the details of the algorithm. We managed complexity by abstracting out all the details and simply giving the module a name.

For real-time systems we need to identify the major processes that the system will consist of. In decomposing a large real-time system we use *process abstraction* [WEG84, p. 16; and FOR85] in a manner similar to the way we used functional (procedural) and data abstraction [LIS86, Chapters 3, and 4]. The processes may include concurrent processes that communicate through shared data or message passing, and distributed processes that only communicate through message passing.

The process abstractions we identify will represent the set of communicating processes that will have to be transformed into Ada constructs. A non-primitive process will transform into one or more Ada packages, and a primitive process to an Ada task. In using process abstractions to decompose the real-time system, we have reduced the complexity at a high level by simply considering a set of process names representing "functions" or "machines" that make up the complete system. Each abstract process will become a device driver (may include interrupt handling) or application process. At the abstract process level in our design we are deferring all details of how these processes must be implemented. We are using process abstraction as a divide-and-conquer approach to manage the complexity of designing a real-time system by identifying the concurrent virtual machines of the model solution.

When we use process abstraction in our design, it is necessary that the set of cooperating sequential (single-thread) processes satisfy two conditions [BEN82, FOR85]:

1. *Safety.* Each process must perform correctly, independent of the other processes in a static domain. An example of this condition includes the requirement of mutual exclusion for shared data and resources. Without mutual exclusion, data values used by one process could be corrupted by another process through interleaving of instructions, and the first process would no longer be performing correctly. Safety properties can be thought of as related to partial correctness for sequential programs. These properties are relatively easy to determine since they are usually implemented as a direct result of the stated requirements.

2. *Liveness.* This condition deals with dynamic properties, and can be compared with total correctness for sequential systems. When a producer sends data to a consumer, the consumer will eventually consume it. When a process (e.g., Ada task) is ready to execute a critical section (e.g., an accept body in an Ada task), it is eventually allowed to do so. The liveness property is more

difficult to determine than the safety property because we are dealing with dynamic events. Our process abstractions may include subtle design errors that can lead to deadlock or starvation [DIJ68, BEN82]. These errors may be extremely difficult to detect because they are usually not reproducible, and we are dealing with a dynamic environment that is constantly changing.

An example of process abstraction was shown in Figure 3-5, where each process is a virtual machine representing a parallel element of the model solution for the robot controller system. The decomposition of the real-time system into the set of abstract processes shown in this figure is not a simple, intuitive, procedure, and guidelines for this partitioning are provided in Part 3. A complete, step-by-step methodology is described in Part 4.

Analysis And Design Tools

Analysis and design tools are necessary in developing large real-time systems. The primary purposes for these tools are (1) to help the designers manage the complexity of the system requirements; (2) to help the designers manage the complexity of the design process at each step in the design methodology; (3) to provide material for design reviews; and (4) to provide material for the required design documentation. The analysis and design tools used with our design methodology are described below.

7.1 Data Flow Diagrams

The data flow diagrams (DFDs) described below are used as one of the primary analysis tools for managing the complexity of the requirements of a large real-time system. The drawing of these diagrams represents the first major step in the design process.

7.1.1 Purpose

The purpose of a DFD is to describe the data flow between the major functional components of the system. These components are determined from the system requirement specifications and represent the first step in decomposing the problem into a set of transforms that operate on the data. The exercise of drawing a set of DFDs is an important first step to gain a thorough understanding of the system requirements. They form the basis for determining the magnitude and complexity of the software to be developed. They are also used to identify concurrency within the system.

7.1.2 Conventions

An example of a DFD is shown in Figure 7-1. This diagram illustrates *transforms* by circles (also referred to as "bubbles"). An arrow pointing to a circle with a data name represents input to that transform, whereas an arrow leaving a circle with a data name represents output from the transform. An abstract data store is represented by two horizontal lines enclosing the name of that data store. Arrows leading into a data store, e.g., from the transform Delete Aircraft to Squadron Aircraft Status, indicate that data is stored. Arrows leaving a data store indicate that data is retrieved. We do not name individual data items for storage and retrieval, unless it is to remove an ambiguity.

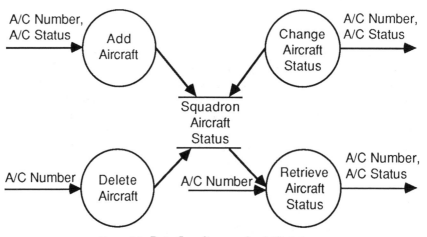

Figure 7-1. Data flow diagram for A/C status.

Arrows and data names are also used to connect transforms, as shown in Figure 7-2. Panel Inputs are sent from the transform Read Panel Input to the transform Validate Panel Input. The broken line going from the transform Receive Axis Ack to Interpret Program Statement indicates that the *event* (or signal) Motion Acknowledge is sent from the former to the latter. In this case Interpret Program

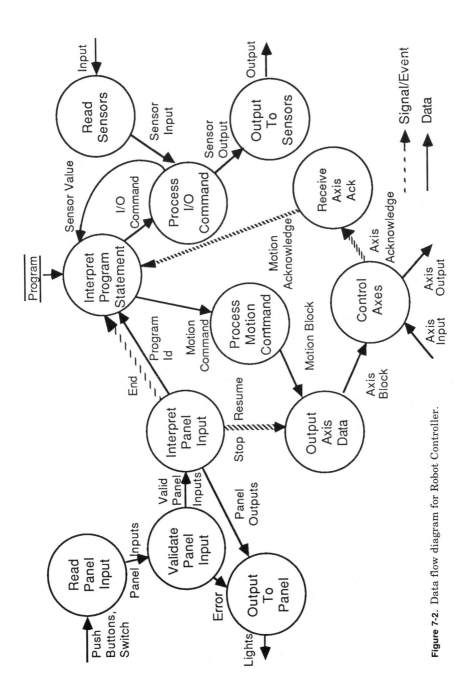

Figure 7-2. Data flow diagram for Robot Controller.

Statement will not operate on the event (an event is not considered data) but will perform actions as a result of the event received.

7.1.3 Transformations

A DFD shows the inputs to and outputs from each transform, and the interfaces between the transforms. The DFD shown in Figure 7-1 illustrates four *data* transforms that operate on the data store Squadron Aircraft Status. Each transform performs a different operation on the elements in the data store, depending on the inputs received. A transform does not always use input data for its operation. Figure 7-2 shows various instances where one process sends a signal (event) to another. For example, the transform Receive Axis Ack sends the signal Motion Acknowledge to the transform Interpret Program Statement. This event triggers certain operations within the latter transform, but it does not use Motion Acknowledge as input data.

7.1.4 Identifying Concurrency

We use the DFD and the process selection rules given in Chapter 9 to identify the concurrent aspects of the system. We first identify single transforms or groups of transforms that can operate independently in time, rather than strictly sequentially. When we group transforms, we look for common functionality between them and whether or not they share data. The four transforms depicted in Figure 7-1 can all operate independently in time, but they access a common data base. If we had a process for each transform, we would have to provide for mutual exclusion to protect the data base. A better approach for this example would be to create a single process for the four transforms with the data base local to this process. Mutually exclusive access to the data base would then be provided by guaranteeing that only one of the four operations could take place at any one time. In Ada this could be implemented with a task that contains four accept bodies within a selective wait. The data base would be declared in the task body. Each accept body represents a critical section, and mutual exclusion of the four operations would be guaranteed.

From the DFD shown in Figure 7-2 we can identify the concurrent processes illustrated by rectangles in Figure 7-3. We have used a set of selection rules to identify the processes. The heuristics for combining transforms into processes are described in Chapter 9.

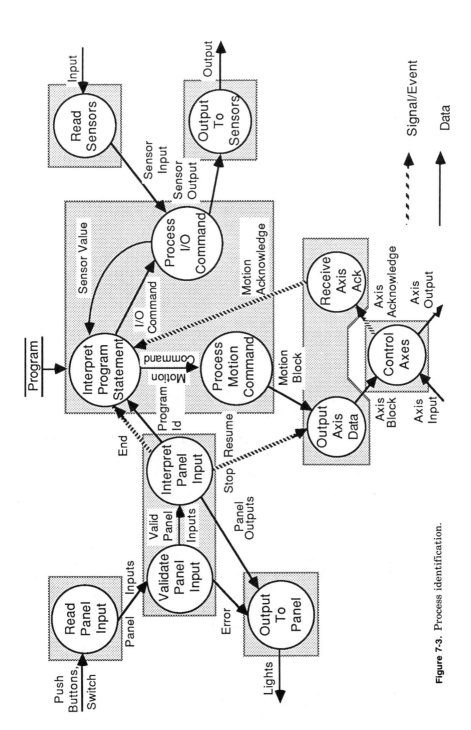

Figure 7-3. Process identification.

7.1.5 Leveling

We are primarily concerned with designing *large* real-time systems, and all the transforms we create will not fit on a single page. We also need a systematic way of refining the details of large, complex transforms. The method of managing this complexity is called *leveling*. Figure 7-4 illustrates a first-level DFD for a simulation program. Each of the transforms in this DFD are quite complex and must be further decomposed. A second-level DFD for the transform Perform Lexical Analysis is shown in Figure 7-5. It is important that a hierarchical numbering system be used to identify the transforms in leveled DFDs. The numbering is used both for identifying lower level transforms and their ancestors, and for arranging paragraphs in large design documents.

When we decompose a transform by leveling, the inputs and outputs of the transform must be consistent (and complete) in the lower level DFD. The inputs and outputs for the four transforms shown in Figure 7-5 are consistent with the ones shown for Perform Lexical Analysis in Figure 7-4. Data items may be decomposed at a lower level, as is shown for Token Kind and Token Value in Figure 7-5.

7.1.6 Correctness

We can use certain guidelines to evaluate the correctness (in a loose sense; we are not proving correctness here) of the DFDs:

1. *Tracing to requirements.* The transforms and data should be easily traceable to the requirement specifications. The functionality displayed in the DFDs should show a high correspondence to the functionality specified in the requirements documentation.

2. *Isolate transforms.* Investigate each transform individually, and its interface to other transforms. We can, at best, hope to detect errors and inconsistencies by evaluating individual transforms. We have very little chance of evaluating a set of leveled DFDs as a whole for a large system.

3. *Sufficient input.* Determine if the inputs to a transform are sufficient to produce the required output.

4. *Parsimony of input.* There should be no extraneous input entering a transform, only the input necessary for the required output.

5. *Missing input or output.* If there is no input to or output from a transform, there is a potential problem with that transform.

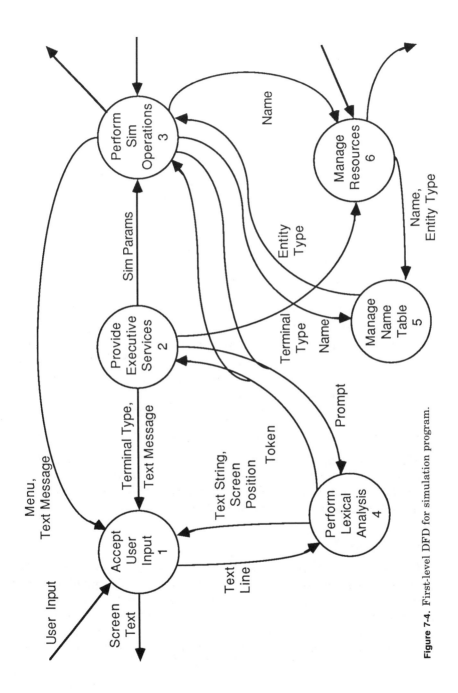

Figure 7-4. First-level DFD for simulation program.

55

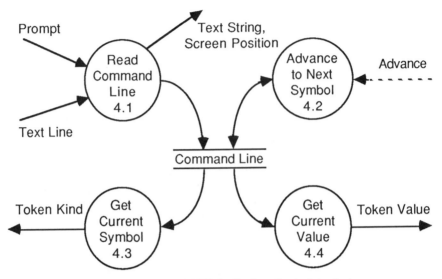

Figure 7-5. Second-level DFD for Perform Lexical Analysis.

6. *Data base connections.* Data stores that show direct connections are most likely in error.

7. *Consistency in leveling.* All the inputs and outputs to a transform must be repeated exactly in the lower level DFD. The data names repeated must appear with identical identifiers, except for possible decomposition of data items.

7.2 Process Structure Charts

We indicated above how we use the DFDs and a set of process selection rules to determine the concurrency of the real-time system. We will now illustrate how we describe graphically the set of cooperating sequential processes and their interfaces.

7.2.1 Purpose

Process structure charts are used to give a language independent graphical representation of the set of cooperating sequential processes that is our design model of the system. These charts include an abstract view of the interfaces between the processes. The process structure charts form the basis for how we will implement the required communication and synchronization between the processes.

7.2.2   Conventions

The conventions described below is a combination of the notation used in MASCOT [ALL81] and DARTS (Design Approach for Real-Time Systems) [GOM84], with our own modifications and extensions.

7.2.2.1   General. An example of a typical process structure chart is shown in Figure 7-6 for a robot controller. The circles designate the independent primitive processes that operate concurrently. Data flows are represented with data names and special symbols describing the coupling between the processes. Access to data stores is shown with arrows just as for DFDs.

7.2.2.2   Interfaces. Special conventions have been used for the interfaces between the concurrent processes. The particular interface we choose depends upon the degree of coupling desired between each pair of processes as follows:

1. A loose coupling is depicted as a "piston" and signifies that a queue is required for handling channel data (e.g., Panel Inputs) passed from one process to another.

2. A slightly tighter coupling is shown as a jagged arrow and illustrates that one process is sending a signal (e.g., End) to another process.

3. A tight coupling is shown as a closing square bracket and signifies that one process is passing a parameter (e.g., Program Id) directly to another process.

4. The tightest coupling between a pair of processes is depicted with an open and a closed bracket as a square "S" shape. This signifies that one process is passing a parameter to another, and that the former is waiting for a reply from the latter (e.g., Axis Block and Axis Acknowledgement).

5. Shared data (pool data) between two or more processes is shown with the data name delineated by a horizontal line on top and bottom (e.g., Sensory I/O Data Store). The arrowheads signify the data flow into or out of the data area.

7.2.2.3   Leveling. Leveling is performed by using off-page connectors when all the processes do not fit on one page. There is, however, no hierarchical decomposition as was the case with DFDs (we only consider primitive processes for our methodology).

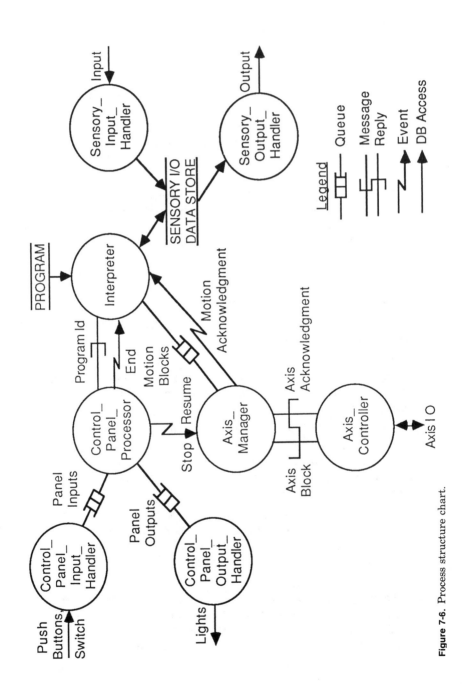

Figure 7-6. Process structure chart.

7.3   Concurrent Process Graphs

Concurrent process graphs (CPGs) contain a graphical description of how the language-independent concurrent processes and their interfaces, as shown in a process structure chart, will be implemented. We are only concerned with an implementation using the Ada programming language here, but CPGs can be used for implementations in any other programming language that includes tasking primitives, or for a programming language and a real-time executive. To emphasize that we have a graphical representation of Ada tasks, we will use the term Ada task graph (ATG) as a synonym for a CPG. CPG can then be used for describing tasks in any implementation language.

7.3.1   Purpose

We use ATGs to show the details of how the concurrent processes will be implemented as Ada tasks, the interfaces between these tasks, and the caller/called decisions that have been made. The heuristics for how we make these decisions are presented in Part 3, Ada Design Principles.

7.3.2   Conventions

An ATG for the robot controller is shown in Figure 7-7. The circles represent Ada tasks that will execute concurrently. An arrowhead that touches a circle represents an entry call to that task (e.g., the task Buffer_Panel_Input contains two entries). If an arrow comes in from the edge without a connection, an interrupt from a device is expected, and a corresponding interrupt entry will be present in the affected task (e.g., Control_Panel_Input_Handler will contain an interrupt entry for the control panel input channel). A small arrow above a line connecting two tasks designates the flow of data between the two tasks. Where the small arrow is missing, a signal (a parameterless entry call in Ada) is sent from one task to another (e.g., Motion Ack from Axis_Manager to Program Interpreter). We note that the shared data area Sensory I/O Data Store shown in Figure 7-6 does not appear in Figure 7-7. Shared data in Ada must be protected and is in this case contained within the task Protect_Sensory_Data.

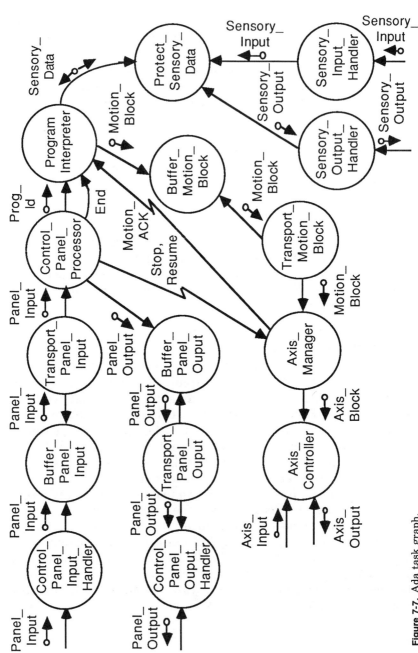

Figure 7-7. Ada task graph.

7.3.3 Leveling

If all the tasks do not fit on a single page, we use off-page connectors. There is no hierarchy of tasks decomposing into subtasks. A different type of leveling can be used if a task is large and decomposes into several subprograms. In this case we can use traditional structure charts to show the calling relationships of the subprograms within each (large) task (structure charts are described below).

7.4 Ada Package Graphs

After all the cooperating tasks and their interfaces have been determined, we have to prepare the proper Ada module architecture. Ada tasks cannot exist as independent compilation units (except as subunits for task bodies), they must be encapsulated within Ada packages or subprograms. Ada package graphs are used to illustrate the design decisions we have made regarding the architecture and encapsulation of the cooperating tasks.

7.4.1 Purpose

Ada package graphs are used to show the design decisions we have made for how the tasks will be specified in the program. Figure 7-8 is a package graph for the robot controller. The solid lines drawn around groups of tasks indicate Ada packages; otherwise the graph is identical to the ATG shown in Figure 7-7. The decision process for how the task groupings should be made is not intuitive; it is based on a set of heuristics which is described in Chapter 10.

7.4.2 Leveling

Since the Ada packaging is obtained by superimposing package structures on the tasks in ATGs, the leveling is the same as for ATGs that do not fit on a single page. We simply use off-page connectors without any kind of decomposition or hierarchy.

7.5 Structure Charts

A task that is too large to contain all its executable code within the task body can be decomposed into subprograms and, possibly, packages. We may also have a problem specification (most likely not a real-time application) whose corresponding design solution is strictly (or largely) sequential. We can use traditional structure charts to show the module structure of a task body that is

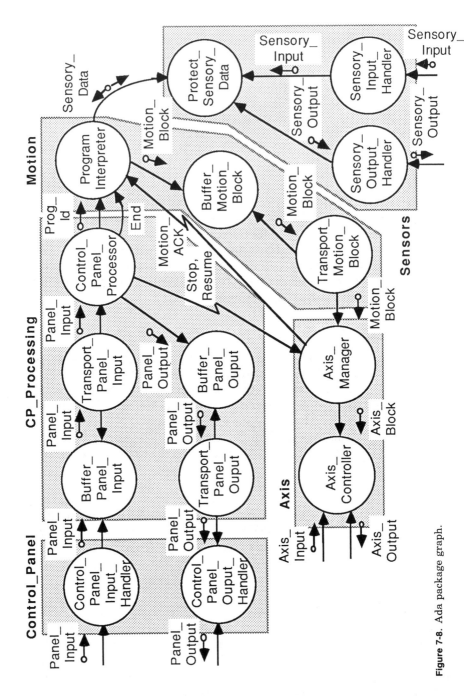

Figure 7-8. Ada package graph.

decomposed into subprograms and packages, or the structure of a large sequential system.

7.5.1 Purpose

The purpose of the structure chart is to describe the data and control flow of a set of subprograms that are executed sequentially, and to show the hierarchical organization of these subprograms.

7.5.2 Conventions

We use graphical conventions that have been slightly modified from those described by traditional structured design [PAG80 and YOU79]. The original intent of structure charts was to show *structural architectural* information [YOU79, p. 55]. In Ada, however, subprograms shown on a structure chart may reside in different packages, and in order to show *architectural* information we must somehow include the package name of a subprogram. The structure chart shown in Figure 7-9 has included the package name that each subprogram is residing in; i.e., it has architectural information in addition to control and hierarchical information. Generic subprograms are treated as *predefined* in traditional structured design with the instantiated name shown in the structure chart.

7.5.3 Leveling

We use the same leveling rules as for traditional structured design with off-page connectors [PAG80, p. 301]. The leveled structure chart shown in Figure 7-10 describes the decomposition of the top-level abstraction Build_Command_Table that is shown with an off-page connector in Figure 7-9. Automated tools are highly recommended for creating and updating structure charts for large systems.

7.6 Program Design Language

A program design language (PDL) is used to translate the design expressed in graphical terms into programming constructs. Process, data, and procedural abstractions have been made prior to the start of the PDL phase, which is tailored to a specific implementation language. The language in our case is Ada, and we use an automated PDL that has an Ada compiler as a "front end." The programming constructs will be legal Ada as specified in the language reference manual [DOD83], and the compiler will perform type checking of all interfaces between packages, subprograms, and tasks. This will

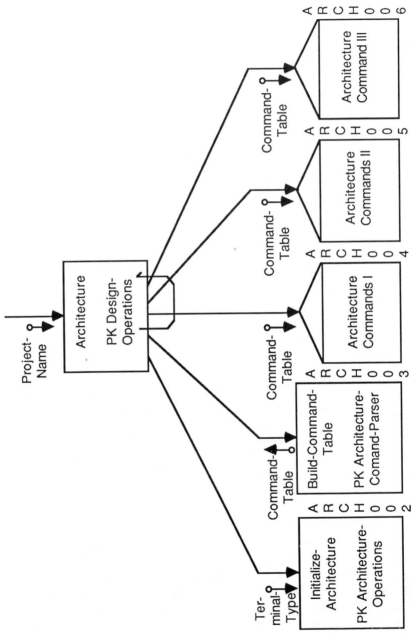

Figure 7-9. Top-level structure chart.

64

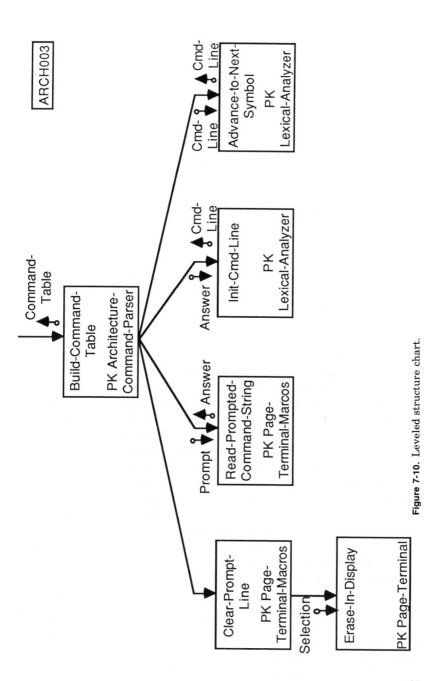

ARCH003

Figure 7-10. Leveled structure chart.

65

reduce the time spent on debugging, since the compiler detects improper uses of interfaces. In addition to its function as a design tool, the PDL provides excellent material for design reviews and reports.

The automated PDL can be a specialized tool such as Byron [INT85], or an Ada compiler such as DEC's VAX Ada. The rationale for choosing one automated PDL over another is related to a particular development project, and is not treated here.

In this section we describe the general usage of a PDL as an automated tool for top-level and detailed design. Using a PDL as part of our design methodology is described in detail in Part 4.

7.6.1 Top-Level Design

The top-level design is normally expected to proceed in a top-down fashion as we create various levels of abstractions to promote the deferring of design decisions. To take full advantage of Ada's type checking abilities, however, the required "helper" packages and subprograms must first be compiled bottom-up and placed in the Ada library (a large program could have several Ada libraries). An example of a top-level design for a set of application packages (to be created top-down) is illustrated with the package graph for the Remote Temperature Sensor (RTS) system shown in Figure 7-11. (A complete specification and solution of the RTS is provided in Appendix A.) The PDL for the package Device_Handlers is shown in Figure 7-12. We note the *with* and *use* of the helper package Definitions which must be in the program library before we invoke the compiler for type checking of the package specification of Device_Handlers. Similarly, for the successful compilation of the package body of Device_Handlers, the helper package containing hardware dependent entities (HDP) must be available in the library. The use of entrance procedures (Transmit_DP, Transmit_CP_ACK, and Read_Temp) promotes information hiding by specifying the corresponding task entries in the package body. These task entries are hidden to all users that *with* the package Device_Handlers. The use of Ada as a PDL also provides for the deferring of design decisions with the use of the *separate* clause.

The actual implementations of the task bodies for TX_Host_Msg, RX_Host_Msg, and DT_Handler are treated as abstractions in the package body of Device_Handlers. The detailed algorithms for these task bodies can be designed later, and are not required for a successful compilation of the top-level design modules.

Specific PDL coding standards must be established for each project. As an example, we have shown interfaces to other packages as

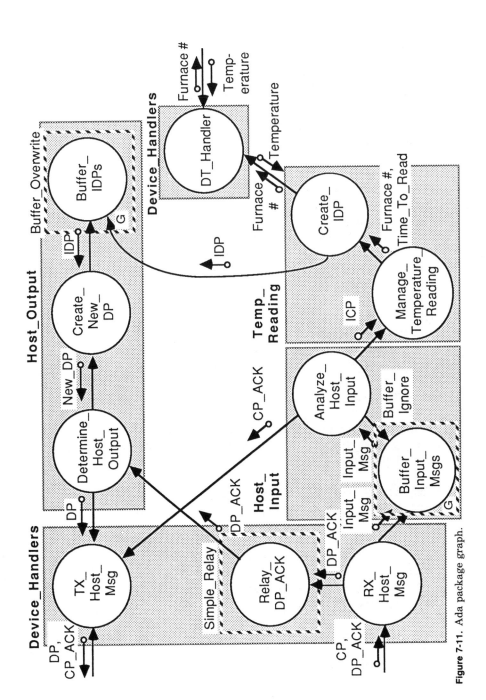

Figure 7-11. Ada package graph.

67

```
with Definitions;  use Definitions;
package Device_Handlers is
  procedure Transmit_DP      (D : in DP_Format);
  procedure Transmit_CP_ACK (C : in Character);
  procedure Read_Temp        (F : in Furnace_Type;
                              T : out Temp_Type);
  pragma Inline (Transmit_DP, Transmit_CP_ACK, Read_Temp);
end Device_Handlers;

with HDP;  use HDP;
package body Device_Handlers is
  task Tx_Host_Msg is
    entry Output_Channel;
    for Output_Channel use at Output_Channel_Adr;
    entry Transmit_DP      (D : in DP_Format);
    entry Transmit_CP_ACK (C : in Character);
  end Tx_Host_Msg;

  task Rx_Host_Msg is
    entry Input_Channel;
    for Input_Channel use at Input_Channel_Adr;
  end Rx_Host_Msg;

  task DT_Handler is
    entry DT_Interrupt;
    for DT_Interrupt use at DT_Interrupt_Adr;
    entry Read_Temp (F : in Furnace_Type; T : out Temp_Type);
  end DT_Handler;

  task body Tx_Host_Msg is separate;
  task body Rx_Host_Msg is separate;
  task body DT_Handler  is separate;

  procedure Transmit_DP (D : in DP_Format) is
  begin
    Tx_Host_Msg.Transmit_DP (D);
  end Transmit_DP;

  -- put in entry calls for remaining entrance procedures

end Device_Handlers;
```

Figure 7-12. Device_Handlers (package specification and body).

"Calls" within comment statements. This has the advantage that we can readily identify package interfaces, but it also means that an additional effort is required to update the comments when changes are made to the interfaces.

7.6.2 Detailed Design

During the detailed design phase we complete the major design decisions that were deferred during the top-level design phase. The simpler algorithms can be specified with complete Ada code in the PDL, or deferred to the coding phase. For more complicated logic we can use properly commented pseudocode with sufficient Ada constructs to allow successful compilation. Figure 7-13 illustrates the use of Ada PDL to supply the design for the task body of TX_Host_Msg that was deferred in the package body of Device_Handlers (see Figure 7-12). The package Device_Handlers is named as the parent in the *separate* clause for the compiler to perform the necessary checking of interfaces. The two entries (Transmit_DP and Transmit_CP_ACK) are implemented with a selective wait statement, and in this case we have used Ada code without any pseudocode. Other design decisions that were deferred during the top-level design phase are completed similarly to the example shown here. Simple algorithms may be deferred further and included during the coding phase. The proper level of detail to be furnished during the detailed design phase is described in the methodology section in Part 4.

7.7 Ada Structure Graphs (Buhr Diagrams)

None of the graphical tools described above show the overall architecture of an Ada program as it will eventually appear as Ada code. We would like to graphically illustrate the package structure and the interfaces between tasks that reside in different packages on the same diagram. The structure and the interfaces in the diagram should be isomorphic to the actual Ada code specified as PDL. A graphical representation that satisfies this requirement has been described in [BUH84], and we are adopting this representation with some extensions and modifications.

7.7.1 Purpose

The purpose of the Ada structure graph is to describe the overall program architecture in detail, including the task structure. It also shows inter-package and intra-package control and data flows, and is

```
separate (Device_Handlers)
task body Tx_Host_Msg is
  Output_Buffer : Character;
  for Output_Buffer use at Output_Buffer_Adr;
begin
  loop
    select
      accept Transmit_DP (D : in DP_Format) do
        for I in D'Range loop
          Output_Buffer := D(I);
          accept Output_Channel;
        end loop;
      end Transmit_DP;
    or
      accept Transmit_CP_ACK (C : in Character) do
        Output_Buffer := C;
        accept Output_Channel;
      end Transmit_CP_ACK;
    or
      terminate;
    end select;
  end loop;
end Tx_Host_Msg;
```

Figure 7-13. Tx_Host_Msg (task body).

a complement to the Ada PDL. Inter-package task visibility is depicted with the use (or absence) of package "entrance procedures" for entry calls.

7.7.2 Conventions

An example of a structure graph is shown in Figure 7-14 for the Remote Temperature Sensor (RTS). The overall package structure is shown with the large rectangles and the package name at the top of the rectangle (Device_Handlers, Host_Output, Host_Input, ASCII_Conversions, and Temp_Reading). Tasks are shown inside each package as parallelograms with entry points at their edges (e.g., TX_Host_Msg is a task inside Device_Handlers and has the entries Output_Channel, Transmit_DP and Transmit_CP_ACK); entrance procedures are shown as small rectangles at the edges of the package (e.g., Transmit_DP, and Transmit_CP_ACK are entrance procedures for the task TX_Host_Msg); nested generic packages or

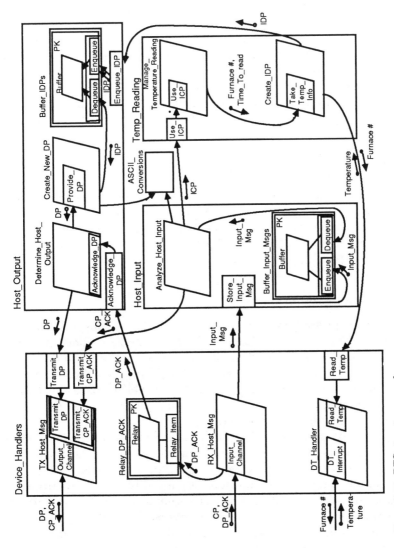

Figure 7-14. RTS structure graph.

71

subprograms are drawn as double rectangles (e.g., Relay_DP_ACK is an instantiation of a generic package inside Device_Handlers).

Inter-package and intra-package control flows are shown with connecting lines and arrowheads, and data flows are shown with small arrows and data names (e.g., the task RX_Host_Msg inside the package Device_Handlers is calling the entrance procedure Store_ Input_Msg in the package Host_Input, and passes the data item Input_Msg as a parameter). Details regarding entry calls can be shown with special notations. For example, the dot by the entry Use_ICP in the task Manage_Temperature_Reading inside the package Temp_Reading signifies that the entry is "guarded."

The isomorphism between the Ada structure graph and the Ada PDL is apparent by comparing Figures 7-12 and 7-14 for the top-level design.

7.7.3 Leveling

Leveling can be used in a hierarchical fashion where one diagram shows all the packages with most of the inside details omitted, and separate pages are used to describe the intra-package interfaces. Another method is to use off-page connectors and create separate pages that will form a large wall chart for design reviews.

7.8 Finite State Machine

For certain systems that can be described in terms of a finite number of states and state changes, we can employ a "black box" called a *finite state machine* (FSM). This concept allows us to defer design decisions and use an abstract automata that embodies all the state conditions and state changes. FSMs have been used effectively in the design of, for example, task scheduling and dispatching, network protocols, and lexical analyzers.

The purpose of an FSM is to localize the events that cause state changes in a system, and the effects on the system of these events. The various states and state changes can be described with a state-transition diagram as shown in Figure 7-15. This diagram illustrates the various states of a concurrent task and the conditions or events that affect changes to these states. For example, a task in a running state will become blocked if it makes a request for a resource that is not currently available.

Another method of describing states and state changes is with state-transition tables such as the one shown in Figure 7-16. In this table the states are listed vertically on the left, and the events that cause state changes are listed horizontally on top of the table. The

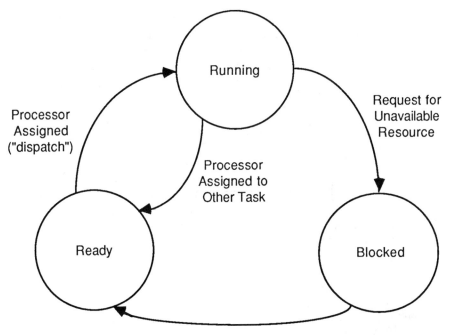

Figure 7-15. Task state-transition diagram.

Events / States	Engine Off	System On	Brake	Resume Speed	System Off
On	Off		Temporarily Suspended		Off
Temporarily Suspended	Off			On	Off
Off		On			

Figure 7-16. Task state-transition table for automobile cruise control.

matrix elements represent the changed states for a given event. For the automobile cruise control shown in Figure 7-16, the state will change from, for example, "temporarily suspended" to "on" when the driver pushes the "resume speed" button. It is not our intent to give a complete treatment of state-transition diagrams and tables here.

Such treatments can be found in References WAR85a, WAR85b, and MAR85. Our primary emphasis here is to describe how we construct FSMs using Ada, as illustrated with the examples that follow. We use state-transition diagrams to manage the complexity of the states and state transitions; the diagrams form the basis for the design of the FSMs.

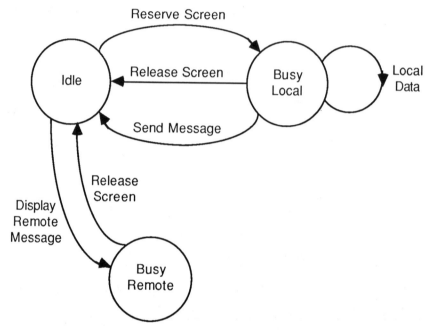

Figure 7-17. State-transition diagram for local/remote screen display.

7.8.1 FSM in Ada Task

We will illustrate how we can construct an FSM in a task as part of a solution to a problem suggested in Reference BUH84, p. 130. The requirement is to have local and remote messages displayed on a screen without any of the messages being overwritten, and with equal-partner contention for the screen. There are three special keys on the keyboard for the operator to RESERVE the screen for a local message to be created and displayed; to RELEASE the screen when the preparation of a local message is discontinued, or a remote message has been displayed; and to SEND the local message that has been created and displayed on the screen. The screen is released and cleared at the completion of the SEND function. The states and transition conditions for the duplex screen display system

```
with Definitions;  use Definitions;

package Event_Control is
  procedure Put_Stroke (Event_or_Char : in Event_or_Char_Type);
           -- accepted anytime

  procedure Put_Message (Message : in Message_Type);
           -- accepted only in 'Idle' state
end Event_Control;


package body Event_Control is

  task State_Manager is
    entry Put_Stroke  (Event_or_Char : in Event_or_Char_Type);
    entry Put_Message (Message : in Message_Type);
  end State_Manager;

  task body State_Manager is separate;

  Procedure Put_Stroke (Event_or_Char : in Event_or_Char_Type) is
  begin
    State_Manager.Put_Stroke (Event_or_Char);
  end Put_Stroke;

  Procedure Put_Message (Message : in Message_Type) is
  begin
    State_Manager.Put_Message (Message);
  end Put_Message;

end Event_Control;
```

Figure 7-18. Specification of state manager FSM.

are shown in Figure 7-17. The PDL for the Event_Control package is shown in Figure 7-18.

The specification contains only the entrance procedures Put_Stroke for events or characters that are accepted anytime, and Put_Message for messages that are only accepted in the Idle state. The package body contains the specification of the task State_Manager. This is the task that contains the FSM; it represents the "black box" concept of an abstract automata we described above. For this part of the top-level PDL we have deferred the design decision of how to implement the FSM by using the *separate*

```
with Screen_Control;
with Message_Control;
separate (Event_Control)

task body State_Manager is
  type States is (Idle, Busy_Local, Busy_Remote);
  State     : States := Idle;
  Msg_Index : Message_Index;
begin
  loop
    select
      accept Put_Stroke (Event_or_Char : in Event_or_Char_Type) do

        case State is

          when Idle =>
            if Event_or_Char = Reserve then
              State := Busy_Local;
              Msg_Index := 1;   -- 1st character in message
            else
              Screen_Control.Ring_Bell;
            end if;

          when Busy_Local =>

            case Event_or_Char is

              when Release =>
                State := Idle;
                Screen_Control.Clear;

              when Send =>
                State := Idle;
                Message_Control.Send_To_Remote;
                Screen_Control.Clear;

              when Legal_Character =>
                Screen_Control.Write (Event_or_Char);
                Message_Control.Collect_Local_Msg (Event_or_Char,
                                                   Msg_Index);
                Msg_Index := Msg_Index + 1;
```

Figure 7-19. Implementation of state manager FSM.

```
            when Reserve =>
               Screen_Control.Ring_Bell;
            end case;   -- Event_or_Char

         when Busy_Remote =>
            if Event_or_Char = Release then
               State := Idle;
               Screen_Control.Clear;
            else
               Screen_Control.Ring_Bell;
            end if;
         end case;   -- State
      end Put_Stroke;

   or
      when State = Idle =>
         accept Put_Message (Message : in Message_Type) do
            State := Busy_Remote;
            Screen_Control.Display (Message);
         end Put_Message;
      end select;
   end loop;
end State_Manager;
```

Figure 7-19 *(continued).* Implementation of state manager FSM.

clause for the task body State_Manager. The implementation of the FSM is contained in the task body of State_Manager and is shown in the PDL in Figure 7-19. The various states are declared with an enumeration type (Idle, Busy_Local, and Busy_Remote), and the state variable (State) is initialized with the value Idle. The FSM is implemented within the selective wait statement with entries for Put_Stroke and Put_Message. The state transitions that can occur for entry calls to Put_Stroke are controlled with an outer case statement for the mutually exclusive states Idle, Busy_Local, and Busy_Remote. A nested case statement controls the transition events for the Busy_Local state. Entry calls to Put_Message are controlled by a guard and are only accepted when the state variable has the value Idle. This implementation of the FSM represents the design decisions that have been made based on the state-transition diagram shown in Figure 7-17. We have not shown the PDL for the helper packages Definitions, Screen_Control, and Message_Control. These helper packages would be required for PDL type checking with an Ada compiler.

7.8.2   FSM in Ada Procedure

The next example illustrates the use of an FSM as part of a design for a lexical analyzer, as outlined in [BOO83, p. 203]. This particular analyzer recognizes identifiers and numbers. The state-transition diagram for the lexical analyzer is shown in Figure 7-20. Initially in the READY state, the analyzer will change its state to recognize either an identifier or a number, depending on the first character of the new token. When a delimiting character is detected, the state is changed to HALTED, and a complete token has been recognized. The FSM must be restarted before another token can be analyzed.

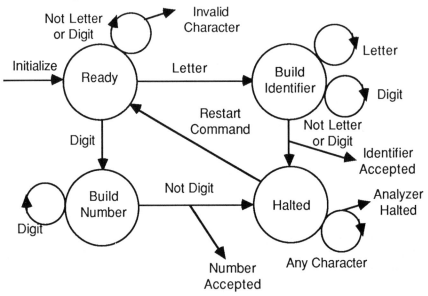

Figure 7-20. State-transition diagram for lexical analyzer.

The top-level PDL for the lexical analyzer is shown in Figure 7-21. The package specification contains the entrance procedures Set_Ready_State and Build_Symbol, and four exceptions. Two of these (Identifier_Accepted and Number_Accepted) signify to the user of the analyzer that the tokens have been completed. One exception (Invalid_Character) notifies the user that an invalid character was detected as the first character of a token. The last exception (Analyzer_Halted) lets the user know that the lexical analyzer must be restarted before another token can be processed. The package body of Lexical_Analyzer contains the various states as an enumeration type (Ready, Build_Identifier, Build_Number, and Halted), the state variable (Present_State) initialized to the value Ready, and the

```
package Lexical_Analyzer is
  procedure Set_Ready_State;
  procedure Build_Symbol (Char : in Character);

  Identifier_Accepted : exception;
  Invalid_Character   : exception;
  Analyzer_Halted     : exception;
  Number_Accepted     : exception;
end Lexical_Analyzer;


package body Lexical_Analyzer is
  type State is (Ready, Build_Identifier, Build_Number, Halted);

  Present_State : State := Ready;

  procedure Set_Ready_State is
  begin
    Present_State := Ready;
  end Set_Ready_State;

  procedure Build_Symbol (Char : in Character) is separate;
end Lexical_Analyzer;
```

Figure 7-21. Specification of lexical analyzer FSM.

implementation of the procedure to restart the analyzer
(Set_Ready_State). The detailed design decisions for the FSM have
been deferred by the *separate* clause for the procedure Build_Symbol.
The implementation of the FSM is shown with Ada PDL in Figure
7-22. The control of the state-transition changes is implemented
with a case statement for the mutually exclusive states Ready,
Build_Identifier, Build_Number, and Halted. The case statement
selector is the state variable Present_State.

7.8.3 General Approach to FSM in Ada

With the examples given above we have shown how we can build
FSMs in Ada. In general, we can use the following Ada constructs:

1. Case statement (for mutual exclusion of states) within subpro-
    gram, within task body without accept statement, or within an
    accept statement in a task body.

```
separate (Lexical_Analyzer)

procedure Build_Symbol (Char : in Character) is
   subtype Alpha is Character range 'A' .. 'z';
   subtype Digit is Character range '0' .. '9';
begin
   case Present_State is

      when Ready =>
          if (Char in Alpha) then
            Present_State := Build_Identifier;
          elsif (Char in Digit) then
            Present_State := Build_Number;
          else
            raise Invalid_Character;
          end if;

      when Build_Identifier =>
          if (Char in Alpha) or (Char in Digit) then
            null;
          else
            Present_State := Halted;
            raise Identifier_Accepted;
          end if;

      when Build_Number =>
          if (Char in Digit) then
            null;
          else
            Present_State := Halted;
            raise Number_Accepted;
          end if;

      when Halted =>
          raise Analyzer_Halted;
   end case;
end Build_Symbol;
```

Figure 7-22. Implementation of lexical analyzer FSM.

2. Selective wait statement in task body with guards for mutual exclusion of state conditions.

3. Any combination or nesting of the above.

4. State values are specified with an enumeration type, and the state variable is declared local to the FSM implementation and is hidden from the users of the FSM.

5. Conditions regarding the state of the FSM can be communicated to the user of the FSM by raising exceptions within the FSM, rather than passing back flags as parameters.

7.9   OOD Diagrams

Described below is yet another graphical tool used in designing large Ada programs. This tool helps us understand the interfaces to the visible part of an abstract data type (ADT) or a resource manager (these are discussed in detail in Chapter 10).

7.9.1   Purpose

The primary purpose of using OOD diagrams is to support object oriented design of large Ada programs. This is done with a graphical representation of a package that encapsulates type definitions and subprograms that represent the operations allowed on objects (data declarations) of the given type. The package is an abstraction of an object in the design (distinct from a data declaration), and the OOD diagram helps us understand what capabilities the design object provides. We need to understand how it is used in order to provide the necessary interfaces, i.e., making calls to the visible subprograms. Understanding how it is constructed is important during the design phase for evaluating the design, and during the maintenance phase for making enhancements or corrections to the design object.

7.9.2   Conventions

An example of an OOD diagram is shown in Figure 7-23. This type of diagram was first introduced by Booch [BOO83]. We have extended the original conventions to include different symbols for type and object specifications, and we have added the specification of exceptions. The large rectangle represents the package Track_Resource. This is the design object that encapsulates a track file (the internal data object) and the operations allowed on the track file. The entities to the left of the package, that cross the package boundary, represent elements that are visible to the users of the package. These elements are declared in the package specification. The ovals (e.g., Track_Count) are type specifications, and the rectangles are subprograms (e.g., Add). Notched rectangles (e.g.,

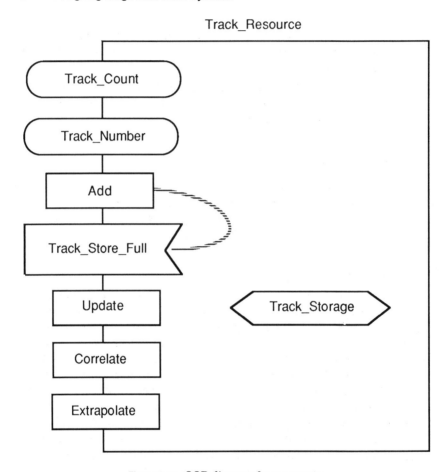

Figure 7-23. OOD diagram for a resource.

Track_Store_Full) represent exceptions, and the dotted line indicates where an exception is raised. The pointed rectangle (Track_Storage) inside the package represents a data object that is hidden from the users of the package. If a pointed rectangle appears across the left boundary of the package, it indicates that the data object is visible to the users of the package. The design implications of this visibility issue are discussed in Chapter 10.

7.9.3 Leveling

OOD diagrams are not used to show the interfaces between packages [except for context dependencies; we described Ada structure graphs (Buhr Diagrams) above for inter-package relations of subprograms and tasks]. The graphical representation of a design object will usually fit on a single page, and we normally will not have to be concerned with multi-page illustrations of a single design object. If we want to show all the internal interfaces and data declarations of the package (i.e., the entities that are declared in the package body and are hidden from the users of the package), we may show this information on a separate page.

CHAPTER

8

Summary

We have described design features, techniques, and tools that apply to large, real-time systems. In Chapter 5 we distinguished between programming-in-the-small, which involves a very small development team, and programming-in-the-large, which is our primary concern and involves several teams of developers. The latter development style is distinguished by a life-cycle approach to software development; extensive planning is required even before the development process starts; a specified design methodology is required for managing the complexity of a large real-time system, and for ensuring a common development approach by the various teams; extensive team coordination is required for effective communication between the team members; documentation is an important part of the development approach; module interfaces must be carefully designed; and formal test procedures are required for a uniform and thorough test approach by all the teams, and for documenting the test results.

In Chapter 6 we described how we use process abstraction to manage the complexity of the concurrency aspects that are inherent in most real-time systems. We described the two properties that determine how successful we are in decomposing our system into a set of cooperating sequential processes: (1) safety—the correctness of an individual process; and (2) liveness—the overall correctness of the set of processes.

In Chapter 7 we described several tools that are used in the top-level and detail design phases. Data flow diagrams are used as an analysis tool to graphically restate the requirements specification, and form the basis for how we determine the set of concurrent processes. Process structure charts provide a graphical representation of the decomposition of the real-time system into a set of (language independent) processes and their interfaces. Concurrent process graphs (or Ada task graphs) depict a complete set of (language dependent) Ada tasks, including intermediaries, data flows, and the caller/called decisions that have been made. Ada package graphs are used to show how the tasks will be encapsulated in Ada module structures. These graphs form the basis for writing Ada code using a program design language. Traditional structure charts are used to show the data flow and control between subprograms that represent a decomposition of a large task or a sequential system. Program design language (PDL) is used to translate the design expressed in graphical terms (in Ada package graphs and subprogram structure charts) into Ada programming constructs. We described how we use PDL for top-level design and detail design, and how we defer major design decisions by using the *separate* clause. Ada structure graphs (Buhr diagrams) provide a pictorial description of the overall architecture, and are isomorphic to the Ada constructs expressed in the PDL. Finite state machines (FSMs) are used as abstract automata that embody all the states and state transitions that pertain to an isolated part of a system. We described how to create FSMs in Ada tasks and subprograms using selective wait and case statements, and how exceptions can be used to communicate conditions about the FSM back to the user of the FSM. State transition tables and diagrams are used as analysis tools to manage the complexity of the state transitions. OOD diagrams are used to illustrate the interfaces and structure of design objects created with the LVM/OOD approach.

Ada Design Principles

Ada is an extremely versatile language with numerous features that can be used in designing large real-time system. In this part we categorize these features to give the designer a chance to pick and choose from the rich variety of Ada design principles available.

After the requirements of the real-time system have been carefully analyzed and understood, the senior designers will start to decompose the system into a set of concurrent processes (assuming the system is inherently concurrent). We describe in Chapter 9 how the decomposition can be performed, how we identify the processes, and how we can characterize the interfaces between the processes.

One of the most important software engineering aspects of Ada is the package *construct. This can be used to support design paradigms such as information hiding, encapsulation, and data abstraction. In Chapter 10 we describe how to use Ada packages for these design paradigms, and we present a taxonomy of Ada packages. We include a set of heuristics for how a task or group of tasks should be packaged.*

The use of generics is expected to greatly enhance the possibility for reuse of general purpose software. In Chapter 11 we describe how to recognize generic functionality during preliminary design, and how to construct generic units that can be placed in an Ada library for general usage within a single Ada program or across programming projects.

Although the emphasis in this book is on real-time systems and concurrency modeling, we also need a design approach for large sequential portions of the functional requirements. This is provided in Chapter 12 with the description of layered virtual machine design.

An important part of traditional structured design included the concepts of coupling and cohesion to be used by designers and for evaluating a software design. In Chapter 13 we expand the traditional coupling and cohesion concepts to include Ada packages and tasks. This will allow us to evaluate large real-time systems written in Ada in terms of these concepts. In Chapter 14 we describe data passed between communicating processes with the concepts of channels and pools.

The tasking model in Ada is based on the rendezvous concept and is a new feature of a modern high-order programming language. A novice Ada designer may embrace this feature without realizing some of the pitfalls associated with its use. In Chapter 15 we describe how to use general tasking paradigms in Ada, and the run time overhead that may occur in using the rendezvous. The caller/called decisions a designer must make are described in Chapter 16 in terms of the asymmetry of the rendezvous and the various tasking paradigms employed. Polling is sometimes required for interfacing with devices that are not interrupt driven, or for accessing status registers. The use of polling in Ada, however, may lead to undesirable effects. Polling and its potentially undesirable effects are discussed in Chapter 17.

One of the advanced features of Ada that is intended to support the creation of fault-tolerant real-time systems is exception handling. The use of this feature can range from implementing go-to structures to detecting bugs. We present a taxonomy of Ada exceptions in Chapter 18 that includes a reasonable set of categories, without the possible misuse of go-to structures.

The specification of Ada includes low-level programming facilities for data representations, record layouts, address association of objects and interrupt entries to hardware addresses, machine code insertion, and interfacing to other programming languages. We describe these features in Chapter 19.

9

Process Identification

In this chapter we present an orderly approach to determining a set of cooperating sequential processes using DFDs and a set of heuristics. The processes we select represent the model of the parallel elements of our system, and their selection must be made with great care. The result of our selection procedure will yield the process abstraction of the real-time system and represents a major design decision.

9.1 Process Selection Rules

The decomposition of a large real-time system starts after the designers have gained a thorough understanding of the requirement specifications. The decomposition process consists of a series of steps that utilize a set of graphical tools as design aids. The guidelines given below are based on an edges-in approach [BUH84], where we first abstract out the processes that are necessary to control the external devices and then determine the processes that make up the "middle-part." The process selection heuristics are used in connection with a set of DFDs that completely describe the requirements of the real-time system. The following rules can be used to identify the concurrent processes (process abstraction) of the real-time system:

1. *External devices.* These devices normally run at widely differing speeds and usually require a separate process for each device or channel. These processes should be designed as simple device drivers with a minimum of executable instructions.

2. *Functional cohesion.* Transforms with closely related functions can be combined into a single process if this will reduce the overhead compared with having each function as a separate process. The implementation of the set of functions as separate modules within the single process will contribute to functional cohesion (highly desirable) both within each module as well as within the process.

3. *Time-critical functions.* Certain functions must be performed within critical time limits, and this implies a separate (high-priority) process for such functions.

4. *Periodic functions.* Periodic functions should be implemented as separate processes that are activated at the proper time intervals. Such functions should not be combined into a single process, because it would quite likely be difficult to program more than one periodic function within the suspend/resume conditions of the process. In Ada, for example, we can specify a periodic interval with a delay statement. The Ada task will be suspended for (at least) the period specified, and it will be difficult to have more than one delay statement representing different periodic functions within the single task.

5. *Computational requirements.* Transforms that are not time critical (and often computationally intensive) can be designed as background processes (low priority) that will consume spare CPU cycles.

6. *Temporal cohesion.* Transforms that perform certain functions during the same time period, or immediately following certain events, can be combined into a single process. Each function should be implemented as a separate module or set of instructions within the process. This contributes to functional cohesion at the module level, but only temporal cohesion within the process.

7. *Storage limitations.* Virtual storage limitations may dictate the creation of additional processes by splitting up any process that is found to be too large. This limitation may apply to processors that use only 16 bits (or fewer) for virtual address calculations. Although not a conceptual issue of concurrent processing, this is frequently a vitally important practical issue.

8. *Data base functions.* Functions that need access to a shared data base can be collected in a single process with mutual exclusion for the access mechanism, and the structure of the data base hidden. This is the concept of a *monitor* [ALL81], and can be implemented in Ada with a task and the selective wait statement.

9.2 Process Interaction

We use the design of a robot controller [GRO86, GOM84] as an example of the creation of a set of concurrent processes using the guidelines given above. The context diagram for the robot controller shown in Figure 9-1 depicts three external devices (control panel, robot, and sensors) and the input and output data that flow between these devices and the software control program (Robot Controller).

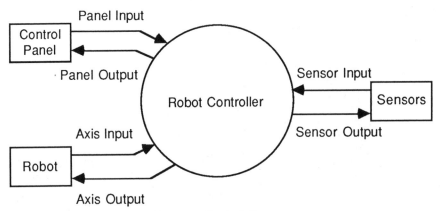

Figure 9-1. Context diagram.

The set of cooperating sequential processes (illustrated by circles) for the Robot Controller is shown in Figure 9-2. This figure represents the process abstraction of the system. At this point in the design we are not concerned with the intricate details of the algorithms of the processes; we are only concerned with the proper representation of the concurrency of the system and with the interfaces between the processes.

9.2.1 Coupling

We determine the proper interfaces between communicating processes by considering the desired coupling between them. The processes shown in Figure 9-2 illustrate a combination of loosely and

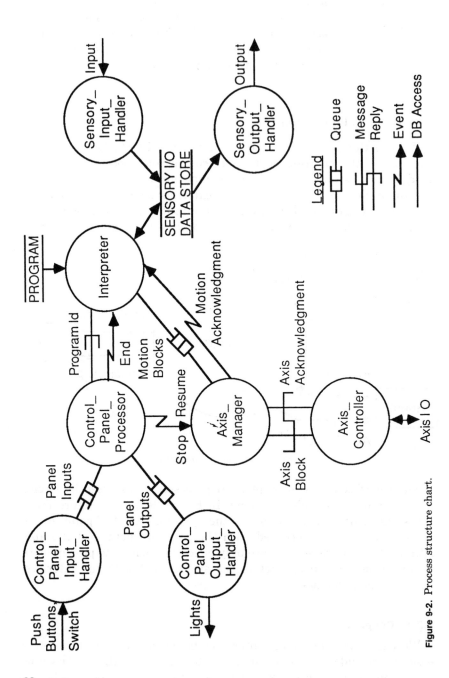

Figure 9-2. Process structure chart.

tightly coupled processes (see Chapter 13). Loosely coupled pairs of processes are Control_Panel_Input_Handler/Control_Panel_Processor, Control_Panel_Processor/Control_Panel_Output_Handler, and Interpreter/Axis_Manager. The loose coupling allows these processes to operate at their own natural speed, in an asynchronous fashion. The Control_Panel_Input_Handler, for example, simply stores panel input in a queue without waiting for the Control_Panel_Processor to finish its processing of any of these inputs.

Tight coupling is required between the Axis_Manager and the Axis_Controller, because the former must wait for a reply (acknowledgement) from the latter before it continues. A less severe form for tight coupling is shown between the Control_Panel_Processor and the Interpreter, where the former is passing a command (Program Id) to the latter. The least restrictive form for tight coupling is where a pair of processes interact via signaling. This is depicted as Control_Panel_Processor sending a signal, "Stop" or "Resume" to Axis_Manager and "End" to Interpreter. Axis_Manager sends "Motion Acknowledgement" to Interpreter.

The processes Interpreter, Sensory_Input_Handler, and Sensory_Output_Handler are coupled through the use of the shared data Sensory I/O Data Store. This form of coupling requires a careful consideration for providing mutual exclusion for access to the shared data to prevent an erroneous program.

9.2.2 Intermediaries

To implement the process structure shown in Figure 9-2, it is necessary to introduce certain intermediary ("agent") processes [BUR85, BAR84]. These processes are also referred to as "third party" processes [YOU82] or "buffered communication" [HOA85].

The effect of having two loosely coupled processes, Control_Panel_Input_Handler and Control_Panel_Processor, is obtained by introducing a buffer and transporter process between them (this is described in detail in Chapter 15). The same effect has been achieved for the process pairs Interpreter/Axis_Manager and Control_Panel_Processor/Control_Panel_Output_Handler.

The protection of the shared Sensory I/O Data Store is obtained by introducing a "monitor" process [ALL81, BRI73, HOA74, BEN82]. This process will guarantee mutually exclusive access to the shared data and prevent erroneous programming.

The intermediary processes that are added to the system will operate on appropriate buffers and queues, and will not only store and retrieve data but will also manipulate the required pointers for proper insertion and removal. The design details of these data structures can be delayed until the detailed program design language (PDL) statements are written.

9.2.3 Language Dependence

Up to this point in the design procedure, the abstraction process has been completely independent of the implementation language and operating system. The process structure shown in Figure 9-2 can be implemented regardless of whether the language is, for example, Ada, C, CMS-2, Fortran, Jovial J73, or Pascal, and regardless of a specific real-time executive. This is, however, as far as we can go without considering the implementation language and associated executive. The introduction of intermediary processes and monitors makes the design language dependent from this point forward. To determine the control between the processes (caller/called relationships), it is necessary to consider the process primitives that are available. For example, the implementation of the robot controller in C, Pascal, or Jovial requires the use of executive service requests to a real-time executive, whereas an implementation in Ada can make use of the Ada tasking model without any service requests. All the remaining steps in the design and implementation process are language dependent. We will present a complete step-by-step methodology that includes the process abstraction described above and the transformation to Ada constructs in Part 4.

Packages

The Ada package construct is the primary mechanism for creating modules in Ada. Packages are passive software elements that are elaborated only each time an Ada program is being prepared for execution. These packages may contain executable statements for initialization, but their primary function is to *encapsulate* active program units such as tasks and subprograms, and constants, type definitions and localized nonportable system features. Packages are used to promote information hiding by providing two separate programming constructs: (1) the package specification, where everything is visible to the users of the package; and (2) the package body, where we can hide information from the users of the package.

In the sections below, we describe how we encapsulate design entities, how packages support data abstraction, and how we can categorize the different types of packages we need in a real-time design.

10.1 Encapsulation Mechanism

Ada packages are used to encapsulate a variety of design entities such as data types, abstract data types (ADTs), tasks and subprograms, nested generic packages, adaptation data, and localized nonportable (hardware-dependent) items. The specification part contains the information that is exported to other users (these users import the information by using the *with* clause). Entrance procedures are provided in the specification for (indirect) access to task entries and subprograms whose specifications and implementations are hidden in the package body. Private data types and their operations are given in the specification part, and the users of the package are restricted to manipulate data objects of that type with only the operations specified. The actual data objects can be declared by the users of the package, or they may be hidden in the package body. How we use this in a design is described below.

Within the package body, we may choose to defer design decisions for the implementations of tasks and subprograms by using the *separate* clause. We may also declare data objects here that are local to the package, and hidden from the users of the package. The package body may contain executable code for the initialization of data objects.

We can consider the package as a *wall* surrounding the declarations and implementations of tasks and subprograms. The specification provides a *hole* in the wall that gives users of the package the minimum information necessary: the interface specification. Several examples of the encapsulation mechanism in Ada are given in Section 10.3.

10.2   Data Abstraction

We described in Chapter 6 how we use data, procedural, and process abstractions to manage complexity of large systems. Ada supports data abstractions eminently by allowing any user-defined data type, and by providing the package construct for encapsulating data types and their operations. We can describe data abstraction with the following elements:

1. *Data type.* A data type has a set of abstract values for objects of that type, and a set of operations allowed on those objects. Examples of data types are rational numbers and track files.

2. *Data structure.* The data structure is the definition of the architecture of the set of values for the type. An example of a data structure is the specification of a track file as an array of records.

3. *Subprograms.* We use subprograms for the implementation of the operations allowed on objects of a given data type. These are typically specified in a package specification as entrance procedures, to hide the actual implementation of the operations.

We can, for example, specify a set of subprograms in a package specification that make calls to one or more task entries that are hidden in the package body.

Operations allowed on objects of a certain type can be classified as follows [LIS86, p. 90]:

a. *Primitive constructors.* Operations that create objects of a given type without using objects of that type as input.

b. *Constructors.* Operations that take objects of a given type as input and create other objects of that type. Examples of these operations include *add* and *multiply*.

c. *Mutators.* Operations that modify a set of objects of a given type. Examples of these operations include *insert* and *delete*.

d. *Observers.* Operations that take objects of their type as input and return results of other types. Examples of these operations include *size*, *member*, *full*, and *empty*.

For most of the abstract data types we create with Ada packages, we expect to have several of these classes of operations included. We may not need primitive constructors, since we can create objects in Ada by a declaration that specifies the data type of the objects. Constructors will include procedures with *in out* or *in* and *out* parameters of the same type, or a function that returns a result of the same type as the input parameters. Mutators will be procedures with *in out* parameters. Observers will be procedures with *in* and *out* parameters of different types, or functions whose results are of a different type than the input parameters.

Several examples of data abstractions in Ada are illustrated in the paragraphs that follow.

10.3 Taxonomy Of Ada Packages

We need to design Ada packages for a variety of categories, as illustrated in Figure 10-1. These categories are described as follows:

1. *Application.* An application-oriented package is one that contains the subprograms and tasks that accomplish the main processing to satisfy the software requirements posed by the problem statement. Application packages are created top-down, and implementation details are deferred using the *separate* clause. An example of an application is shown in Figure 10-2 for a temperature reading package used in a remote temperature sensor

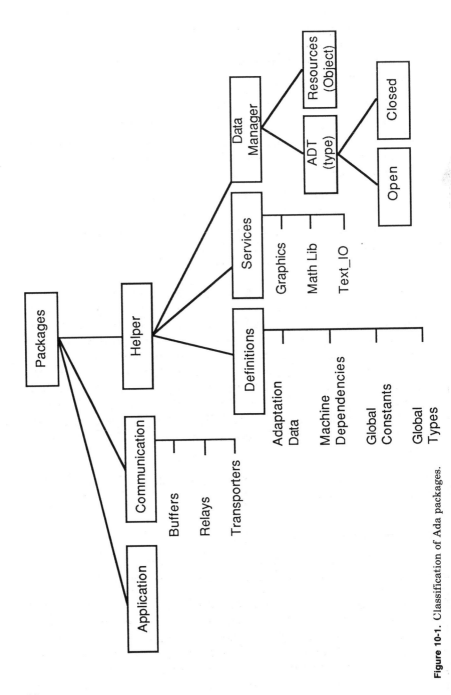

Figure 10-1. Classification of Ada packages.

```
with Definitions;  use Definitions;

package Temp_Reading is
  procedure Use_ICP (I : in ICP_Type);
  pragma Inline (Use_ICP);
  --  Calls
      --  Host_Output.Enqueue_IDP
      --  Device_Handlers.Read_Temp

end Temp_Reading;

package body Temp_Reading is
  task Manage_Temperature_Reading is
    entry Use_ICP (I : in ICP_Type);
    --  Calls
        --  Create_IDP.Take_Temp_Info
  end Manage_Temperature_Reading;

  task Create_IDP is
    entry Take_Temp_Info (F : in Furnace_Type;
                          T : in Read_Time);
    --  Calls
        --  Device_Handler.Read_Temp
        --  Host_Output.Enqueue_IDP
  end Create_IDP;

  task body Manage_Temperature_Reading is separate;
  task body Create_IDP                 is separate;

  procedure Use_ICP (I : in ICP_Type) is
  begin
    Manage_Temperature_Reading.Use_ICP (I);
  end Use_ICP;

end Temp_Reading;
```

Figure 10-2. Application package: Temperature Reading.

system (see case study in Appendix A). The specification part includes an entrance procedure for the visible package interface, and the calls that are made to operations in other packages. The pragma Inline is used to make sure that only one call is made via the entrance procedure, rather than two separate calls: first to the entrance procedure, and then to the task entry.

The package body encapsulates the specification of the two tasks Manage_Temperature_Reading and Take_Temp_Info. We have deferred the design decisions of how we want to implement these tasks by using the *separate* clause for the two task bodies.

2. *Communication.* A communication-oriented package is one whose primary purpose is to provide for data transfers between the application packages. They affect the caller/called relationships of the processes that have been identified for the application packages. Communication packages are typically generic units that provide buffers, relays, and transporters (see Chapter 15). If the required packages are not already available as library units, they will be created bottom-up before the application packages are designed.

Figures 10-3, 10-4, and 10-5 include examples of a generic buffer, relay, and transporter, respectively. The package specifications contain the entrance procedures (if any), and the package bodies contain the task specifications. If the task implementation is simple, we include the task body as shown for the transporter in Figures 10-4 and 10-5. The more complicated task implementations are deferred as shown for the buffer task in Figures 10-3 and 10-4.

3. *Helper.* A helper package is one that provides a set of services to "help" an application package accomplish its function. The Helper category includes previously developed software such as executive service routines, in addition to packages that provide needed information, such as a definitions package.

The most important use of a helper package is to provide a set of services that allow us to defer detail. When we are designing the main processing modules (the application packages) to satisfy the software requirements, we should not have to pause (either logically or literally) to address minor details of how to accomplish major processing functions. Rather, we should assume the availability of "virtual machines" (see Chapter 12) that can easily accomplish the high-level functions we require. If these virtual machines are not already available, we create at least the required package specifications bottom-up before we design the application packages that will use them. The details of the virtual machines can be supplied later.

The helper category can be divided into the following subcategories:

a. *Definitions.* A definitions package is developed to provide localized machine dependencies, adaptation data, and other global constants and types required by the application

```
generic
  Size : in Natural := 20;
  type Item is private;

package Generic_Buffer is
  procedure Enqueue (I : in Item);
  procedure Dequeue (I : out Item);
  pragma Inline (Enqueue, Dequeue);
end Generic_Buffer;

package body Generic_Buffer is
  task Buffer is
    entry Enqueue (I : in Item);
    entry Dequeue (I : out Item);
  end Buffer;

  task body Buffer is separate;

  procedure Enqueue (I : in Item) is
  begin
    Buffer.Enqueue (I);
  end Enqueue;

  procedure Dequeue (I : out Item) is
  begin
    Buffer.Dequeue (I);
  end Dequeue;

end Generic_Buffer;
```

Figure 10-3. Communication package: Generic Buffer.

packages. An example of a definitions package for a track file application is shown in Figure 10-6. The package specification contains type definitions, adaptation data constants, and data structures. There is usually no package body for this type of helper package.

b. *Services.* A service package may already be available as a library package such as Text_IO for input/output functions, or a mathematics library for general mathematical functions, e.g., Sin and Cos. Other service packages may have to be developed to support the application packages, e.g., a set of graphics routines. An example of a service package is shown in Figures 10-7 and 10-8 for a track file monitor. The

```
generic
  Size : in Natural := 20;
  type Item is private;
  with procedure Consumer (C : in Item);

package Generic_Relay is
  procedure Enqueue (I : in Item);
  pragma Inline (Enqueue);
end Generic_Relay;

package body Generic_Relay is
  task Buffer is
    entry Enqueue (I : in Item);
    entry Dequeue (I : out Item);
  end Buffer;

  task Transporter is
    -- Calls
      -- Buffer.Dequeue
      -- Consumer
  end Transporter;

  task body Transporter is
    X : Item;
  begin
    loop
      Buffer.Dequeue (X);
      Consumer (X);
    end loop;
  end Transporter;

  task body Buffer is separate;

  procedure Enqueue (I : in Item) is
  begin
    Buffer.Enqueue (I);
  end Enqueue;

end Generic_Relay;
```

Figure 10-4. Communication package: Generic Relay.

operations on the track file are given in the package specification as entrance procedures. An exception to indicate that

```
generic
  type Item is private;
  with procedure Producer (P : out Item);
  with procedure Consumer (C : in  Item);

package Transporter is
end Transporter;

package body Transporter is
  task Transport_Item is
    -- Calls
      -- Producer
      -- Consumer
  end Transport_Item;

  task body Transport_Item is
    X : Item;
  begin
    loop
      Producer (X);
      Consumer (X);
    end loop;
  end Transport_Item;
end Transporter;
```

Figure 10-5. Communication package: Generic Transporter.

the track store is full is also declared here. This exception will be raised by the implementation of the operation to add a track, and must be handled by the user of this package.

The implementation of the monitor operations is shown in Figure 10-8, including the implementation of the entrance procedures. The track file is protected by a monitor task, and the entrance procedures make calls to the entries in the monitor task. Two additional tasks are specified in the package body, and all the task implementations have been deferred by using the *separate* clause.

c. *Data manager.* A data manager is developed to provide the required data type abstractions and the operations allowed for a given type. Such a manager can be further subdivided into abstract data types (ADTs) and resources [YOU82, p.119] or object managers:

```
with Calendar;  use Calendar;
package Definitions is

  type Coordinates is range -100_000 .. 100_000;
                                  -- Needed for Proximity

-- Adaptation data

  Update_Periodic          : constant Duration := 1.0;
  Display_Periodic         : constant Duration := 5.0;
  Maximum_Number_Of_Tracks : constant := 200;
  Proximity                : constant Coordinates := 1000;
  Speed                    : constant := 200;

-- Type definitions

  type Track_Count    is range 0 .. Maximum_Number_Of_Tracks;
  subtype Track_Number is Track_Count range 1 .. Track_Count'Last;

  type Track_Record is
    record
      X, Y   : Coordinates;
      Update : Time;
    end record;

  type Track_File is array (Track_Number range <>) of Track_Record;

end Definitions;
```

Figure 10-6. Helper package: Definitions.

i. *Abstract data types (type managers).* Users of an ADT allocate their own data stores, and it could be several of these data stores in a single program. ADTs may employ "open" (visible) types or use the *private* construct to create "closed" (hidden) data types. A data manager is shown in Figure 10-9 as an open ADT for a rational numbers manager. This is a type manager as opposed to the resource or object manager that is described below. The type declaration for the rational numbers is given in the package specification and is "open" to the users of the package. An object for the rational numbers is not declared either in the package specification or body; the users will declare their own objects. There

```
with Definitions;  use Definitions;
package Track_File_Monitor is

  procedure Latest_Track_File (Tracks : out Track_File;
                               Number_Of_Tracks : out Track_Count);
  procedure Add_Track     (X, Y : in Coordinates);
  procedure Update_Track (X, Y : in Coordinates;
                          Track_ID : in Track_Number);

  Track_Store_Full : exception; -- raised by Add_Track

  -- Calls
    -- Raw_Data_Buffer.Dequeue
    -- Track_Services.Update
    -- Track_Services.Correlate
    -- Track_Services.Extrapolate

end Track_File_Monitor;
```

Figure 10-7. Helper package: Services.

may be several such objects in a single program, and this is one of the primary differences from a resource or object manager. In the latter there is only a single object in a program. Another major difference is that for an ADT (type manager) the object to be manipulated must be passed as one of the parameters in the entrance procedures. This is not the case for a resource (object manager), since the object is declared within the resource package body and is hidden from the users of the package.

A data manager is shown as a *closed* ADT (type manager) in Figure 10-10. In this example the type specification for the track file is declared *private*, and its structure is hidden ("closed") from the users of the package. Another example of a closed ADT is shown for the rational numbers manager in Figure 10-11. The type for the rational numbers is declared private, as opposed to the open ADT shown in Figure 10-9, where the type structure was visible to the package users.

  ii. *Resources (object managers).* A resource provides a single data store that is shared by the users of the resource. An example of a generic resource or object manager is shown in Figure 10-3. The generic

```
package body Track_File_Monitor is

---------- Monitor -------

  task Monitor is
    entry Latest (Tracks           : out Track_File;
                  Number_Of_Tracks : out Track_Count);

    entry Add     (X, Y : in Coordinates;
                  Full : out Boolean);

    entry Update (X, Y    : in Coordinates;
                  Track_ID : in Track_Number);

    entry Correlate (X, Y : in Coordinates);

    entry Extrapolate;

    -- Calls
      -- Track_Services.Update
      -- Track_Services.Correlate
      -- Track_Services.Extrapolate
  end Monitor;


----- Extrapolation_Timer -----

  task Extrapolation_Timer is
    -- Calls
      -- Monitor.Extrapolate

    -- Delays for appropriate extrapolation interval and tells
    -- Monitor that it is time to extrapolate
  end Extrapolation_Timer;

----- Transport_Coordinates -----

  task Transport_Coordinates is
    -- Calls
      -- Raw_Data_Buffer.Dequeue
      -- Monitor.Correlate
```

Figure 10-8. Implementation of service package.

```
      -- Transports a set of coordinates from the
      -- buffer to the track file Monitor
   end Transport_Coordinates;

   task body Monitor               is separate;
   task body Extrapolation_Timer   is separate;
   task body Transport_Coordinates is separate;


----- Entrance Procedures -----


   procedure Latest_Track_File (Tracks           : out Track_File;
                                Number_Of_Tracks : out Track_Count) is
   begin
     Monitor.Latest (Tracks, Number_Of_Tracks);
   end Latest_Track_File;


   procedure Add_Track (X, Y : in Coordinates) is
     Full : Boolean;
   begin
     Monitor.Add (X, Y, Full);
     if Full then
       raise Track_Store_Full;
     end if;
   end Add_Track;


   procedure Update_Track (X, Y     : in Coordinates;
                           Track_ID : in Track_Number) is
   begin
     Monitor.Update (X, Y, Track_ID);
   end Update_Track;

end Track_File_Monitor;
```

Figure 10-8. Implementation of service package.

parameters include the size of the buffer (default value
is 20 elements) and the type of the elements to be buffered. The package specification contains the entrance
procedures, and the pragma Inline to ensure that the
calls to the entrance procedures are translated as direct

```
package Rational_Numbers is
  type Rational is
    record
      Numerator   : Integer;
      Denominator : Positive;
    end record;

  function Equal (X, Y : Rational) return Boolean;
  function "+"   (X, Y : Rational) return Rational;
  function "*"   (X, Y : Rational) return Rational;
end Rational_Numbers;

package body Rational_Numbers is
  procedure Same_Denominator (X, Y : in out Rational) is
  begin
    -- reduces X and Y to the same denominator
  end Same_Denominator;

  function Equal (X, Y : Rational) return Boolean is
    U : Rational;
    V : Rational;
  begin
    U := X;
    V := Y;
    Same_Denominator (U, V);
    return (U.Numerator = V.Numerator);
  end Equal;

  function "+" (X, Y : Rational) return Rational is ... end "+";

  function "*" (X, Y : Rational) return Rational is ... end "*";
end Rational_Numbers;
```

Figure 10-9. Data manager: open ADT.

calls to the task entries by the compiler. The package
body contains the task specification and the implementations of the entrance procedures. The task body is
declared as a stub. The implementation of the buffer
task body is shown in Figure 10-12. This implementation can be used with either the generic buffer specified
in Figure 10-3 or the generic relay specified in Figure
10-4 by furnishing the proper parent name.

```
with Definitions;  use Definitions;
package Track_Services is

    type Track_File is private;

    procedure Add (Tracks : in out Track_File;
                   X, Y   : in Coordinates);

    -- raise exception, rather than Full as parameter

    Track_File_Full : exception;


    procedure Update (Tracks       : in out Track_File;
                      X, Y         : in Coordinates;
                      Track_Number : in Track_Count);

    procedure Correlate  (Tracks : in out Track_File;
                          X, Y   : in Coordinates);

    procedure Extrapolate (Tracks : in out Track_File);

private
    -- track file is defined here,
    -- rather than in the Definitions package
end Track_Services;
```

Figure 10-10. Data manager: closed ADT.

We note in Figure 10-12 the declaration of the object Buf, which is the actual buffer. This buffer is hidden from the users, and the users do not declare their own buffer stores. We note in Figure 10-3 that the users of the generic package do not pass the buffer object as a parameter in the entrance procedures.

The example shown in Figure 10-13 illustrates how we use a private type from a closed ADT to declare an object in a user program. The specifications in the closed ADT Track_Services are imported by the *with* clause, and the object for the track file is declared as

```
Track_Storage : Track_Services.Track_File;
```

```
package Rational_Numbers is
  type Rational is private;
  function Equal (X, Y : Rational)                 return Boolean;
  function "+"   (X, Y : Rational)                 return Rational;
  function "*"   (X, Y : Rational)                 return Rational;
  function "/"   (N : Integer; D : Positive) return Rational;
private
  type Rational is
    record
      Numerator   : Integer;
      Denominator : Positive;
    end record;
end Rational_Numbers;


package body Rational_Numbers is
  procedure Same_Denominator (X, Y : in out Rational) is
  begin
    -- reduces X and Y to the same denominator
  end Same_Denominator;

  function Equal (X, Y : Rational) return Boolean is
    U : Rational;
    V : Rational;
  begin
    U := X;
    V := Y;
    Same_Denominator (U, V);
    return (U.Numerator = V.Numerator);
  end Equal;

  function "+" (X, Y : Rational) return Rational is ... end "+";

  function "*" (X, Y : Rational) return Rational is ... end "*";

  function "/" (N : Integer; D : Positive) return Rational is
    R : Rational;
  begin
    R.Numerator   := N;
    R.Denominator := D;
    return R;
  end "/";  -- to create rational numbers
end Rational_Numbers;
```

Figure 10-11. Data manager: closed ADT.

```
separate (<parent name>)

task body Buffer is
  subtype Index_Type is Positive range 1 .. Size;
  subtype Count_Type is Natural  range 0 .. Size;

  Buf    : array (Index_Type) of Item;
  Insert : Index_Type := 1;
  Remove : Index_Type := 1;
  Count  : Count_Type := 0;
begin
  loop
    select
      when Count < Size =>
        accept Enqueue (I : in Item) do
          Buf (Insert) := I;
        end Enqueue;
        Insert := (Insert mod Buf'Last) + 1;
        Count  := Count + 1;

    or
      when Count > 0 =>
        accept Dequeue (I : out Item) do
          I := Buf (Remove);
        end Dequeue;
        Remove := (Remove mod Buf'Last) + 1;
        Count  := Count - 1;
    or
      terminate;
    end select;
  end loop;
end Buffer;
```

Figure 10-12. Resource (object manager): Generic Buffer implementation.

The example shown in Figure 10-14 shows how we import
the services of various helper and other application packages, and how we can handle an exception raised in one of
the helper packages (the design aspects of exception handling will be discussed in detail in Chapter 18).

```
with Track_Services;  use Track_Services;
separate (Track_File_Monitor)
  task body Monitor is

   Track_Storage : Track_Services.Track_File;

  begin
    loop
      select
        accept Latest (Tracks : out Track_File) do
          Tracks := Track_Storage;
        end Latest;
      or
        accept Add (X, Y : in Coordinates;
                    Full : out Boolean) do

          Handle_Track_Store_Full:
          begin

            Track_Services.Add (Track_Storage, X, Y);
            Full := False;

          exception
            when Track_Services.Track_Store_Full =>
              Full := True;
          end Handle_Track_Store_Full;

        end Add;
      or
        accept Update (X, Y : in Coordinates;
                       Track_ID : in Track_Number) do
          Track_Services.Update (Track_Storage, X, Y, Track_ID);
        end Update;
      or
        accept Correlate (X, Y : in Coordinates) do
          Track_Services.Correlate (Track_Storage, X, Y);
        end Correlate;
      or
        accept Extrapolate do
          Track_Services.Extrapolate (Track_Storage);
        end Extrapolate;
      end select;
    end loop;
  end Monitor;
```

Figure 10-13. Using a private type from a closed ADT (Track_Services).

Our taxonomy addresses specifically the design of large real-time systems. A taxonomy of reusable software components, based on packages and generics, has been proposed by Booch [BOO87].

10.4 Packaging Rules

A set of heuristics can be used as an aid in creating application packages. The first five rules listed below apply to how a task or group of tasks should be packaged. The last two apply to packaging in general.

1. *Encapsulation module.* Tasks can reside in subprograms, tasks, and packages. Nesting of tasks is not recommended, since the debugging process can be extremely complex. This leaves us the choice between placing tasks in packages or subprograms. The only tasks recommended for placement within a subprogram are tasks used as simulators or for special debugging purposes. These tasks should then be placed in the main procedure for maximum control of the debugging process. The recommended placement of tasks is within packages, unless a specification requirement makes it mandatory to put a task within a subprogram.

2. *Functionality.* Tasks can be grouped within the same package if their functionalities are related.

3. *Reusability.* Special purpose tasks, e.g., buffers, transporters, and relays, that can be used by several units within the program (or by other programs) should be placed in packages as library units. These packages should be generic, if possible, for maximum reusability.

4. *Coupling.* Tasks should be placed in packages such that the coupling is minimized with respect to data types, operations, and constants that are imported from the encapsulating package. The issue of task coupling is further discussed in Chapter 13.

5. *Visibility.* The package structure should provide for minimum visibility of task entries. Task specifications should be hidden in package bodies, and entrance procedures provided for interactions between tasks that reside in different packages. Special considerations must be given to whether entrance procedures should handle conditional or timed entry calls, or if the task specification should be moved to the package specification to provide these services directly.

```
package Operator_Interface
  -- Calls
    -- External_Devices.Get_Data_From_Operator
    -- Track_File_Monitor.Add_Track
    -- Track_File_Monitor.Update_Track
end Operator_Interface;

package body Operator_Interface is
  task Interface is
    -- Calls
      -- External_Devices.Get_Data_From_Operator
      -- Track_File_Monitor.Add_Track
      -- Track_File_Monitor.Update_Track
  end Interface;

  task body Interface is separate;

end Operator_Interface;



with Definitions;  use Definitions;
with Text_IO;       use Text_IO;
with Track_File_Monitor;
with External_Devices;

separate (Operator_Interface)
  task body Interface is
    X, Y : Coordinates;
    Track_ID : Track_Number;
    Add_Track_Indicator : constant Track_Number := 0;
  begin
    Interface_With_Operator:
    loop
      Handle_Track_Store_Full:
      begin
        External_Devices.Get_Data_From_Operator (X, Y, Track_ID);

        if Track_ID = Add_Track_Indicator then
          Track_File_Monitor.Add_Track (X, Y);
        else
          Track_File_Monitor.Update_Track (X, Y, Track_ID);
        end if;
```

Figure 10-14. Application package making use of helper and other application packages.

```
exception
  when Track_File_Monitor.Track_Store_Full =>
    Put_Line ("Track store full.");
  end Handle_Track_Store_Full;
 end loop Interface_With_Operator;
end Interface;
```

Figure 10-14 (continued). Application package making use of helper and other application packages.

6. *Dependency.* The chosen package structure should result in a minimum dependency (use of *with* clauses) between the packages. It is desirable to confine *with*ing to package bodies, rather than package specifications.

7. *Recompilation.* The chosen package structure should result in a minimum amount of recompilation when any of the packages are changed. This is closely associated with the dependency issue described above. Minimum recompilation will occur when the required *with*ing is performed by the subunits (for tasks or subprograms) rather than by the package specification or body that encapsulate the tasks or subprograms.

8. *Object orientation.* Every effort should be made to construct application packages that represent *objects* of the type described in Chapters 5 and 12.

9. *Data stores.* A data store that appears on a DFD should be protected by a monitor task which is encapsulated in a package.

11

Generics

Generic packages and subprograms in Ada are used as templates from which programs of similar functionality can be constructed. These templates are written only once, but are used repeatedly by each program that needs a specific kind of functionality. Examples of generic functions include queueing, sorting, message handling, and finding roots of various mathematical functions. The advantages of using generics in Ada include (1) a higher probability of correctness—there is less code to write and test; and (2) easier maintenance—changes are made only in the generic units rather than throughout the program. The new instantiations are automatically created when the program is recompiled.

There is even the potential for more compact source code when we use generics. An algorithm such as a "swap" routine for different types of objects may be instantiated, for example, for type Color and type Integer. It is likely that an optimizing compiler will recognize that the underlying representations of the types are identical and therefore use the same code body.

The most promising design implications for creating generic units are the areas of reusability and extendibility. Reusable software, in the form of generic packages or subroutines, is obtained from an Ada library and instantiated with the proper actual generic parameters in the application program being designed. An ideal design situation would be to construct our whole application program from generic units, similar to the way hardware is designed. Extendibility pertains to the ease with which software can be modified to reflect changes in the requirements. Generic Ada units can be extended by making the necessary modifications and replacing the old library units with the modified units. The old application programs that use the generic units will have to be recompiled. The instantiations need not be modified, unless the generic parameters have been changed. Another design implication of using generics is that our methodology will not be strictly top-down. The generic units must be in the Ada library before we can instantiate them in our application programs. Generic units for a given application program will be created bottom-up, before we proceed top-down with the application program that instantiates them.

The following paragraphs do not describe the detailed programming syntax and semantics of Ada generics. The emphasis in this chapter is on how to recognize generic functions in a preliminary design, how to construct Ada generic programs, and restrictions that apply to the parameters used. Details of the syntax and semantics of Ada generics can be found in the LRM [DOD83] and in texts such as References YOU82, BOO83, BAR84, and SHU84.

11.1   Generic Functionality

The primary purpose of identifying generic functions is to construct general purpose library units that can be used by any program that needs a function that is similar to the one encapsulated in the generic unit. This almost always involves the specification of a pattern (or template) of an algorithm for dealing with entities that are similar but different. The user program simply provides a set of actual parameters and the generic templates are instantiated at compile time. A general rule to follow when trying to recognize generic functionality is that every instance of a specific problem is identifiable with a small set of parameters.

The following criteria can be used to recognize generic functions in a preliminary design:

1. *Similar purpose.* If the purpose is, for example, to sort an array, a single algorithm can be constructed to sort arrays of integers, floating point values, records, etc. A generic sorting routine can be constructed to handle a multitude of sorting requirements of a similar kind for different data types. Other examples of functions with a similar purpose include handling of variable-length

messages, determining roots of mathematical functions, providing queueing mechanisms for buffers with different size and element types, and providing input/output routines for different data types. Examples of generic units for functions of similar purpose are illustrated below, and are further discussed in Section 11.2 with regard to the kind of parameters used. An attempt to classify software components in terms of data abstractions has been made by Booch [BOO87].

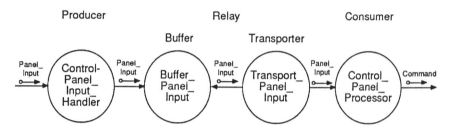

Figure 11-1. Buffer-Transporter intermediary.

2. *Intermediaries.* Intermediaries used as buffers, transporters, and relays (see Chapter 15) represent general purpose functions and can be implemented as generic library units. An example of such an intermediary is a combination of a buffer and transporter task placed between a producer/consumer pair as shown in the Ada task graph in Figure 11-1. The producer (Control_Panel_Input_Handler) and the consumer (Control_Panel_Processor) need to operate asynchronously and have been uncoupled by introducing a buffer-transporter intermediary (constituting a relay) between them. The buffer acts as a pure server. It receives panel inputs from the producer and passes them to the transporter when the transporter makes a request. This allows the producer to accept panel input via interrupts and to pass them on to the buffer without waiting for any processing of the input to be done by the consumer. The transporter is a pure caller. It first calls the buffer for more panel input. If none is available, it waits until the buffer has received the next input from the producer. After the transporter has received the panel input, it passes it on by calling the consumer. The consumer processes the input at its own speed, independent of the rate at which it comes from the producer.

The generic buffer-transporter unit is shown in Figure 10-4. There are three generic parameters provided: "Size" for the length of the buffer, "Item" for the type of elements to be buffered, and the procedure "Consumer" which will be called by the transporter. The generic package (Generic_Relay) specification contains only the procedure Enqueue which is an entrance procedure. The package body contains the specification of the buffer task and the transporter task, and the task body of the transporter. The details of the buffer task have been deferred by using the *separate* statement and are supplied later as the subunit shown in Figure 10-12 (by providing Generic_Relay for the parent name). The following instantiation:

```
package CP_Relay is new Generic_Relay
   (Size    => 56,
    Item    => Character,
    Consumer => CP_Processor.Take_CP_Input);
```

is for buffering of 56 characters that will be sent to the consumer CP_Processor.Take_CP_Input.

The generic package Generic_Relay can be used to uncouple any producer/consumer pair of processes by instantiating with an appropriate set of actual parameters for "Size," "Item," and "Consumer." Various combinations of intermediaries (buffers, transporters, and relays) can be identified during preliminary design and translated into appropriate general purpose generic units (see Chapter 15).

11.2 Constructing Generic Units

The construction of generic units depends upon the parameters required to instantiate the library templates. Allowable parameters include data values and objects, data types, and subprograms. Generic program units are limited to packages and subprograms. Generic tasks are not allowed. A generic program unit is created in the same way as non-generic packages, and subprograms are created except that the reserved word *generic* followed by the formal parameters precede the specification part.

Special care is needed in the creation of generic units in order to restrict the operations to those applicable to the type of the generic parameters. For example, if we have:

```
type Index is (< >);
```

then incrementing objects of type Index must not use "+", but rather Index'Succ, since the type is discrete. Part of the art of writing generic units is to make the minimum essential assumptions in the unit's body, in order to make the unit as broadly applicable as possible.

After the data abstractions have been determined for a generic application, we have to decide whether the operations should be encapsulated in a package, or if a single subprogram will suffice. The next step is to determine the appropriate generic parameters. In the example shown in Figure 11-2 we decided that the operations required to manipulate a stack include "Pop" and "Push" and that these operations should be encapsulated in a package rather than in two separate generic procedures. We thereby encapsulate (or hide) the data structure along with the procedures that operate on it. This creates an abstract data type of the form *object manager* or *resource* as described in Chapter 10. The parameters required to make this a general purpose package are the size of the stack and the type of the elements that will belong to the stack. The instantiations shown in Figure 11-2 illustrate the use of this generic package for a stack of integers and of boolean values. It can also be instantiated for any user-defined type. The instantiation shown in (a) uses "positional" notation for the actual parameters, whereas (b) uses "named association."

The three different kinds of parameters that are used to construct generic units—objects, types, and subprograms—are discussed below.

11.2.1 Generic Object Parameters

Data objects can be declared as generic parameters similar to ordinary subprogram parameters, but the mode can only be either *in* or *in out*. Generic object parameters cannot have the mode *out*. An *in* parameter acts as a constant whose value is provided by the actual parameter during instantiation. This is illustrated by "Size" as shown in Figure 11-2. The value of "Size" is provided as shown in the instantiations to be 200 and 100 for integer and boolean types, respectively. This is the default mode for generic object parameters, and *in* can be omitted just as for subprogram parameters. An *in* parameter cannot be of limited private type since assignment is not allowed for this type, and the mechanism of giving the value to the generic parameter is treated as assignment. This is different from using *in* parameters in subprograms where limited types are allowed.

An example of an *in out* generic object parameter is shown in Figure 11-3. "Counter" acts as a variable renaming the corresponding actual parameter, i.e., "Calls" for the instantiations given in the same figure. The generic function allows us to count the number of times the Sin or Cos functions are called without modifying these

```
generic
  Size : Positive;
  type Item is private;

package Stack is
  procedure Push (E : in Item);
  procedure Pop  (E : out Item);
  Overflow  : exception;  -- raised in Push
  Underflow : exception;  -- raised in Pop
end Stack;

package body Stack is
  Space : array (1 .. Size) of Item;
  Index : Integer range 0 .. Size := 0;

  procedure Push (E : in Item) is
  begin
    if Index = Size then
      raise Overflow;
    end if;
    Index := Index + 1;
    Space (Index) := E;
  end Push;

  procedure Pop (E : out Item) is
  begin
    if Index = 0 then
      raise Underflow;
    end if;
    E := Space (Index);
    Index := Index - 1;
  end Pop;

end Stack;
```

Instantiations:

a. package Int_Stack is new Stack (200, Integer);

b. package Boolean_Stack is
           new Stack (Size => 100, Item => Boolean);

Figure 11-2. Generic stack package.

```
generic
  type Domain is limited private;
  with function F (X : Domain) return Domain;
  Counter : in out Integer;

function Instrument (X : Domain) return Domain;

function Instrument (X : Domain) return Domain is
begin
  Counter := Counter + 1;
  return F (X);
end Instrument;



with Instrument;
with Math_Pack; -- defines Sin and Cos

procedure Compute is
  Calls : Integer := 0; -- number of calls

  function Sin is
          new Instrument (Float, Math_Pack.Sin, Calls);

  function Cos is
          new Instrument (Float, Math_Pack.Cos, Calls);

begin

  -- A very large number of calls
  -- to Sin and Cos.
  -- Print message for number of calls

end Compute;
```

Figure 11-3. Generic object parameter of *in out* mode.

functions and without creating a global variable that could be updated from every place the functions were invoked (this would require lots of additional code).

```
generic
  type Object is private;

  procedure Exchange (X, Y : in out Object);

  procedure Exchange (X, Y : in out Object) is
    Temp : Object;
  begin
    Temp := X;
    X    := Y;
    Y    := Temp;
  end Exchange;



  Instantiations:

    a.  procedure Swap is new Exchange (Float);

    b.  procedure Swap is new Exchange (Color);

    c.  procedure Swap is new Exchange (Tracks);
```

Figure 11-4. Generic swap procedure.

11.2.2 Generic Type Parameters

In the example shown in Figure 11-2, the type of elements on the stack—"Item"—is a generic type parameter. The instantiations shown in the same figure illustrate the use of the actual parameters "Integer" and "Boolean" for the elements that belong to the two stacks. In Figure 11-3, "Domain" is a type parameter that is used in the generic function "Instrument" and is instantiated with the actual parameter "Float." Another example is shown in Figure 11-4, where "Object" is a formal generic type parameter and the three instantiations include the actual parameters "Float," "Color," and "Tracks" for the respective types of the objects that need to be exchanged. A complete set of different types that can be used as generic parameters include the following:

```
type T is
  limited private;      -- No operations
  private;              -- Assignment and equality comparison
  (< >);                -- Operations for discrete types
  range < >;            -- Integer types
  delta < >;            -- Fixed point types
```

```
digits < >;            -- Floating point types
access;                -- Access (pointer) types
array (Index) of Item; -- Array types
```

Type checking is performed by the compiler, and attributes and operations must correspond for actual and formal parameters. Binding of generic parameters take place at compile time as opposed to subprogram parameters, which are bound at run-time. A generic formal parameter may depend upon a previously declared formal parameter which is also a type. This is illustrated in Figure 11-5 for a generic array type. The "Index" parameter is used to specify the size of the array, and the "Floating" parameter to specify the elements in the array. The index type of the actual array type parameter (Integer Vector and Day Vector) must be consistent with the actual parameter for the (formal) "Index."

```
generic

  type Index is (< >);
  type Floating is digits < >;
  type Vector is array (Index range < >) of Floating;

function Sum (S : Vector) return Floating;

function Sum (S : Vector) return Floating is
  Result : Floating := 0;
begin
  for I in S'Range loop
    Result := Result + S(I);
  end loop;
  return Result;
end Sum;


  Instantiation:

    a.  function Sum_Vector is new Sum (Integer, Real, Vector);

    b.  function Sum_Vector is new Sum (Day, Real, Vector);
```

Figure 11-5. Generic type parameter dependency.

11.2.3 Generic Subprogram Parameters

Subprograms in Ada cannot be passed as parameters (in subprograms) at execution time, but they can be passed as generic parameters. Passing subprograms is sometimes useful in mathematical applications. In the example illustrated in Figure 11-3, "Math_Pack.Sin" and "Math_Pack.Cos" are passed as actual parameters in the instantiations shown. These parameters replace the generic function "F" that is used inside the generic function "Instrument."

A generic subprogram parameter is specified by preceding the subprogram specification with the reserved word *with*. Note that this is a different usage of *with* from the one employed to import library units.

```
generic
  type Item is private;
  type Index is (< >);
  type Vector is array (Index range < >) of Item;
  with function "<" (X, Y : Item) return Boolean;

procedure Quicksort (V : in out Vector);


  Instantiation:

    function "<" (L, R : String) return Boolean is
    begin
      -- user defined
      return ... ;
    end "<";

    procedure String_Sort is new
        Quicksort (Character, Natural, String, "<");

  Name : String (1 .. 5) := "Byron";

  String_Sort (Name);
```

Figure 11-6. Operator as generic parameter.

Another use of passing subprograms as parameters is to supply operations that are performed on objects of a certain type inside generic subprograms. The example shown in Figure 11-6 represents a generic specification of a *quicksort* procedure. The private type

"Item" is augmented by the "<" operator supplied as a generic formal parameter in order to provide the meaning of "less than." To instantiate the generic procedure, three type names and the "<" operator must be supplied as actual parameters. The instantiation shown is for sorting a string of characters with the user defined comparator "<". The object declaration is for a string of length 5, and the call to "String_Sort" will sort "Name" in ascending order.

Generic subprogram parameters can be specified with a default for the actual subprogram. If the actual parameter is omitted in the instantiation, the default subprogram is used inside the generic unit. The default can be specified with a box ("< >"), having the effect that a default subprogram must be visible at the point of instantiation. Both the name and specification of the default subprogram must match those of the generic formal parameter. The instantiation shown in the first example in Figure 11-7 has the effect of specifying the (default) predefined operator "<" for a "String" type.

In the second example the default subprogram parameter is specified with a name rather than with a box. The named subprogram must be visible at the point of declaration in the generic unit, and must have parameters and modes corresponding to those of the generic formal subprogram parameter. The instantiation shown in the second example has the effect that the library unit "Increment" is used as the default procedure for "Step." Note the two uses of *with* in this example: "with Increment;" is used to import the library unit, and "with procedure Step ...;" is used to specify the generic formal subprogram parameter.

11.2.4 Generic Parameter Restrictions

Certain restrictions apply to generic parameters as follows:

1. *Object parameters.* The only modes permitted are *in* and *in out.* Object parameters with *out* mode are not permitted. An *in* generic parameter can not be of a limited private type since assignment is not allowed for this type.

2. *Type parameters.* Type parameters are restricted to the classes listed above in Section 11.2.2. The generic discrete type (< >) includes any integer type, but excludes all the arithmetic operations that are specific to integers since the formal parameter may be an enumeration type.

   For array types the actual parameters supplied with an instantiation must satisfy certain matching rules:

a.
```
generic
   type Item is private;
   type Index is (< >);
   type Vector is array (Index range < >) of Item;
   with function "<" (X, Y : Item) return Boolean is < >;

procedure Quicksort (V : in out Vector);

   Instantiation:

      procedure String_Sort is
         new Quicksort (Character, Natural, String);
```

b.
```
with Increment;
generic
   with procedure Step (X : in out Integer) is Increment;

procedure Use_Step (Y : in out Integer);

procedure Use_Step (Y : in out Integer) is
begin
   . . .
   Step (Y);
   . . .
end Use_Step;


   Instantiation:

   procedure New_Step is new Use_Step;
```

Figure 11-7. Default subprogram parameters.

a. The actual and formal arrays must have the same dimensions.

b. The index and component types must be the same.

c. If the formal array type is unconstrained, the actual type must also be unconstrained. Constraints on the actual parameter apply to the formal as well, but constraints implied by the formal type mark are ignored.

If the generic type parameter is declared as a private type, the only operations available on objects of that type are assignment and comparison for equality or inequality. If the generic type is declared as *limited private*, then no operations are available for objects of that type. The actual parameters for a limited private type may be any type except an unconstrained array type.

An actual generic parameter may be a subtype, but an explicit constraint is not allowed. The actual parameter is restricted to being a type mark and cannot be a subtype indication.

Formal generic record types and task types are not allowed. This is to enhance the matching capability of the compiler. The internal structure of records is somewhat arbitrary and it would be difficult to perform matching between the actual and formal generic parameters. The matching of formal and actual task types would be even more involved than for record types.

3. *Subprogram parameters.* Actual and formal generic subprogram parameters must satisfy the same matching rules as for renaming [BAR84, pp. 117, 205]. Any constraints implied by the actual parameter are imposed on the formal, but any constraints implied by the formal subprogram are ignored.

If default declarations [BAR84, p. 206] are used with the formal subprogram parameters, the subprogram itself must not have any parameters that depend on the formal types preceding the declaration. The default subprogram can, however, be an attribute:

```
with function Next (X : T) is T'Succ;
```

A restriction that applies to generic parameters in general is that a formal generic parameter cannot be used in places where an expression has to be static. Examples of this kind of expression include alternatives in a case statement or variant, the range in an integer type definition, and the number of digits in a floating type definition.

The same restrictions apply to the mixing of named association and positional notation for actual generic parameters as for actual subprogram parameters. If a parameter is omitted (a default is specified in the generic unit), subsequent parameters must be listed using named association only.

11.2.5   Exception Handling

Generic units are written as general, reusable software components. The designers of these units do not know a priori all the different ways in which the components will be used and must provide a measure of protection against operations that are not allowed. These operations could include removing an item from an empty stack or queue, pushing an item onto a full stack, or adding an item to a full queue. Undefined operations should be accounted for by declaring exceptions in the specification part that is visible to the users. Appropriate comments should be included to describe the nature of the exceptions and where they are raised.

The users of the generic components must include the necessary exception handlers and take appropriate action if an undefined operation is attempted. The generic stack package shown in Figure 11-2 includes the two exceptions Overflow and Underflow, with comments indicating where the exceptions are raised. The users of this stack package must include the appropriate exception handlers for the two declared exceptions.

12

Decomposing Large Tasks

We described the general concepts of virtual machines and objects in the context of programming-in-the-large in Chapter 5. In Chapter 6 we demonstrated how we use process abstraction to create a set of cooperating sequential processes as a model solution for a large real-time system. These processes represent a top layer of virtual machines that will execute in parallel as Ada tasks. In this chapter we describe the design principles that apply to the decomposition of large Ada tasks into a set of virtual machines and objects that perform the sequential execution within each task. This also applies to a large sequential program that is not inherently concurrent. We can simply consider the complete program as a single, large Ada task.

12.1 Virtual Machines (Functional Abstraction)

A virtual machine in the form of an Ada task is a sequence of abstract, high-level instructions that solve a problem that corresponds to a set of specified requirements. The machine should solve the problem in a simple, straightforward manner, minimizing both data manipulation and data flow between parts of the machine. Its logical complexity should be low and its "instruction set" should be simple. Virtual machines allow for a hierarchical decomposition of the problem based on functional abstraction.

In order to design a complex program, we cannot simply start at the beginning and specify every step to be accomplished at the level of detail allowed by current programming languages. We would have to sequentially specify thousands of instructions. In a concurrent system, we would have to specify the interactions of simultaneous sequences of such instructions. This is nearly impossible; we would simply get lost in the detail. Instead, we like to think about abstract processing steps that at the first level of decomposition of the problem are closely related to the problem to be solved. For an air traffic control application, for example, an important element is the track file, the storage for the location, velocity, and identification of all aircraft being controlled. For this application, we might think of steps such as the following:

1. Determine the number of aircraft in this sector.

2. Correlate tracks with other aircraft in the track file.

3. Determine new course to avoid collision.

These steps are abstractions of the processing, ignoring or deferring the details of how the abstract steps are to be implemented. If we had a machine that could directly execute such instructions, our problem would be easy to solve!

We do not have such an actual machine, however, so our task is to create such a machine. The instructions of this first-level virtual machine may be very complex. Therefore, in the implementation of the individual instructions of the virtual machine, we reapply the same principle of envisioning a (now lower level) virtual machine. For example, to create the instruction "correlate tracks with other aircraft in the track file," we might have a lower level virtual machine with instructions such as:

1. Obtain the next track from the track file.

2. Determine the distance between the track from the track file and the new track.

3. Place the new track into the track file as a separate entry.

We would, as necessary, reapply the same notion to construct yet lower level virtual machines—hence layered virtual machines.

Some of the instructions of the virtual machines that we are building have a special characteristic; they are related to a data structure and provide operations on the data structure. For example, the instructions "obtain the next track from the track file" and "place the new track into the track file as a separate entry" operate on the track file data structure. The instructions are providing a service—operations on the track file.

In order to allow the virtual machine to deal with abstract data, it is important to hide the actual implementation of the methods for storing the track file, exporting only the operations on the track file. This is accomplished by encapsulating the data structure (the track file) together with the operations (the "instructions" noted above) that manipulate the data structure. This creates a track file object. The details of how the object manipulates the data structure are hidden from the virtual machine.

The creation of the virtual machine thus makes use of the operations of the object. In fact, it is often the needs of the various virtual machines in a system that dictate the operations that will be defined on the object. It is this interaction between the virtual machine and object that leads to a *parallel concern* with virtual machines and objects.

12.2   Objects (Data Abstraction)

An object provides the set of operations necessary to manipulate a data structure. The operations are determined by the application, although certain data structures will always have some general purpose operations. For example, a track file will have a correlate operation (application-specific), while a stack will always have push and pop operations (general purpose). The operations are visible; the data structure is hidden.

Objects allow for a hierarchical decomposition of the problem based on data abstraction. They allow the virtual machines to operate on abstract data, thereby narrowing attention to the problem to be solved.

An object may operate on a data structure as simple as a queue, a first-in–first-out linear list. The operations would be insert and remove. It might operate on a priority ordered linear list, with the same operations but more complex internal processing. Or it might operate on some very complex data structure or provide complex operations on the elements of the data structure.

The processing necessary to correlate a track in a track file, or insert a value in a semi-balanced tree in priority order, may be very complex. How are such operations on an object designed and constructed? By using the methods of layered virtual machines, specifying the abstract functional steps to solve the problem. This is exactly the use of a virtual machine. Here the problem to be solved is to correlate the track, or insert while keeping the tree balanced.

An object may make use of a lower level object. For example, a simulation program may have an event list, with typical operations of "insert event" and "get next event." The event list will be ordered by time (typically as a linked list), with a number of different events scheduled (in priority order) at any given time. It may well be desirable, when designing the mechanism for handling access to events by time order, to ignore (abstract away, or defer) the detail of how events are handled and stored by priority order. The mechanism for doing so is to construct an object that operates on a (hidden) data structure for events in priority order. Then the (concrete) implementation of the (abstract) data structure of the event list depends upon an abstract viewpoint of a prioritized list. We thus see that there is a layering of abstract objects as well as a layering of virtual machines.

12.3   Virtual Machine and Object Interactions

Designing software involves a parallel concern with algorithms and data structures. The design of the objects and the virtual machines are largely independent. When we are concerned with the functional processing of the system, we should not be concerned with the details of data structures. We should be concerned with the steps taken to meet the program requirements.

When we are designing data structures and operations, we need not be concerned with how they will be used. We should be concerned with localization of operations on the data and the completeness and consistency of the set of operations. However, there is an important manner in which the virtual machines and the objects are intimately linked: the needs of the virtual machine may dictate operations of the object. As we first design an object, we attempt to anticipate the likely uses (operations) of the object. But as we further refine our virtual machines, we will often discover other operations required, or uncover timing issues that may influence the characteristics of the hidden data structure—hence parallel consideration of virtual machines and objects.

12.4   Graphics

The use of graphics is important to the development of designs. The process of documenting a design, and having it reviewed by others, is an important component of the design process for large systems. Since virtual machines represent the steps to be accomplished to solve the problem, structure charts are an effective representation of the interactions between higher and lower level machines. Each module in a structure chart tree (except the leaves) is implemented by a lower level virtual machine.

Objects and their interactions are effectively shown with object oriented design (OOD) diagrams, with the operations of the object being the exported subprograms of the object.

12.5 Summary

Virtual machines and objects provide a mechanism for the decomposition of large tasks or inherently sequential systems. Appendix B is a tutorial case study amplifying these ideas and illustrating the use of graphics. Appendix C applies the ideas to a simplified version of a real programming problem, applying our standard approach of using top-level and detailed design PDL.

The use of structure charts and OOD diagrams as design tools was described in Chapter 7. The functional abstraction is represented graphically by the structure chart, and the data abstraction by the OOD diagram, as shown in Figure 12-1. The hierarchical structure of virtual machines shown in Figure 12-2 illustrates the layers of instruction sets (functional abstractions) that solve the problem. In the same figure we also note how an object (data abstraction) makes use of a lower level object to perform its function.

Functional Abstraction	Data Abstraction
Algorithms <u>VIRTUAL MACHINE</u> • Steps to solve problem • Layered, using lower-level machines and objects 	Algorithms may make use of data abstractions.
Data Structures Complex operations on data structures may be implemented through use of functional abstraction.	<u>OBJECT</u> • Operations on an object • Structure of data is hidden • Layered, using lower-level machines and objects

Figure 12-1. Two forms of abstraction.

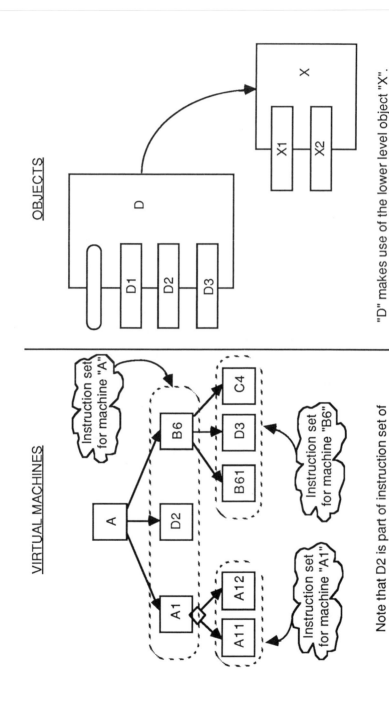

OBJECTS

D

D1

D2

D3

X

X1

X2

"D" makes use of the lower level object "X". For example, D2 may call X1 (in addition to internal subprograms).

VIRTUAL MACHINES

Instruction set for machine "A"

A

A1

D2

B6

A11

A12

B61

D3

C4

Instruction set for machine "B6"

Instruction set for machine "A1"

Note that D2 is part of instruction set of machine "A". It is treated as a primitive -- not further partitioned.

Figure 12-2. Virtual machines and objects.

13

Coupling and Cohesion

The traditional concepts of coupling and cohesion [YOU79, PAG80] have been used extensively with structured design methods to provide a guideline for creating good software designs. In this chapter we expand the traditional concepts to include coupling and cohesion for Ada tasks and packages and apply the expanded concepts to the design of Ada real-time systems.

13.1 General

A generally accepted paradigm for good design is that strong cohesion (internal binding) within individual modules promotes low coupling, tends to minimize the rippling effect that can occur when modifications are made to a module, and promotes high maintainability [PAG80, DEM78, YOU79]. It also supports a high degree of modularity by isolating functionality and data abstractions to individual software modules.

The discussion that follows includes a brief review of coupling and cohesion as they are used in structured design, and how these concepts should be modified or extended to account for the Ada programming constructs.

13.2 Coupling

The level of coupling between modules can be evaluated from good to bad as follows (see [PAG80, or YOU79] for details):

1. *Data coupling.* Data is passed by parameters only.

2. *Stamp coupling.* Data structures are passed as parameters, even though a module may only need a single component of the structure.

3. *Control coupling.* The internal logic of a module is controlled by a flag passed to it by another module.

4. *Common coupling.* Two or more modules refer to the same global data area.

5. *Content (pathological) coupling.* One module alters statements or data within another module.

These measures of coupling apply to modules as defined in [MYE78]; a module is a set of executable program statements that satisfies the following three criteria:

1. It is a closed subroutine.

2. It has the potential of being called by any other module in the program.

3. It has the potential of being separately compiled.

The programming constructs in Ada that are used to create software components are subprograms (procedures and functions), tasks, and packages. These units can have separate specification and body components which add to the complexity of evaluating Ada constructs (with regard to coupling) within the narrow module definition given above.

13.2.1 Ada Subprograms

Non-nested subprograms can be considered modules, but nested subprograms are not, since they cannot be called from any other module in the program. Subprograms declared in a package body are not modules, since they are not visible to other modules. The traditional coupling concepts can thus be applied to Ada subprograms.

13.2.2 Ada Tasks

Tasks are not callable, only task entries can be called by other modules. This implies that the set of instructions executed within an Ada rendezvous might be considered a module. This set of instructions cannot, however, be separately compiled, and it does not satisfy the strict module definition. It would be useful to be able to evaluate a concurrent design in terms of interdependencies between tasks, but the traditional coupling concepts and module definitions are inadequate for this purpose, and the coupling concept will have to be extended to specifically include Ada tasks.

By relaxing the strict definition of a module to include Ada tasks, we can consider coupling at two levels: (1) between subprograms and tasks and (2) strictly between tasks. Coupling between subprograms and tasks (subprograms calling task entries or tasks calling subprograms) can be evaluated with the traditional concepts used for modules. One exception might be common coupling which is a poor, but still acceptable, form for coupling in structured design. In a concurrent design, the use of shared, unprotected, data may produce an erroneous program and is not acceptable. Subprograms in Ada tasks should not have direct access to common (shared) data and must access the data via a protecting task:

```
task Protect is
  entry Read  (I : out Item);
  entry Write (I : in Item);
end Protect;

task body Protect is
  Shared : Item := Initial_Value;
begin
  loop
    select
      accept Write (I : in Item) do
        Shared := I;
      end Write;
    or
      accept Read (I : out Item) do
        I := Shared;
      end Read;
    or
      terminate;
    end select;
  end loop;
end Protect;
```

This example shows the use of a protective task to provide the required mutual exclusion for the common data ("Shared") to prevent erroneous programming, and does not represent common coupling as applied to structured design.

The overall coupling between a set of tasks can be evaluated by introducing a new term: concurrency coupling. This type of coupling does not fit in the hierarchy between data and content coupling (listed above) since it does not apply to a pair of tasks, but, rather, to a set of tasks:

- *Concurrency coupling.* A concurrent system is loosely coupled if the task interactions are well balanced in terms of caller/called decisions, and the use of intermediary tasks [BUH84, HIL82, PYL85]; cyclic task dependencies have been eliminated; polling used is desirable [GEH84]; the amount of busy wait has been minimized; instructions within the rendezvous have been minimized; and appropriate modes have been used for the parameters passed.

Concurrency coupling can include both tightly coupled and loosely coupled pairs of tasks:

1. *Tightly coupled.* Ada tasks are tightly coupled through the rendezvous mechanism with various degrees of tightness:

   a. The least amount of coupling in a rendezvous is where a task calls a parameterless entry to signal a specific event. The caller in this case does not wait for a reply, and the accept body does not contain any executable statements:

   ```
   task Accept_Signal is
     entry Start;
     entry Stop;
   end Accept_Signal;
   ```

```
task body Accept_Signal is
begin
  loop
    select
      accept Start;
      -- other statements
    or
      accept Stop;
      -- other statements
    or
      terminate;
    end select;
  end loop;
end Accept_Signal;
```

b. A slightly higher amount of coupling during a rendezvous is
   where a task calls an entry with *in* or *out* parameters only.
   The accept body contains only the necessary instructions to
   read or copy the *in* or *out* parameter(s):

```
. . .
accept Write (I : in Item) do
  Shared := I;
end Write;
. . .
accept Read (I : out Item) do
  I := Shared;
end Read;
. . .
```

c. The tightest coupling during a rendezvous occurs where a
   task calls an entry with *in out* or *in* and *out* parameters. In
   this case the caller is expecting a reply and the rendezvous
   will last until the required actions have been taken in the
   accept body to determine values for the *in out* or *in* and *out*
   parameters:

```
task Tracker is
  entry Init (I : in Track_Info);
  entry Read (T : in Track_Id; I : out Track_Info);
  entry Change (T : in    Track_Id;
                I : in out Track_Info);
end Tracker;
```

```
task body Tracker is
  Data : Track_Info;
begin
  . . .
  accept Change (T : in     Track_Id;
                 I : in out Track_Info) do
    -- Use T to locate the correct Track.
    -- Calculate new track info based on
    -- input track info.
    -- Return new track info to caller.
  end Change;
  . . .
end Tracker;
```

2. *Loosely coupled.* Any number of intermediary tasks can be created between a pair of producer and consumer tasks to uncouple this pair. Intermediary tasks can be used in various combinations, with a typical combination being a buffer/transporter (see Chapter 15). Examples of intermediary tasks are:

   a. *Buffer task.* This is strictly a server task with entries to store items (typically in a queue) as they are received from the producer, and entries to provide items to the consumer:

```
task Buffer is
  entry Take_Item    (I : in Item);
  entry Provide_Item (I : out Item);
end Buffer;

task body Buffer is
  Queue : Buffer_Type;
begin
  loop
    select
      accept Take_Item (I : in Item) do
        -- Insert I in Queue.
      end Take_Item;
      -- Update insert index.
    or
      accept Provide_Item (I : out Item) do
        -- Assign next element in Queue to I.
      end Provide_Item;
      -- Update remove index.
    or
```

```
      terminate;
    end select;
  end loop;
end Buffer;
```

b. *Transporter task.* This is strictly a caller which gets an
    item from a producer or intermediary, and passes the item
    on to the consumer (possibly via an intermediary):

```
task Transporter;

task body Transporter is
  Local_Item : Item;
begin
  loop
    Producer.Provide_Item (Local_Item);
    Consumer.Take_Item (Local_Item);
  end loop;
end Transporter;
```

c. *Relay task.* The relay task waits at an accept statement
    until it receives an item from a producer. It then transfers
    the item to a consumer (or intermediary) via an entry call:

```
task Relay is
  entry Take_Item (I : in Item);
end Relay;

task body Relay is
  Local_Item : Item;
begin
  loop
    accept Take_Item (I : in Item) do
      Local_Item := I;
    end Take_Item;
    Consumer.Take_Item (Local_Item);
  end loop;
end Relay;
```

The uncoupling of the producer and consumer is accomplished by
introducing one or more of these intermediaries between them, for
example, a producer-buffer-transporter-consumer (PBTC) or a
producer-transporter-buffer-transporter-consumer (PTBTC). Of these
two examples the PTBTC model provides a looser coupling between

the producer and consumer than the PBTC, but an additional task with associated run time overhead has been introduced. This uncoupling of Ada tasks represents a buffering mechanism that provides the desired degree of buffering and asynchronism between the concurrent processes [HOA85, p. 238], and is used in conjunction with the rendezvous mechanism that provides tight (synchronous) coupling between two tasks.

13.2.2.1 Design Evaluation. A concurrent Ada design can be evaluated with regard to coupling at two levels. First, it can be evaluated by considering the interactions between the complete set of tasks in the system. This includes the caller/called decisions made, the use of intermediary tasks, cyclic dependencies, possible use of polling and associated "busy wait," and the amount of processing that takes place within each rendezvous. Second, it can be evaluated by considering the coupling between pairs of tasks. Two loosely coupled Ada tasks represent an asynchronous behavior in the concurrent design and may be desirable. A loose coupling is accomplished by introducing intermediary tasks such as buffers, transporters, and relays. The Ada rendezvous, on the other hand, represents various degrees of tight coupling dependent on whether or not the entries are called with parameters, and the mode of such parameters. This type of coupling is quite acceptable in an Ada design and represents the synchronization mechanism for communicating processes.

13.2.3 Ada Packages

Ada packages are not modules in the strict sense, since they are not callable. Packages constitute an extremely important part of Ada design constructs, however, and it is highly desirable to be able to evaluate the use of packages in an Ada design. It has been proposed [HAM85] that the traditional coupling concepts be extended to include the use of Ada packages as follows:

1. *Definition coupling.* Two modules are definition coupled if they use a common definition that is global to both of them. This would be the case if they both *with* the same package, or use a resource that is defined in the package that contains both modules.

2. *Package coupling.* Two modules are package coupled if they both import the same package (by *with*ing), but do not use any common elements within the package.

Of these two new forms of coupling, the former represents a better (looser) interdependence than data coupling, since data may not actually be shared. The two modules may simply import a common type from the same package. Package coupling appears to offer the ultimate in loose coupling since neither data nor types are shared by the two modules importing the package. It is questionable, however, that this is a desirable way to structure a package. It should probably be split up into two or more packages, and have each module *with* the package that contains the elements it needs. An exception to this guideline is a widely used, very general purpose package such as a package of mathematics or graphics routines.

It should be noted that the two new forms of coupling apply to modules as defined above (including Ada tasks), but do not apply to coupling between packages.

Suggestions for good package design have been made in Reference BOO83 and include the modeling of abstract data types. Such packages should provide only the necessary and sufficient services required to implement the specific model. A module that imports one of these packages would utilize all or most of the services provided in it. Guidelines for constructing packages that will minimize the overall coupling of the program include [BOO83, p. 193]:

1. *Named collections of declarations.* Objects and types are exported, but not other program units.

2. *Groups of related program units.* Program units are exported, but not objects or types.

3. *Abstract data types.* Objects, types, and their operations are exported.

4. *Abstract state machines.* Objects, types, and their operations are exported. State information is maintained in the package body (actually in the subprogram or task body contained within the package body).

These guidelines can be used as an aid to a qualitative evaluation of package designs. A quantitative measure of Ada package design has been proposed in Reference HAM85, but it is currently not available as an automated tool.

13.3   Cohesion

Cohesion is a measure of the strength of functional associations between elements within a module. Strong cohesion is desirable for a good software design because it makes the code easy to understand

and modify, and it supports low coupling between modules. Module cohesion (from high to low) can be characterized as follows [PAG80]:

1. *Functional cohesion.* The module consists of a single problem-related function.

2. *Sequential cohesion.* Output data from one activity (set of instructions) serve as input data to the next activity.

3. *Communicational cohesion.* Elements contribute to activities that use the same input or output data. The order of execution of the activities is not important.

4. *Procedural cohesion.* Different and possibly unrelated activities are (usually) executed in some order with control flowing from one activity to the next.

5. *Temporal cohesion.* Unrelated functions are executed at a particular time during the processing sequence. Activities are closely related to those in other modules, creating a tight coupling.

6. *Logical cohesion.* The module contains a number of activities of the same general kind. A specific activity is picked out of the "grab bag."

7. *Coincidental cohesion.* The module contains a number of completely unrelated activities.

These measures of cohesion apply without restrictions to Ada subprograms. Ada tasks and packages, however, require special considerations and are further discussed below.

13.3.1 Ada Tasks

Even though an Ada task is not callable (the entries are called), its structure is sufficiently close to a procedure that it should be considered a module. For a task with no entries the cohesion rules apply just as they do for procedures. When entries are included, the picture is not so clear. For a task with several entries we could have procedural and logical cohesion for the implementation of the various rendezvous activities on the one hand. On the other, the implementation of a finite state machine using selective wait statements within a task could be considered functional cohesion. The cohesion rules would apply to each separate rendezvous activity within a task. An Ada task may consist of several accept bodies (or subprograms) that perform their functions within a given time period (periodic or cyclic task). This would represent functional cohesion at the accept body (or subprogram) level and temporal cohesion at the task level. Temporal cohesion could thus be acceptable for an Ada concurrent design.

We have also found it useful to introduce a new term for task cohesion in Ada: timed sequential cohesion. This refers to a code section that is executed when a particular event takes place, e.g., a rendezvous or expiration of a delay, and represents a break in the normal, sequential flow of execution. This type of cohesion is used in Ada for synchronization between communicating tasks, to have the effect of periodicity or to model cyclic events, and is quite acceptable.

13.3.1.1 Design Evaluation. The traditional cohesion rules for structured design can be used to evaluate cohesion within Ada task bodies. This evaluation is not as straightforward as for subprograms, because of the complications arising when the selective wait is used. The selective wait may result in procedural, temporal, or logical cohesion which could be acceptable in a task body, but not in a subprogram. Temporal cohesion would be acceptable at the task level where the task body consists of several accept bodies that together represent a periodic or cyclic task. The individual accept bodies would have functional cohesion, whereas the task would have temporal cohesion.

13.3.2 Ada Packages

The cohesion rules outlined above apply to activities (i.e., sets of executable instructions) within a module. Ada packages may have a sequence of executable statements following the optional *begin* in the package bodies, but these statements are used for object initialization and are not considered an "activity" in the same sense for which the cohesion rules apply. The evaluation of the internal structure of Ada packages will not be concerned with binding within activities, but rather with the effect it has on the overall design, e.g., for the units that *with* the package. The evaluation of the proper use of packages will be concerned with the coupling concepts of the modules using the packages, rather than with "cohesion" within a given package.

Channels And Pools

When we describe a set of communicating processes, we also need to consider the data items that are passed between the processes or manipulated by the processes. A convenient way to describe the data and associated activities is to adopt the *channel* and *pool* concepts defined in MASCOT (Modular Approach to Software Construction Operation and Test) [BIR85, PYL85]. MASCOT is a real-time software development approach where activities (operations) are associated with one of two data characteristics: (1) Channels represent data passed in a certain order between communicating processes. The data items are simply consumed, they are not manipulated. Channels provide a medium for data transferred between communicating processes. (2) Pools describe data that is shared between communicating processes. This type of data can be considered as a data base that is manipulated, but not consumed or passed between the processes.

For any set of communicating processes we can describe all the activities associated with data items passed between the processes, or shared among the processes, in terms of virtual machines for channels and pools. The paragraphs that follow describe how we construct these virtual machines in Ada.

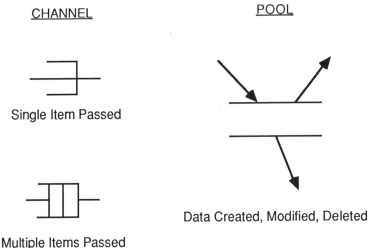

CHANNEL   POOL

Single Item Passed

Multiple Items Passed

Data Created, Modified, Deleted

Figure 14-1. Channels and pools.

14.1 Ada Channels

Virtual machines for channels in Ada are typically implemented as buffer, relay, and transporter tasks (see Chapter 13). The graphical representation of single and multiple channel items is shown in Figure 14-1. This representation is a slight modification of the original MASCOT graphic notation and gives us an immediate clue to the kind of virtual machine required for the appropriate channel interface. The tasks inserted as intermediaries between producer/consumer task pairs are virtual machines to effect the proper level of coupling as described in Chapter 13. The intermediary tasks provide the service of consuming the data items as they are received from the producer and subsequently passed to the consumer. The proper handling of these data items will normally require a queue which can be implemented as a circular buffer, unless only a single data item is required to be passed. An example of a virtual machine for a channel in Ada is shown in Figure 14-2. This is a simple relay for a single data item, implemented as a generic package. The generic parameters include the type of the data item to be relayed, and the subprogram that represents the consumer. The actual relay is implemented as a task with an entry for receiving the data item, and a call to the consumer. A more sophisticated relay is shown in Figure 10-4 for multiple data items. An additional generic parameter is added for the size of the buffer required (default size is 20), and the relay is implemented as two separate tasks: a buffer task for storing the data items that arrive from the producer and a transporter task for getting the data items

```
generic
  type Item is private;
  with procedure Consumer (C : in Item);

package Simple_Relay is
  procedure Relay_Item (I : in Item);
  pragma Inline (Relay_Item);
end Simple_Relay;

package body Simple_Relay is
  task Relay is
    entry Relay_Item (I : in Item);
  end Relay;

  task body Relay is
    X : Item;
  begin
    loop
      accept Relay_Item (I : in Item) do
        X := I;
      end Relay_Item;
      Consumer (X);
    end loop;
  end Relay;

  procedure Relay_Item (I : in Item) is
  begin
    Relay.Relay_Item (I);
  end Relay_Item;

end Simple_Relay;
```

Figure 14-2. Single-item channel relay.

to the consumer one item at a time. The implementation of the
buffer task has been deferred by using the separate clause in the
package body. A general purpose buffer implementation is illustrated in Figure 10-12. The task body contains the actual buffer
storage (Buf), and the indexes required for maintaining the ordering
in the circular FIFO queue. The insertion into and removal from
the queue are guarded such that a user cannot insert an item in a
queue that is full, or remove an item from an empty queue.

Slight variations from the implementations shown above can be coded and collected in an Ada library as a set of channel objects that can be reused for any application of communicating processes.

14.2 Ada Pools

Virtual machines for pools in Ada are built to protect data shared between communicating processes, and are typically implemented as monitors [HOA74]. The graphic representation of a pool that is shared between two or more processes is shown in Figure 14-1 and is identical to the notation we use for showing data bases on a DFD. When we build the virtual machine, the shared data storage is declared in the body of a monitor task, and access to this data is provided by a set of entrance procedures that represent the operations allowed on the data. An example of a monitor for an Ada pool is shown in Figures 10-7 and 10-8 for the protection of a track file. The allowed operations (entrance procedures) include Latest_ Track_File which provides the track file object and how many tracks are contained in it; Add_Track for addition of a track to the track file; and Update_Track for an update of the position of a given track. An exception is raised by Add_Track if the track store is full, and the caller to Add_Track must include an exception handler for this condition. The implementation of the monitor task hidden inside the package body of Track_File_Monitor is shown in Figure 14-3. Storage for track file (Track_Storage) is declared in the task body, and the allowable operations are implemented within a select statement. The select statement guarantees mutual exclusion for the accept bodies and thus protects the locally declared track file from corruption by multiple, simultaneous callers.

Ada pools can be implemented for specific data bases, as was shown above for the track file, or for general purpose applications using generics. Typical generic parameters will include the size of the data base, the type of the key used for access to the data base, and the type of the data elements to be created, modified, and deleted.

```ada
with Track_Services;  use Track_Services;
separate (Track_File_Monitor)
  task body Monitor is

    Track_Storage : Track_File (Track_Number);
    Last_Track : Track_Count := 0;

  begin
    loop
      select
        accept Latest (Tracks : out Track_File;
                       Number_Of_Tracks : out Track_Count) do
          Tracks := Track_Storage (1 .. Last_Track);
          Number_Of_Tracks := Last_Track;
        end Latest;
      or
        accept Add (X, Y : in Coordinates; Full : out Boolean) do
          Full := Last_Track = Track_Count'Last;
          if Last_Track < Track_Count'Last then
            Last_Track := Last_Track + 1;
            Track_Services.Update (Track_Storage, X, Y, Last_Track);
          end if;
        end Add;
      or
        accept Update (X, Y : in Coordinates;
                       Track_ID : in Track_Number) do
          Track_Services.Update (Track_Storage, X, Y, Track_ID);
        end Update;
      or
        accept Correlate (X, Y : in Coordinates) do
          Track_Services.Correlate (Track_Storage, X, Y);
        end Correlate;
      or
        accept Extrapolate do
          Track_Services.Extrapolate (Track_Storage);
        end Extrapolate;
      end select;
    end loop;
  end Monitor;
```

Figure 14-3. Pool monitor task implementation.

15

Tasking Paradigms

When we use the Ada tasking model to design a set of cooperating sequential processes, it is important that the proper coupling is attained for each producer/consumer pair. Tight coupling is obtained by using the rendezvous directly, whereas loose coupling is obtained by introducing intermediary tasks between a producer/consumer pair. There is a run time penalty, however, when intermediary tasks are introduced into our design. The more tasks introduced, the higher the penalty in the form of additional task control blocks, task scheduling and dispatching time, and context switching time. These concepts and concerns are discussed in the following paragraphs.

15.1 Producer/Consumer Coupling

The proper level of coupling (asynchronicity) between a producer and consumer is a very important design issue and must be decided before the caller/called decisions for the set of tasks can be completed. We decide the proper coupling levels by examining the functional requirements, and the descriptions of the specific hardware devices required for the system.

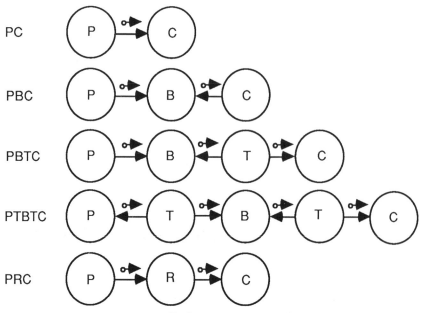

Figure 15-1. Producer/consumer coupling.

15.1.1 Tight Coupling

Figure 15-1 illustrates various paradigms for how the proper coupling can be obtained. Tight coupling is obtained via the Ada rendezvous (PC) without introducing any intermediary tasks. The various levels of tight coupling depend on whether parameters are passed in the entry call, and, if so, the mode of the parameters. These levels of tight coupling were discussed in detail in Chapter 13 and are not repeated here. If the PC paradigm is used between a producer and consumer, the two tasks cannot operate asynchronously and are highly dependent. During the rendezvous, the calling task is suspended and cannot resume execution until the rendezvous is completed. The calling task is not even guaranteed to regain possession of the processor immediately after the completion of the rendezvous. The task scheduling mechanism is non-deterministic and implementation dependent. The advantage of a direct rendezvous between the producer and consumer is that no intermediary tasks are introduced with an associated run time overhead.

15.1.2 Loose Coupling

When a loose coupling is required between a producer/consumer pair, we introduce intermediary tasks. Figure 15-1 illustrates four different paradigms for loose coupling:

1. *PBC.* By placing a buffer task between the producer and consumer, the producer sends an item by calling the buffer, and continues its execution when the item has been accepted by the buffer task (when it regains possession of the processor). The consumer calls the buffer to receive the next item. By separating the producer and consumer with a buffer task, they can each operate at their respective speeds, but they must rendezvous with the buffer task. An example of a generic buffer specification is shown in Figure 10-3, and the implementation in Figure 10-12 (with Generic_Buffer for the parent name).

2. *PBTC.* If we do not want the consumer to have to wait for the rendezvous with the buffer task in the PBC paradigm, we can introduce a transporter task between the buffer and consumer. The consumer is now *called*, rather than being the *caller*. The consumer will now accept the next item from the buffer via the transporter without having to call the buffer task directly. An example of a generic transporter specification and implementation is shown in Figure 10-5. The transporter is a pure caller (details of caller/called relations are given in Chapter 16), and the calls to be made are given as generic parameters.

3. *PTBTC.* If we also do not want the producer to be tied up in a rendezvous with the buffer task, we introduce another transporter task between the producer and the buffer, making the producer a called task. Both the producer and the consumer are now free to operate asynchronously with even less coupling than for the PBC paradigm. When it is ready, the producer sends the next item to the buffer via the transporter task. When the consumer is ready to process the next item, it gets it from the other transporter task without having to rendezvous directly with the buffer task.

4. *PRC.* The functions of a buffer and transporter can be combined into a relay. The producer sends the next item to the relay via a rendezvous, and the consumer accepts the next item from the relay when it is ready to process that item. An example of a generic relay specification is shown in Figure 10-4 and contains declarations for a buffer task and transporter task. The transporter calls the consumer which is supplied as a generic parameter. The implementation of the relay buffer is shown in Figure 10-12 (with Generic_Relay for the parent name).

15.2   Run Time Overhead

Any Ada task introduced into our design has associated with it a run time overhead. This overhead includes task activation and termination, task scheduling and dispatching, context switching, propagation of exceptions, selection of an open entry in a selective wait statement, queueing management of entry calls, and allocation of task control blocks. This kind of overhead is not unique to Ada, however; similar overheads are experienced when using any programming language *and* a real-time executive that contains tasking primitives.

The overhead described here alerts us to the fact that we cannot blindly introduce any number of Ada tasks into our design. We must analyze our concurrent design in terms of a trade-off between the required/desired asynchronicity between producer/consumer pairs, and how much run time overhead can be tolerated. To properly evaluate our concurrent design, we must measure the various overheads associated with using the Ada tasking model via suitable benchmark programs. The measurements must be made on the system we expect to use as the target machine, and the planned production compiler. For critical timing requirements, at least, it will not be sufficient to make estimates based on relative speed or results obtained on another system. The run time support supplied with an Ada compilation system will be highly implementation dependent with regard to levels of optimization [HAB80, HIL82] and execution efficiency.

An example of a set of measured overhead activities for a fictitious Ada implementation is shown in Table 15-1 [BUR87]. The measurements are given both as absolute values in microseconds and as normalized values relative to the time for a procedure call. These values should give an indication of whether or not, for example, a PTBTC paradigm can be tolerated in our design. Benchmarks for these kinds of measurements can be obtained from the Ada Software Repository [CON87] or by contacting ACM SIGAda's Performance Issues Working Group (PIWG).

15.3   Periodic Tasks

The implementation of the Ada tasking model is radically different from the traditional cyclic executive previously used for multitask programs [MAC80]. The cyclic executive is designed to execute tasks within time frames and in a fixed order. The order is determined by the preparation of a "task list" prior to program execution. This approach is drastically different from the Ada tasking model

TABLE 15-1. Overhead Associated with Ada Tasking
Activities and Task Paradigms

	Overhead	
Activity/Paradigm	μs	Normalized
1. Task activation and termination	2010	183
2. Task created via an allocator	150	14
3. Procedure call	11	1
4. PC (two context switches)	500	45
5. PBC	1220	111
6. PBTC	1700	155
7. PTBTC	2240	204
8. PRC	900	82
9. Conditional entry call		
No rendezvous	170	15
With rendezvous	30	3
10. Timed entry call		
No rendezvous	250	23
With rendezvous	30	3
11. Selective wait with terminate	127	12
12. Exception in a block	220	20
13. Exception in a procedure	220	20
14. Exception during rendezvous	960	87

where the task execution order is non-deterministic. Periodic tasks
can be designed in Ada if the following features are included in the
run time support:

1. The expiration of a delay will guarantee a scheduling event.

2. Different priorities can be assigned to individual tasks with the
    pragma Priority.

3. The highest priority task is selected to execute next, as a result
    of the scheduling event.

A periodic task in Ada can be implemented using the delay statement, but we must take precautions to control the potential for
cumulative drift. The following example illustrates the implementation of a periodic Ada task:

```
with Definitions; use Definitions;
with Calendar;    use Calendar;

task body Periodic_Timer is
  Next_Time : Time := Clock + Update_Periodic;
```

```
begin

  Periodic_Loop: loop
    delay Next_Time - Clock;

    -- do whatever is to be done periodically

    Next_Time := Next_Time + Update_Periodic;
  end loop Periodic_Loop;

end Periodic_Timer;
```

This task executes in a context where the capabilities of Calendar have been made available with the *with* clause. The *use* clause provides immediate visibility to the type Time and the functions Clock, "+," and "-." The periodic interval Update_Periodic is specified in the package Definitions and treated as an adaptation parameter.

Next_Time is always the "next" time that the periodic event is to occur and hence is always incremented by Update_Periodic. The amount of delay is expressed as the difference between the scheduled next time and the clock in order to compensate for two things:

1. The time taken to "do whatever is to be done periodically."

2. The time taken by other system activities. Remember that the delay is a *minimum* time, not an exact time.

The method above will produce cyclic events repeating on the *average* each Update_Periodic seconds. If the expression in the delay statement becomes zero or negative, the task will continue to execute without any suspension, and will thus "catch up" in the cycle of periodic executions. As long as the duration of each interval (including the cyclic function and other system processing) is less than Update_Periodic, there will be no cumulative drift away from the desired average frequency of occurrence.

Caller/Called Decisions

When we described Ada task graphs in the section on design tools, we noted that these graphs are used to illustrate the complete set of interacting Ada tasks, their interfaces, and the caller/called relations between them. We said nothing about how to determine these relations, however, and that is the topic of this chapter.

Making proper decisions about calling and called tasks in Ada is extremely important because of the asymmetry inherent in the tasking model [SHU88], the complexity that can result if improper decisions are reached [SHU88, BUH84, BUR85], and the potential for a polling bias [GEH84]. We attempt to remove the mystery of how to make these decisions by presenting a set of heuristics that can apply to most of our concurrent designs.

16.1 Asymmetric Rendezvous

The Ada tasking model is different from other models previously used to build real-time systems. It is based on the rendezvous concept [ICH79] to provide a procedure-like interface between two tasks. The rendezvous approach has never previously been employed in a widely used programming language or executive to implement a major real-time system. The rendezvous has several characteristics that will influence system design: (1) It is a single mechanism for synchronization and communication; (2) it provides for simultaneous two-way transmission of information; (3) it allows instructions to be executed on behalf of two cooperating tasks; and (4) it is an asymmetric process, providing capabilities for a *calling* task (which issues an entry call) different from a *called* task (which accepts an entry call).

The aspect of asymmetry is of particular importance for the design of task interaction. The rendezvous is asymmetric in three ways:

1. The calling task must know the name of the called task (and its entries), but not vice versa.

2. A call may occur in a subprogram (either subordinate to a task or in a separate package) or initialization part of a package body, while the acceptance of a call must occur only in the sequence of statements of a task body.

3. A calling task may call only one other task. It may be on only a single entry queue of tasks waiting for a call to be accepted. A called task, on the other hand, may wait for any of many different types of calls. It may have many queues of callers (one queue for each entry) waiting for its attention.

The first kind of asymmetry allows the programming of general purpose library or service tasks. The second kind has an effect on modularization. The third kind of asymmetry is fundamental to the Ada tasking model and is concerned with which task will have greater control over the rendezvous.

The called task, using the select statement with guards, has more control over its fate than does a calling task. The called task, however, has a degree of non-determinism since it must be prepared to respond to a call to any of the accepts in the select statement. This distinction has led Pyle [PYL85] to differentiate between active (calling) tasks and passive (called) tasks. He states [PYL85, p. 96]: "The programmer using tasks will mainly write active tasks, taking advantage of previously written passive tasks." Burns [BUR86, p. 204] feels that tasks "should not act as both passive and active tasks. ..." His approach is to use active tasks to satisfy the application (what we have called application tasks), and passive tasks to provide controlled access to resources. This may not be completely true since many tasks may have both calling and called aspects, but it is certainly true that programmers must learn "... how to design programs the Ada way" [YOU82, p. 338]. In the heuristics that follow for making caller/called decisions, we allow the construction of tasks that are pure callers (active), pure servers (passive), and hybrids (a mixture of active and passive).

16.2 Intermediary Tasks

In Chapter 15 we described how we introduce intermediary tasks to attain the proper coupling between each producer/consumer pair. By convention, the caller/called relations for these intermediaries are as follows:

1. *Buffer task.* A buffer task is always a pure server and contains exactly two entries, one for enqueueing and one for dequeueing items. Buffer tasks never make calls to other Ada program units. This is illustrated in Figure 16-1a by having both the control arrows pointing to the circle representing the buffer task.

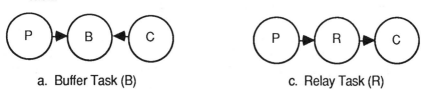

    a. Buffer Task (B)   c. Relay Task (R)

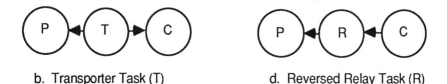

  b. Transporter Task (T)   d. Reversed Relay Task (R)

Figure 16-1. Caller/called relations of intermediaries.

2. *Transporter task.* A transporter task is always a pure caller; it contains no entries. It first makes a call to receive an item, and then makes a second call to pass on the item it received. This is illustrated in Figure 16-1b by the two control arrows leaving the circle representing the transporter task. A transporter task can be considered to be a single-item buffering mechanism, since the item it receives from the producer is kept internal to the task until it is delivered to the consumer.

3. *Relay task.* A relay task is a hybrid: it contains an entry for receiving items, and makes calls to dispose of these items. This is illustrated in Figure 16-1c with one control arrow pointing

toward and another pointing away from the circle representing the relay task. For single items to be passed between a producer and consumer, a single task is sufficient for the relay. For multiple items a buffer is required, and the relay will then consist of a buffer task and a transporter task. The direction of items passed through a relay can be reversed as shown in Figure 16-1d.

By using these conventions for intermediary tasks, we have reduced the complexity of making caller/called decisions for the complete set of tasks. We next consider the application tasks.

16.3 Application Tasks

For application tasks we suggest the following guidelines:

1. *Device drivers.* Device drivers can be pure servers or hybrids for interrupt driven devices. These drivers will contain entries for the interrupt handling and, possibly, an entry for the interface with other application tasks. It may alternately make a call to the interfacing application tasks, and thus become a hybrid. For devices that require polling, hybrid tasks or pure callers are the most likely choice. These drivers will poll the devices via calls to see if they are ready for input or output. They may contain entries for the interfaces with the other application tasks, or they may make calls to these tasks.

2. *Controlling tasks.* Tasks that need to control a rendezvous are called. The control is typically implemented with guarded entries, nested rendezvous, exception handling with inner frames, and the use of the Count attribute.

3. *Busy tasks.* Busy tasks are called. "Busy" is here referring to tasks that can interact with several other tasks, i.e., there are several entries specified within a single task. If a busy task is allowed to make calls to other busy tasks, severe delays could be experienced for the calling task.

4. *Complex tasks.* Algorithmically complex tasks are callers. This will reduce their complexity compared with making them called tasks. A call within a task represents an abstraction of a portion of the algorithm and thus reduces the complexity of that task body.

5. *Service tasks.* Tasks with functions that provide the equivalent of executive services should be pure servers, like the buffer tasks described above.

6. *Avoid hybrids, if possible.* If the choice (in conjunction with the heuristics given above) is between a hybrid or a pure caller or server, avoid the hybrid. This will enforce the notion of active or passive tasks discussed above and advocated by Pyle and Burns.

With this collection of rules as a general guide for making caller/called decisions, we have drastically reduced the number of possible interactions between a set of cooperating sequential Ada tasks. There is still the potential for polling, however, which is the topic of Chapter 17.

17

CHAPTER 7

Polling

Polling is the repeated checking (looping) to determine if a specific event has taken place, or if a given condition has become true. Polling is normally used to interface with devices that are not interrupt driven; we typically examine registers repeatedly for a change in a device state. An example of a roll call polling system [DOL78] is shown in Figure 17-1. This represents a method of serving several users (stations), that may or may not have messages, in a cyclic order. Typical applications of polling schemes include data link protocols for multipoint lines and local-area networks (LANs). We are not attempting to analyze polling systems here (see, for example, Reference TAK86); we are taking the limited view of how the polling effect can be, and should be, implemented in Ada. We will see below that polling may occur in Ada when we use the conditional entry call or a selective wait with an *else* clause. Polling is often wasteful of resources and should be avoided if possible.

17.1 Polling in Ada

We will follow Gehani's general description of polling in Ada associated with the use of the Ada tasking model [GEH84, p. 149], but first we present an example of polling within an Ada task that is

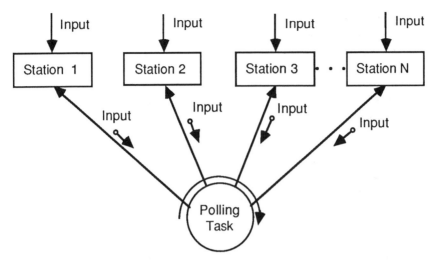

Figure 17-1. Polling system for multiple stations.

independent of the rendezvous. The example shown in Figure 17-2 illustrates a polling mechanism for accessing a particular bit in a device status register. The device could, for example, be a display for text or graphics. The polling mechanism is localized to the while loop, where the Ready_Bit (bit 7 in the status register) is repeatedly checked to see if the device is ready to accept another character. This kind of polling is used with devices that are not interrupt driven and can be considered a "benign" form of polling. We will now contrast this with the potentially harmful effects of polling associated with the Ada rendezvous.

Following Gehani [GEH84, p. 149], we can identify two polling effects that are directly related to the use of the Ada rendezvous:

1. *Rendezvous polling.* Rendezvous polling takes place when one task is repeatedly attempting to rendezvous with another task. This is accomplished with a conditional entry call, or within a task body with a selective wait with an else clause. The first example in Figure 17-3 illustrates an attempt to rendezvous via a conditional entry call. The else clause contains a null statement that in this case does not represent busy wait. Busy wait is here defined as no useful work being performed between the attempted rendezvous. We are assuming here that useful work (represented by the ellipse) is performed after the select statement and before another rendezvous is attempted. We should avoid this type of rendezvous in our task design, if we can, since it is very easy to introduce busy wait. Aside from the busy wait issue, there is also the potential that the task that is performing

```
task Display_Character is
  entry Put (C : in Character);
end Display_Character;

task body Display_Character is
  type Status_Array is array (0 .. 15) of Boolean;
  Status_Register : Status_Array;

  for Status_Register use at 8#177600#;
  for Status_Array'Size use 16;

  Ready_Bit : Boolean renames Status_Register (7);
                    -- we want to access bit 7

  Hdw_Buffer : Character;
  for Hdw_Buffer use at 8#077404#;

  Local_Char : Character;
begin
  loop
    accept Put (C : in Character) do
      Local_Char := C;    -- save the char until device is ready
    end Put;

    while not Ready_Bit loop
      null;  -- busy wait
    end loop;

    Hdw_Buffer := Local_Char;
  end loop;
end Display_Character;
```

Figure 17-2. Polling: accessing a bit in a status register.

the polling may prevent a higher priority task from gaining possession of the processor.

2. *Information polling.* Information polling takes place when one task is repeatedly rendezvousing with another task while waiting for a state change to happen. An example of information polling is shown in Figure 17-3, where the task is repeatedly rendezvousing with Resource_Manager.Request until the Resource_ Free flag changes state from False to True. There is no busy wait associated with this example, and the polling mechanism is acceptable. A synchronization point is established

1. *Rendezvous Polling:*

```
...
loop
  select
    Task_Name.Entry ( ... );
  else
    null;
  end select;
  ...
end loop;
...
```

2. *Information Polling:*

```
...

Resource_Free := False;

while not Resource_Free loop
  Resource_Manager.Request (Resource_Free);
  ...
end loop;

...  -- resource is now free and we can continue
```

Figure 17-3. Rendezvous and information polling.

each time the two tasks rendezvous, and other tasks may thus gain control of the processor.

17.2 Eliminating Undesirable Polling

We have noted that polling in Ada may involve undesirable busy wait, and it has been argued that using the tasking primitives in Ada leads to a bias toward rendezvous polling [GEH84, p. 149]. It is also possible that a task that is repeatedly trying to rendezvous with another task may prevent a higher priority task from gaining possession of the processor. When undesirable polling is discovered in a concurrent design, we attempt to rewrite the code that represents the unwanted effects. For the rendezvous polling shown in

...

```
loop
  select
    accept Update (X   : in X_Coordinate; Y   : in Y_Coordinate;
                   V_X : in Velocity;      V_Y : in Velocity) do
      -- save new coordinates and velocities
    end Update;

  else
    -- calculate new position using old coordinate and velocities
  end select;

  -- display point on screen

end loop;
```

...

Figure 17-4. Example of desirable polling: no busy wait.

Figure 17-3, for example, it would be preferable that the task make a simple entry call rather than a conditional entry call:

```
...
loop
  Task_Name.Entry ( ... );
  ...
end loop;
...
```

If the called task is not immediately available for a rendezvous, the calling task is suspended until the rendezvous can take place. No busy wait is expended here, but more importantly, the calling task will be suspended until the rendezvous can take place. This synchronization point will allow other tasks the possibility of gaining access to the processor, which they may not with the rendezvous polling shown in the first example in Figure 17-3. In some cases the use of the else clause in rendezvous polling is justified, as shown in Figure 17-4 (adapted from [GEH84, p. 151]). In this case, calculations (that are an effective alternative to the rendezvous) are performed if the rendezvous is not immediately available, and this does not represent busy wait. An example of an empty else clause that does not represent busy wait is shown in Figure 17-5. The empty

```
...

loop
  select
    accept Update ( ... ) do
      ... -- save new data
    end Update;

    -- calculate new values

  else
    null;   -- no busy wait;   use old data
  end select;

  -- display data (new or old)

  delay X;    -- we are modifying the polling effect
end loop;
```

Figure 17-5. Acceptable polling: no busy wait.

else clause is included here to force the display of old data if new data is not immediately available through the Update entry. Even though the else clause in the select statement is a null, there is useful work performed by displaying data before the next rendezvous is attempted. The polling effect is also modified somewhat by the delay statement. This increases the chance that new data will be available before the next polling attempt.

It is sometimes difficult to completely eliminate busy wait in rendezvous polling, as shown in Figure 17-6a for an elevator manager [GEH84, p. 153, and WEL81]. The task is rendezvous polling for entry calls to any of the floors, using a family of entries. For a small building we could rewrite the task body as shown in Figure 17-6b. The number of floors must be known when the task is written, however, and repeating the accept statements would only make sense for a small number of floors.

In general, the use of an empty else clause in a select statement should be avoided since it may lead to busy wait and needless postponement of execution of other tasks. If the algorithm cannot easily be rewritten to avoid the use of the empty else clause, an attempt should be made to substitute a delay statement with a short time interval. This will cause the task performing the rendezvous polling to become suspended and allow the other tasks a chance to gain possession of the processor.

```
with Definitions;
task Elevator_Manager is
  entry Up    (Definitions.Floors);
  entry Down (Definitions.Floors);
end Elevator_Manager;

task body Elevator_Manager is
begin
  loop                                    loop
    ...                                     ...
    for I in Definitions.Floors loop        select
      select                                  accept Up (1) do .. end;
        accept Up (I) do                    or
          ...                                 accept Up (2) do .. end;
        end Up;                             or
      or                                      ...
        accept Down (I) do                  or
          ...                                 accept Down (1) do .. end;
        end Down;                           or
      else                                    accept Down (2) do .. end;
        null;  -- busy wait                 or
      end select;                             ...
    end loop;                               end select;
    ...                                     ...
  end loop;                               end loop;
end Elevator_Manager;

  (a) Polling with Family of Entries          (b) No Polling
```

Figure 17-6. Rendezvous with a family of entries.

Exceptions

The capability to declare, raise, and handle exceptions is a feature of Ada that has never previously been implemented in a widely used high-order programming language. Exceptions have been included in Ada to promote the creation of defensive, fault-tolerant real-time programs. The exception handling facility is intended to treat not only error conditions, but also any exceptional, expected condition that may require a recovery attempt before normal execution continues.

The syntax and semantics of exception declaration, raising, and handling are specified in the language reference manual [DOD83] and are not our concern here. Our main objective in the paragraphs that follow is to describe *how we use* Ada exceptions in designing our real-time systems. Since the use of exceptions incurs run time overhead, we also discuss how we can eliminate unnecessary exception handling.

18.1 Taxonomy of Ada Exceptions

Various suggestions have been made regarding the use of exceptions in Ada, ranging from traditional error handling to controlling program flow [BUH84, ICH84, AUS85]. The categories described below are considered of equal importance; no implicit priority should be attached to the order in which they are presented. Using exceptions for controlling program flow is not considered appropriate for the design of real-time systems, and is thus not included in the taxonomy given below. Following Ausnit et al. [AUS85, p. 95], we will discuss the following categories:

1. Anticipated conditions

2. General purpose software

3. Hardware failures

4. Invalid input data

5. Unanticipated errors (bugs)

18.1.1 Anticipated Conditions

This category applies to situations that are expected to occur during the normal execution of the real-time program. These exceptions are not the result of software bugs, and their occurrences are not a surprise to our software. The handlers we design for these exceptions have specific names; *others* is not used. An example of the handling of an exception in this category is shown in Figure 18-1 as a nested handler for the predefined Numeric_Error or Constraint_Error. It is expected that an overflow may occur when the counter Lost is incremented in the outer exception handler. The outer exception is of another category that is described in the next section.

Another example of an anticipated situation is shown in Figure 18-2 for the allocation of asynchronous serial numbers (ASNs). As the allocated ASN reaches its maximum allowable value, the incrementing past this value will raise the predefined exception Constraint_Error. We capture this exception with a local handler and set the value back to the starting value, thus having the effect of a wraparound. We have already noted that the use of exceptions are associated with run time overheads, and we will later show how we can have the identical effect of a wraparound for this example without using an exception.

18.1.2 General Purpose Software

One of the primary uses of the package construct in Ada is to be able to create general purpose software that can be shared by many users. We cannot guarantee that all the users will use these packages properly. We protect the general purpose software by raising

```
with Definitions;  use Definitions;
with Text_IO;      use Text_IO;
with User_Interface;
with Asynch_Comm_Buffer;
separate (ACI_Buffer)

   -- Task body for ACI handler
    -- Processing of the characters:
    -- 1.  Remove from hdw buffer and put in interface buffer;
    -- 2.  Maintain 'lost count' for each intermediate buffer
    --     when full;
    -- 3.  Pass appropriate char to intermediate buffer when
    --     possible;
    -- 4.  Maintain max value when 'lost count' overflows;

  task body ACI_Handler is
    Lost : array (Kbd_Index) of Natural := (others => 0);
              -- Number of chars lost for each kbd

    procedure Process_Char is
      Input : Asynch_Comm_Manager.Element; -- each element has two
                                           -- components
    begin
      -- From H/W buffer
      Asynch_Comm_Manager.Get (Asynch_Comm_Manager.Buffer, Input);

      -- To user interface buffer (for specified kbd)
      User_Interface.Put (User_Interface.Buffer ( ... ), ... )
      Lost ( ... ) := 0;

    exception
      when Asynch_Comm_Manager.Underflow =>  -- Hdw buffer empty
        null;
      when User_Interface.Overflow =>        -- Interm. buffer full
        begin
          Lost ( .. ) := Lost ( ... ) + 1;
          Put_Line ("Lost char in Process_Char");
        exception
          when Numeric_Error|Constraint_Error =>
            Put_Line (" Numeric_Error or Constraint_Error
                                        in Process_Char");
            Lost ( ... ) := Natural'Last;
                            -- Maintain max count of lost chars
        end;
    end Process_Char;
    ...
  end ACI_Handler;
```

Figure 18-1. Anticipated overflow condition.

```ada
package ASN is
  type Serial_Number is private;

  procedure Get_ASN (ASN : out Serial_Number);

private
  Max_Numbers : constant := 1_000_000;
  type Serial_Number is range 1 .. Max_Numbers;
end ASN;


package body ASN is

  task ASN_Manager is
    entry Get_ASN (ASN : out Serial_Number);
  end ASN_Manager;

  task body ASN_Manager is
    Counter : Serial_Number := 1;
  begin
    loop
      accept Get_ASN (ASN : out Serial_Number) do
        ASN := Counter;
      end Get_ASN;

      begin
        Counter := Counter + 1;
      exception
        when Constraint_Error =>
          Counter := 1;
      end;
    end loop;
  end ASN_Manager;


  procedure Get_ASN (ASN : out Serial_Number) is
  begin
    ASN_Manager.Get_ASN (ASN);
  end Get_ASN;

end ASN;
```

Figure 18-2. Using exception to provide wraparound.

```
generic
  type Index_Type is range <>;
  type Element_Type is private;    --Element in the buffer

package Buffer_Module is
  type Buffer is limited private;

  procedure Dequeue (B : in out Buffer; E : out Element_Type);
  procedure Enqueue (B : in out Buffer; E : in  Element_Type);
  function Empty (B : in Buffer) return Boolean;
  function Full  (B : in Buffer) return Boolean;

  Underflow : exception;  -- raised in Dequeue
  Overflow  : exception;  -- raised in Enqueue

private
  type Buf_Type is array(Index_Type) of Element_Type;
  type Buffer is
    record
      Head : Index_Type := Index_Type'First;  -- remove
      Tail : Index_Type := Index_Type'First;  -- insert
      Buf  : Buf_Type;                         -- array of elements
    end record;
end Buffer_Module;


package body Buffer_Module is
  procedure Dequeue (B : in out Buffer; E : out Element_Type)
                                               is separate;
  procedure Enqueue (B : in out Buffer; E : in Element_Type)
                                               is separate;
  function Empty (B : in Buffer) return Boolean is separate;
  function Full  (B : in Buffer) return Boolean is separate;
end Buffer_Module;
```

Figure 18-3. Protection of special purpose software.

exceptions when a misuse is detected. An illustration of this kind of
protection is shown in Figure 18-3 for a first-in–first-out queue manager for sequential processing. We are preventing users from getting an item from an empty queue (exception Underflow is raised in
Dequeue), and from putting items into a full queue (exception Overflow is raised in Enqueue). The users must provide handlers for
these exceptional conditions.

```
separate (Buffer_Module)

   procedure Dequeue (B : in out Buffer; E : out Element_Type) is
   begin
     if Empty (B) then
       raise Underflow;
     end if;

     E := B.Buf (B.Head);
     B.Head := (B.Head mod B.Buf'Last) + 1;
   end Dequeue;
```

```
separate (Buffer_Module)

   procedure Enqueue (B : in out Buffer; E : in Element_Type) is
   begin
     if Full (B) then
       raise Overflow;
     end if;

     B.Buf (B.Tail) := E;
     B.Tail := (B.Tail mod B.Buf'Last) + 1;
   end Put;
```

```
separate (Buffer_Module)

   function Empty (B : in Buffer) return Boolean is
   begin
     return (B.Head = B.Tail);
   end Empty;
```

```
separate (Buffer_Module)

   function Full (B : in Buffer) return Boolean is
   begin
     return (((B.Tail mod B.Buf'Last) + 1) = B.Head);
   end Full;
```

Figure 18-3 *(continued)*. Protection of special purpose software.

18.1.3 Hardware Failures

The operational performance of hardware devices is commonly measured as mean time between failure (MTBF), and these devices are expected to eventually fail. Such failures should not affect the entire real-time system. We would like to be able to detect the failures, attempt to recover and continue execution, and maybe to report the failures. Figure 18-4 illustrates how we can detect a hardware failure (for a digital thermometer) and continue normal execution. The task is waiting for an interrupt from the digital thermometer (accept DT_Interrupt;) within a select statement. If a response has not been received within Max_DT_Response_Time seconds, the exception No_Response_From_DT is raised. By placing the handler inside the task loop, execution will continue normally past the handler. In this case we are not reporting the failure to respond; that could be done with a call to Put_Line of package Text_IO or with a special message sent to the host.

18.1.4 Invalid Input Data

This is a category slightly different from protecting general purpose software. The program units in this category analyze input data supplied by the callers, and if it is determined that the input is invalid, an exception is raised and propagated to the caller. The caller must include the appropriate handlers and take corrective action.

The package shown in Figure 18-5 is used to convert ASCII string messages to the equivalent integer values. If a data error is recognized in attempting the assignments in the procedure Analyze_ Message, the predefined exception Constraint_Error or Numeric_ Error is captured in the local exception handler. This handler raises the exception Invalid_Message which is propagated back to the caller. The caller must take the appropriate action to recover from the invalid input data.

As a general design issue, an anticipated predefined exception should never be propagated directly to the caller. An appropriate handler for the predefined exception should be available in the called task or subprogram and should raise a *user-defined* exception that is propagated back to the caller. The caller would be too far removed from the point at which the predefined exception is raised to be able to perform any kind of constructive recovery.

```
separate (Device_Handlers)

task body DT_Handler is
  DT_Buffer_Furnace : Furnace_Type;
  for DT_Buffer_Furnace use at DT_Buffer_Furnace_Adr;

  DT_Buffer_Temp : Temp_Type;
  for DT_Buffer_Temp use at DT_Buffer_Temp_Adr;

  Max_DT_Response_Time : constant Duration := 10.0;
begin
  loop
    Handle_No_Response:
    begin
      accept Read_Temp (F : in Furnace_Type;
                        T : out Temp_Type) do
        DT_Buffer_Furnace := F;

        select
          accept DT_Interrupt;
        or
          delay Max_DT_Response_Time;
          raise No_Response_From_DT;
        end select;

        T := DT_Buffer_Temp;
      end Read_Temp;

    exception
      when No_Response_From_DT =>
        null;  -- we want to continue task execution
    end Handle_No_Response;
  end loop;
end DT_Handler;
```

Figure 18-4. Detecting a hardware error in the Digital Thermometer.

18.1.5 Unanticipated Errors (Bugs)

The detection of unanticipated bugs is important in any software system. For real-time processing we would always like to recover from an exceptional condition and continue normal execution. For a software bug, however, the best we can do is to report the subprogram or task where the bug was detected, and to repair the program as part of the maintenance phase. An example of the detection of a

```
with Definitions;  use Definitions;
package Message_Analyzer is
  procedure Analyze_Message (Message   : in  Message_Type;
                             Furnace   : out Furnace_Type;
                             Frequency : out Frequency_Type);


  Invalid_Message : exception;  -- raised in Analyze_Message
                                -- for invalid input message
end Message_Analyzer;


package body Message_Analyzer is
  procedure Analyze_Message (Message   : in  Message_Type;
                             Furnace   : out Furnace_Type;
                             Frequency : out Frequency_Type) is
  begin
    Furnace   := Integer'Value (Message (1 .. 2));
    Frequency := Integer'Value (Message (3 .. 5));

  exception
    when Numeric_Error | Constraint_Error =>
      raise Invalid_Message;
  end Analyze_Message;

end Message_Analyzer;
```

Figure 18-5. Invalid input data.

bug in a procedure is shown in Figure 18-6. We are capturing the
exception with *others*, since we do not know the cause of the exception. There is no direct way to recover from this type of condition,
and we simply print a message identifying the procedure where the
exception occurred. A similar example is shown in Figure 18-7 for
detection of a bug in a task.

18.2 Overhead

There is usually a run-time overhead associated with using exceptions (at least when an exception is raised and handled), and it is
beneficial to eliminate unnecessary exceptions, or to redesign the
most time consuming ones. An example of how we can eliminate an
exception entirely is shown in Figure 18-8 as an alternate solution
to the design we showed for the same function in Figure 18-2.
Rather than capturing the Constraint_Error exception and resetting

```
with Text_IO;   Use Text_IO;
with A;

procedure X is
   -- local data declarations
begin
   -- some processing

   A.B ( ... );

   -- more processing

exception
   when others =>    -- we won't know the type of exception, or
                     -- where it was raised
     Put_Line (" Unknown exception in procedure X");
end X;
```

Figure 18-6. Reporting a bug detected in a procedure.

Counter back to its starting value, we are using the *mod* function for the identical effect of wraparound. This allows us to eliminate the exception handling entirely within the task body of ASN_Manager. The trade-off in this case is the elimination of the use of an exception, but we are introducing the *mod* function which is executed each time through the loop. The exception would only be raised each time the maximum value of the ASN is exceeded.

When we discussed the overhead associated with using the tasking activities and task paradigms in Chapter 15, we noted that the exception handling during a rendezvous was about five times higher than for exception handling in a block or a procedure (see Table 15-1). Time-critical tasks must thus be evaluated carefully to determine if exception handling can be tolerated for task rendezvous. Here, again, is the unfortunate trade-off we have to make between the use of advanced programming facilities and the added overhead experienced during program execution.

```
with Text_IO;      use Text_IO;
with Definitions;  use Definitions;
with User_Interface;

procedure Kbd_Driver is

  Max_String : constant := 30;
  subtype Text is String (1 .. Max_String);

  Kbd_1 : Text := "Analog is used for FM Voice   ";
  ...

  task Use_UIB;

  task Simulate_Kbds is
    entry Take_Char (Id : in Kbd_Index; C : in Character);
  end Simulate_Kbds;

  task body Use_UIB is
    Char : Character;
    Lost : Natural;
  begin
    Put_Line (" Start of Use_UIB");
    for J in Kbd_Index loop
      for K in Text'Range loop
        User_Interface.Read_Kbd (J, Char, Lost);
        Put (Char);
        if Lost > 0 then
          Put (Natural'Image (Lost));   -- Chars lost
        end if;
      end loop;
      Put_Line ("  End Of Buffer");
    end loop;
  exception
    when others =>
      Put_Line ("Unknown exception in Use_UIB");
  end Use_UIB;
  ...
end Kbd_Driver;
```

Figure 18-7. Reporting a bug detected in a task.

```ada
package ASN is
  type Serial_Number is private;

  procedure Get_ASN (ASN : out Serial_Number);

private
  Max_Numbers : constant := 1_000_000;
  type Serial_Number is range 1 .. Max_Numbers;
end ASN;


package body ASN is

  task ASN_Manager is
    entry Get_ASN (ASN : out Serial_Number);
  end ASN_Manager;

  task body ASN_Manager is
    Counter : Serial_Number := 1;
  begin
    loop
      accept Get_ASN (ASN : out Serial_Number) do
        ASN := Counter;
      end Get_ASN;

      Counter := (Counter mod Serial_Number'Last) + 1;
             -- could also use "mod Max_Number"
    end loop;
  end ASN_Manager;

  procedure Get_ASN (ASN : out Serial_Number) is
  begin
    ASN_Manager.Get_ASN (ASN);
  end Get_ASN;

end ASN;
```

Figure 18-8. Eliminating unnecessary exception.

Low-Level Interfacing

Ada is a high-order programming language intended to be used for real-time embedded systems. This implies that there is a requirement to interface with hardware devices, and our software design efforts will include development of device drivers and interrupt handlers. Our program will need access to hardware buffers, status registers, and interrupt locations. From a language designer's point of view, there is a dilemma between providing high-level constructs for a logical representation of functional, data, and process abstraction, and also providing low-level constructs for real-time systems programming that allow access to the underlying, physical, machine.

The traditional approach to low-level interfacing is to write a set of assembly language routines that can be accessed from a high-order language like Pascal, Fortran, or C. These low-level routines are either part of an operating system, or they are written specifically by a specialist, a systems programmer, for a specific project and suite of hardware. The designers of Ada solved the dilemma of including high-level constructs for low-level interfacing by separating the logical and physical representations [ICH84]:

1. The logical properties of data items are specified first. Algorithms using these data items only deal with abstract logical

properties; they are not aware of the physical properties of the underlying machine.

2. The physical properties of the data items may be explicitly specified by the programmer, or chosen by default by the compiler.

The various ways in which an Ada programmer can map logical program entities to physical machine representations are described in the following paragraphs. We also describe how we can interface between Ada and other languages such as Fortran, Pascal, or C.

19.1   Representation Clauses

Representation clauses are used to specify how the types we define are to be mapped onto the underlying machine. We can also associate data objects, subprograms, task units, packages, and task entries with specific addresses. The following representation clauses are described below:

1. Enumeration type representation clauses

2. Length clauses

3. Record representation clauses

4. Address clauses

19.1.1   Enumeration Type Representation Clauses

An enumeration representation clause can be used to specify the internal representations of the literal values for an enumeration type. The commands for a channel program, for example, can be specified as follows:

```
type Channel_Commands is (Read, Write, Transfer_To_Loc,
                          Seek_Track, Search_Id, Search_Key);
for Channel_Commands use (16, 18, 19, 21, 30, 42);
```

We have here associated each symbolic command with a corresponding numeric value. A Write command, for example, has the value 18 (decimal). If we did not associate the symbolic names with numeric values, the compiler would assign a set of default values.

The attributes Succ (successor), Pred (predecessor), and Pos (position) are defined based on the logical type specification and are not affected by non-contiguous values given in the enumeration representation clause. The sequence of values must be strictly increasing.

```
package Processor_Status_Longword is

   type Flag is (Off, On);
   for Flag use (0, 1);  -- enumeration values

   subtype Priority is Integer range 0 .. 31;
   for Priority'Size use 5;  -- 5 bits; length clause

   type Mode is (Kernal, Executive, Supervisor, User);
   for  Mode use (0, 1, 2, 3);  --  enumeration values
   for  Mode'Size use 2;  -- 2 bits; length clause

   type PSL is     -- Processor Status Longword
      record
         Carry_CC    : Flag;     -- carry (borrow) condition code
         Overflow_CC : Flag;
         Zero_CC     : Flag;
         Negative_CC : Flag;
         TTE         : Flag;     -- trace trap enable
         IOTE        : Flag;     -- integer overflow trap enable
         FUTE        : Flag;     -- floating underflow trap enable
         DOTE        : Flag;     -- decimal overflow trap enable
         IPL         : Priority; -- interrupt priority level
         PAM         : Mode;     -- previous access mode
         CAM         : Mode;     -- current access mode
         EIS         : Flag;     -- executing on the interrupt stack
         IFPD        : Flag;     -- instruction first part done
         TTP         : Flag;     -- trace trap pending
         CM          : Flag;     -- compatibility mode
      end record;
```

Figure 19-1. Specification of DEC VAX-11 Processor Status Longword.

19.1.2 Length Clauses

A length clause is used to specify the amount of storage associated with a given type. For the channel commands given above, we can specify the number of bits required for the internal values:

```
for Channel_Commands'Size use 6;
```

The number of bits is specified using the attribute Size. The attribute Storage_Size can be used to specify the number of storage units to be reserved in connection with an access type or subtype, and the

```
for PSL use  -- record component layout
  record at mod 4  -- align on every 4'th storage unit
                   -- assume storage unit = 8 bits
      Carry_CC    at 0 range 0 .. 0;
      Overflow_CC at 0 range 1 .. 1;
      Zero_CC     at 0 range 2 .. 2;
      Negative_CC at 0 range 3 .. 3;
      TTE         at 0 range 4 .. 4;
      IOTE        at 0 range 5 .. 5;
      FUTE        at 0 range 6 .. 6;
      DOTE        at 0 range 7 .. 7;
                                      -- 8 spare bits
      IPL         at 2 range 0 .. 4;
                                      -- 1 spare bit
      PAM         at 2 range 6 .. 7;
      CAM         at 3 range 0 .. 1;
      EIS         at 3 range 2 .. 2;
      IFPD        at 3 range 3 .. 3;
                                      -- 2 spare bits
      TTP         at 3 range 6 .. 6;
      CM          at 3 range 7 .. 7;
  end record;

  for PSL'Size use 32;   -- 32 bits; length clause

  PSLW : PSL;
  for PSLW use at 16#00A0#;

end Processor_Status_Longword;
```

Figure 19-1 *(continued).* Specification of DEC VAX-11 Processor Status Longword.

number of storage units reserved for the activation of a task object of a given task type [DOD83, p. 13-12].

19.1.3 Record Representation Clauses

A record representation clause is used to specify the order, position, and size of record components. This is illustrated in Figure 19-1 with a representation of a VAX-11 (Digital Equipment Corporation) Processor Status Longword (PSL) [LEV80, pp. 257 and 278]. The types Flag, Priority, and Mode are specified for use by the individual record components of PSL. The record component layout is declared by specifying the bit position(s) within a given storage unit.

The interrupt priority level (IPL), for example, is represented by bits 0 through 4 of the third storage unit. The physical layout of the PSL is shown in Figure 19-2. The record component layout is used in conjunction with the enumeration representation and the length clauses as shown here, and with the address clauses as described below.

19.1.4 Address Clauses

Address clauses are used to associate objects and interrupt entries with hardware addresses. This kind of feature has never before been specified in a widely used high-order programming language, and it remains to be seen how efficiently it can be implemented. We will also have to expect that the various software vendors will make their own interpretation of how this feature should be implemented. The LRM merely specifies the address clauses without any references to how they should be implemented.

19.1.4.1 Objects. An example of an address clause for an object is shown in Figure 19-1 with the declaration following the record component layout:

```
PSLW : PSL;   -- an object of type PSL
for PSLW use at 16#00A0#;   -- object associated with an
                            -- address
```

We first declare the object, then we associate it with a hardware address. We should avoid having literal values sprinkled throughout our code and should use symbolic addresses instead:

```
PSLW : PSL;
for PSLW use at PSL_Address;
```

The hardware dependent symbolic addresses can be collected in one or more packages for easy identification of non-portable items.

Another example of an address clause for an object is shown in Figure 19-3 for a digital thermometer handler. Two distinct hardware buffers (DT_Buffer_Furnace and DT_Buffer_Temp) are declared and associated with symbolic hardware addresses (DT_Buffer_Furnace_Adr and DT_Buffer_Temp_Adr, respectively). The value of the furnace number (F) received via the entry call is placed in the digital thermometer furnace buffer (DT_Buffer_Furnace). The task waits for an interrupt from the digital thermometer and retrieves the value of the temperature of the furnace from the digital

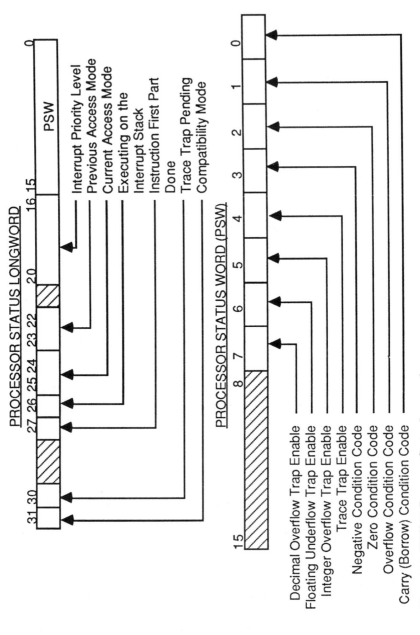

Figure 19-2. VAX-11 Processor Status Longword.

PROCESSOR STATUS LONGWORD

PSW

Interrupt Priority Level
Previous Access Mode
Current Access Mode
Executing on the
Interrupt Stack
Instruction First Part
Done
Trace Trap Pending
Compatibility Mode

PROCESSOR STATUS WORD (PSW)

Decimal Overflow Trap Enable
Floating Underflow Trap Enable
Integer Overflow Trap Enable
Trace Trap Enable
Negative Condition Code
Zero Condition Code
Overflow Condition Code
Carry (Borrow) Condition Code

```ada
separate (Device_Handlers)

task body DT_Handler is
  DT_Buffer_Furnace : Furnace_Type;
  for DT_Buffer_Furnace use at DT_Buffer_Furnace_Adr;

  DT_Buffer_Temp : Temp_Type;
  for DT_Buffer_Temp use at DT_Buffer_Temp_Adr;

  Max_DT_Response_Time : constant Duration := 10.0;
begin
  loop
    begin  -- exception handler
      accept Read_Temp (F : in Furnace_Type;
                        T : out Temp_Type) do
        DT_Buffer_Furnace := F;

        select
          accept DT_Interrupt;
        or
          delay Max_DT_Response_Time;
          raise No_Response_From_DT;
        end select;

        T := DT_Buffer_Temp;
      end Read_Temp;

    exception
      when No_Response_From_DT =>
        null;  -- we want to continue task execution
    end;  -- exception
  end loop;
end DT_Handler;
```

Figure 19-3. Object address clauses.

thermometer temperature buffer (DT_Buffer_Temp). This value (T) is returned to the caller of the task entry.

19.1.4.2 Interrupts. In addition to being able to associate buffers, channels, and registers with hardware addresses in Ada, we can also link task entries to interrupt locations. We have already included this feature in the example shown in Figure 2-1 without describing the effect of the address association. When we have associated a

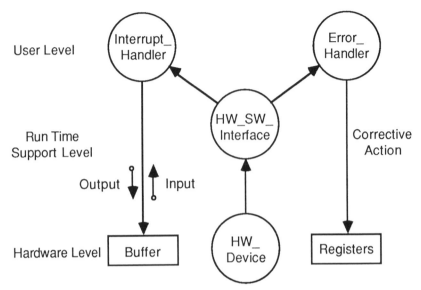

Figure 19-4. Model of interrupt handling.

task entry with an interrupt location, and the interrupt occurs, control is transferred to the task containing the entry. The accept body is then executed as it would for a normal rendezvous, and we may think of the interrupt handling as interfacing with a mythical hardware task.

Vectoring of the interrupt to the task entry is no simple process and is highly implementation dependent. One model of this process is shown in Figure 19-4. The model contains three separate levels of concern:

1. At the user level we write the interrupt handler as a task and associate the entry with an interrupt location. An example is shown in Figure 19-5 for a keyboard handler. We are here using the attribute Address to associate the task entry with the symbolic interrupt address (Kbd_Interrupt'Address), and the program buffer with the hardware buffer (Kbd_Data'Address).

    In this model we also have to provide an error handler to account for the possibility that our interrupt handler is busy when another interrupt occurs. The error handler may have to take corrective actions to reset certain bits in the hardware registers.

2. At the run time support level there is an interface task between the hardware and our software at the user level. This interface will first determine if the interrupt handler is immediately

```
with Hardware_Interface;

task Kbd_Handler is
  entry Kbd_Input;
  for Kbd_Input use at
              Hardware_Interface.Kbd_Interrupt'Address;
end Kbd_Handler;


task body Kbd_Handler is
  Kbd_Buffer : Character;
  for Kbd_Buffer use at
              Hardware_Interface.Kbd_Data'Address;
  Local_Input : Character;
begin
  loop
    accept Kbd_Input do
      Local_Input := Kbd_Buffer;
    end Kbd_Input;

    -- process character obtained from Kbd_Buffer

  end loop;
end Kbd_Handler;
```

Figure 19-5. User level device handler.

available to accept the current interrupt. If it is, the interface task will provide for the necessary context switching, task scheduling of the interrupt handler, and transfer of control to the task entry of the interrupt handler. If the interrupt handler is not immediately available to accept the current interrupt, the interface task provides for the equivalent functions for the error handler, which is expected to take appropriate corrective action. A rough sketch of the interface task is illustrated in Figure 19-6. Various optimization schemes may be incorporated to speed up the handling of interrupts.

3. At the hardware level we have the mythical hardware task which sends the interrupt to the interface task. Also at this level are the hardware buffers and registers. The interrupt handler will access the buffers for input or output, and the error handler will manipulate the registers to take corrective action.

```
task body Kbd_Interface is
begin
  loop
    ...
    accept Interrupt_From_Kbd_Task;
      ...
      select
        Kbd_Handler.Kbd_Input;
      else
        Kbd_Error_Handler.Recovery_Entry;
      end select;
      ...
    end Interrupt_From_Kbd_Task;
    ...
  end loop;
end Kbd_Interface;
```

Figure 19-6. Runtime support level H/W-S/W interface task.

We have here only described a single model for how the interrupt handling may be handled in an actual implementation. Different software vendors will most likely employ different approaches for this implementation, and we will have to understand their approach before we can design our interrupt handlers using Ada.

19.2   Machine Code Insertions

The specification of Ada allows the use of machine code insertions in procedure bodies [DOD83, p. 13-14]. The only constructs allowed in connection with machine code insertions are the code statements, *use* clauses, comments, and pragmas. Exception handlers are not allowed. The use of machine code is, of course, highly implementation dependent and should be avoided whenever possible. Each implementation may impose additional restrictions over those specified in the language reference manual. Some implementations may not provide this feature at all.

The code statements have the following format:

```
code statement ::= type_mark'record_aggregate;
```

The base type of the type mark of a code statement must be declared within a predefined library package called Machine_Code. This package provides record declarations for the instructions of the target machine and must be imported in the context of the procedure that contains the machine code statements. The following example is from the Ada reference manual [DOD83, p. 13-14]:

```
M : Mask;
procedure Set_Mask;
pragma Inline (Set_Mask);
procedure Set_Mask is
   use Machine_Code;
begin
   SI_Format'(Code => SSM, B => M'Base_Reg, D => M'Disp);
   -- M'Base_Reg and M'Disp are implementation-specific
   -- predefined attributes
end Set_Mask;
```

The pragma Inline instructs the compiler to produce in-line code, rather than a closed procedure, whenever the procedure is used.

19.3 Interfacing to Other Languages

To promote software reusability, the pragma Interface is specified to allow Ada programs to call subprograms written in another language. The following example is taken from the Ada reference manual [DOD83, p. 13–15]:

```
package Fortran_Library is
   function Sqrt (X : Float) return Float;
   function Exp  (X : Float) return Float;
private
   pragma Interface (Fortran, Sqrt);
   pragma Interface (Fortran, Exp);
end Fortran_Library;
```

For the square root and exponential functions required, we have declared Ada functions in the usual manner. The bodies of these Ada functions are not supplied, however, and the pragma Interface is informing the compiler to establish linkage conventions to the equivalent Fortran functions. The actual object code will be provided later during the normal link editing process. We must supply the pragma for each Ada subprogram that is using a module in another language, and all communication with the called Ada subprograms must be achieved via parameter passing and/or function results. The pragma Interface is not defined for generic subprograms. Certain restrictions may be placed on the allowable forms and placements of parameters and calls.

There is no requirement specified in [DOD83] that an implementation must support interfaces to certain languages, and some vendors may choose not to support any.

Summary

In this part we have described general Ada design principles that can be used for real-time and sequential systems. In Chapter 9 we included heuristics for how to decompose a large real-time system into a set of cooperating sequential processes. We described a graphic notation for depicting interfaces between concurrent processes, and we described how we introduce intermediaries to reduce the coupling between concurrent processes.

In Chapter 10 we discussed the use of Ada packages as an encapsulation mechanism and how to create data abstractions. We also presented a taxonomy of Ada packages for design usage:

1. Application packages

2. Communication packages

3. Helper packages

    a. Services

    b. Definitions

    c. Data managers

        i. Abstract data types (ADTs) (type managers)

- Open ADT
- Closed ADT

    ii.   Resources (object managers)

Chapter 11 contains a description for how to determine potential generic units during preliminary design and how to construct generic units. The three different kinds of parameters associated with generic units are:

1. Object parameters
2. Type parameters
3. Subprogram parameters

In Chapter 12 we illustrated how to design large sequential portions of a real-time system (or a complete sequential system) using layered virtual machines. This approach makes use of the following concepts and tools:

1. Create top-level virtual machine.
2. Construct support packages.
3. Create data managers.
4. Illustrate design with object-oriented design diagrams.
5. Show hierarchy with structure charts.
6. Create lower level virtual machines and data managers.

Coupling and cohesion have been used in traditional structured design as a guide for creating good software designs. We have expanded these principles in Chapter 13 to include Ada packages and tasks. The additional coupling concepts include:

1. Definition coupling (for Ada packages)
2. Package coupling (for Ada packages)
3. Concurrency coupling (for the Ada tasking model)

In Chapter 14 we described data passed between communicating processes in terms of channels and pool. A channel represents data that is created by a producer and passed on to a consumer, without any kind of manipulation. A pool, on the other hand, is not consumed but is manipulated. Pools in Ada must be protected with mutual exclusion for access by the communicating processes.

When we create a set of communicating processes in Ada, we must provide the proper level of asynchronism between them. This is accomplished by introducing intermediary tasks. We described various tasking paradigms in Chapter 15 in terms of loose and tight coupling between producer/consumer pairs. We also discussed the additional run time overhead that is associated with introducing intermediary tasks. The asymmetric caller/called relations of Ada rendezvous have an effect on which task is the caller and which task should be called. In Chapter 16 we specified caller/called conventions for intermediary tasks and provided guidelines for application tasks. Busy tasks should be called to give them control of the rendezvous choices. Algorithmically complex tasks should be callers. This will reduce the complexity of the task body by introducing simple abstractions to replace portions of the algorithm.

Polling in Ada can be implemented using the tasking model, and in Chapter 17 we described rendezvous polling for a task that is repeatedly attempting to rendezvous with another task. Information polling is defined for a task that is repeatedly rendezvousing with another task, for example, by accessing a status bit in a register.

In Chapter 18 we presented a taxonomy for the use of exception handling in Ada. The recommended categories include:

1. Anticipated conditions

2. General purpose software

3. Hardware failures

4. Invalid input data

5. Unanticipated errors (bugs)

In Chapter 19 we described the use of the following representation clauses:

1. Enumeration type representation clauses

2. Length clauses

3. Record representation clauses

4. Address clauses

    a. Objects

    b. Interrupts

We also discussed the potential use of machine code insertion, and how to interface from Ada to software written in other programming languages.

Ada Real-Time Design Methodology

In this part we will specify a complete Ada real-time design methodology which uses the tools and design principles described in Parts 1 to 3. The methodology uses elements from Modular Approach to Software Construction Operation and Test (MASCOT) [BIR85, ALL81], Design Approach for Real-Time Systems (DARTS) [GOM84], structured design [YOU79, PAG80, MEL86], object-oriented design [ABB83, BOO86], and layered virtual machines [DIJ68, ALL81]. These are general, programming language–independent concepts and methodologies that we have adapted to Ada real-time implementations. Our methodology applies to the design of both concurrent and sequential systems.

The central focus of our integrated approach is that any program is a virtual machine that accomplishes all the required functionality. The appropriate way to construct such a machine is to build it with abstraction specifications of lower level machines; hence we have the concept of layered virtual machines. These machines include data objects and their operations, as well as the abstract functions that the machines perform. We thus have an object-oriented approach.

The part of our methodology that applies to the concurrent aspects of the design is to identify those major software modules that will execute in parallel. The parallelism may be actual in multiprocessor systems, or apparent with the concurrent processes competing for the use of a single processor. We use process abstraction *to identify concurrent actions and decompose the system into parallel machines that can operate simultaneously (see Chapters 5, 6, and 9). Each of the concurrent processes is a primitive element, with sequential execution of its instructions.*

The part of our methodology that applies to the sequential aspects of the design is to decompose each primitive process into smaller software components that can then be designed in detail, coded, and tested. This decomposition breaks the larger problem into smaller pieces using data *and* procedural *abstractions (see Chapters 5, 6, 10, and 12).*

In Chapter 21 we give a background of the major language independent design methodologies that we have used in developing our Ada-specific methodology. We describe our step-by-step design approach in Chapter 22 using a robot controller to illustrate the various graphical tools employed. Informal and formal design reviews are discussed, as well as proper documentation of a large real-time system. Suggestions are made for how the methodology can be used for implementation languages other than Ada. In Chapter 23 we describe how we use Ada as a program design language for top-level and detail design. Chapter 24 contains a summary of Part 4.

21

Background

In this chapter we describe the traditional language independent software design concepts and methodologies that we have adapted for use with our Ada-specific real-time design methodology.

21.1 MASCOT

MASCOT (Modular Approach to Software Construction Operation and Test) was originally developed in England in the early 1970s and is a widely used real-time design methodology in the United Kingdom [SIM79, BIR85, p. 41]. It includes a formal approach that is independent of hardware configurations and a specific programming language. The methodology supports the complete life cycle, and the design approach is intended to create a highly modular system that is straightforward to implement and maintain.

The design approach in MASCOT is centered around the creation of data objects and the *activities* that operate on these objects. The data objects are of two types:

1. *Channels.* Queues containing data objects that are consumed (data is simply passed through; it is not modified).

2. *Pools.* Data bases of non-consumed data objects that are created, modified, and deleted.

Activities are single-thread concurrent processes with the following characteristics:

1. *Operations.* They operate on channels and pools.

2. *Graphical notation.* They are represented as a set of networking nodes in an Activity-Channel-Pool (ACP) diagram. Interfaces between the activities are illustrated with Intercommunication Data Areas (IDAs) as shown in Figure 21-1.

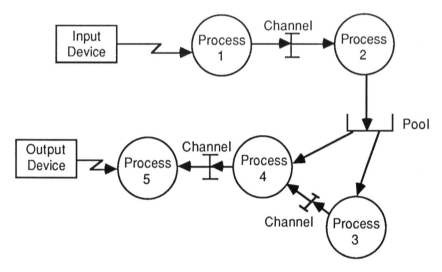

Figure 21-1. Activity-channel-pool network in MASCOT.

3. *Functional entities.* They represent functional entities that have a close correspondence with the items in the requirements specification.

The basic design approach is to start with a set of DFDs and define a set of co-operating asynchronous activities from the data flows. The IDAs for the channels and pools are identified to describe the communication between the activities. The resulting ACP network represents the top-level design of the system. An example of an ACP is shown in Figure 21-1.

We have adopted the MASCOT approach of describing the concurrent processes as a network architecture, with appropriate interfaces between the processes. We do not use the exact graphic notation for the interfaces as shown in Figure 21-1; we use a slightly modified version as described below. MASCOT does not provide specific guidelines for how to create a set of activities (processes) that operate concurrently.

21.2 Design Approach for Real-Time Systems (DARTS)

DARTS represents a formal design methodology for real-time systems. It is based on MASCOT and includes an enhanced graphical notation for illustrating concurrent processes and their interfaces. We have adopted this graphical notation with minor modifications, as shown in Figures 21-2 and 21-3. DARTS also includes a set of rules for how to create the concurrent processes from DFDs. We have adopted this set of heuristics with some extensions (see the process selection rules in Chapter 9).

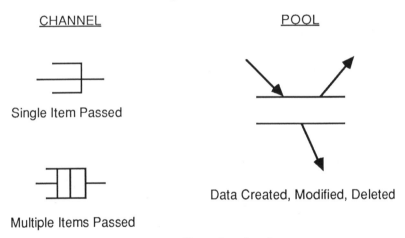

Figure 21-2. Channels and pools.

The DARTS approach consists of the following steps:

1. *Data flow diagrams.* Draw DFDs for the complete system.

2. *Determine concurrency.* Use the DFDs and a set of rules to determine a set of concurrent processes.

3. *Define interfaces.* Define appropriate interfaces between the concurrent processes for the channels and pools in the system.

4. *Defer design decisions.* Defer design decisions by specifying a set of interface modules, e.g., process communication modules and process synchronization modules. Appropriately named abstractions are used to specify the modules.

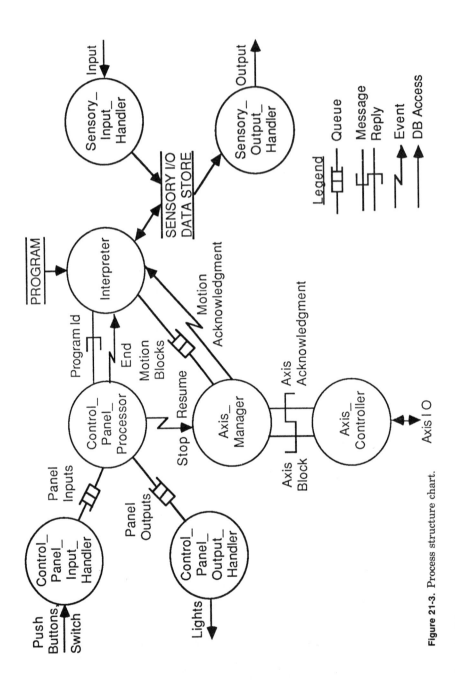

Figure 21-3. Process structure chart.

204

5. *Decompose complex processes.* Use structured design (graphically represented with structure charts) to decompose each single-thread process that is complex or large.

6. *Finite state machines.* Augment the detailed design with FSMs for state transition oriented processes.

The first three of these steps are commensurate with our methodology. As a fourth step we create appropriate Ada communication packages as described in Chapter 10. These packages are typically generic. To decompose large tasks, or systems that are primarily sequential, we use the layered virtual machine approach as described in Chapter 12. We do employ the concept of finite state machines and implement them as Ada tasks and subprograms.

21.3 Structured Design

The original structured design approach as presented in [YOU79 and PAG80] was intended for large sequential systems and did not include real-time concepts. The primary design strategies included transform analysis as a bridge between data flow diagrams and structure charts, and transaction analysis to decompose a large transaction-oriented sequential processing system. The concepts of coupling and cohesion were used as guidelines for creating good designs.

The traditional structured design approach has been extended by Ward and Mellor to include real-time features for both the system analysis and the design phases. The approach is called Structured Development for Real-Time Systems, and is documented in a three-volume book series [WAR85a, WAR85b, and MEL86]. The first volume describes analysis tools used for real-time systems, such as adding control flows to DFDs and distinguishing between time-continuous and time-discrete behavior. The second volume presents modeling techniques for analyzing a real-time system using DFDs with data and control flows, and state-transition diagrams and tables. It also describes a context schema for analyzing external interfaces. The third volume contains a set of heuristics for designing a real-time system.

We have adapted the following structured design concepts for our methodology:

1. *Data flow diagrams.* DFDs with control flows to indicate events or signals are used in the analysis phase.

2. *Structure charts.* Structure charts are used in the creation of layered virtual machines for the functional decomposition of

large Ada tasks. The names of the subprograms include the package that encapsulates them.

3. *Coupling and cohesion.* We have extended the traditional concepts to include coupling and cohesion for Ada tasks and packages.

4. *Context schema.* We are using the context diagram to illustrate the external interfaces to the real-time control program we have to design.

5. *State-transition diagrams.* State-transition diagrams and tables are used in the construction of finite state machines.

6. *Heuristics.* Several of the heuristics presented in Reference MEL86 are used as part of the process selection rules (see Chapter 9), and in the design evaluation guidelines (see Chapter 26).

21.4 Object-Oriented Design

Object-oriented design has been considered as the most important software development approach [ABB83, BOO86, EVB85] for Ada since the advent of structured design [YOU79]. It does not represent a complete software development *methodology* for real-time systems, however; it is a *concept* that supports modern software design paradigms. The term "object" means many things to many people, and we need to formally define this term before we can analyze various parts of our methodology in an object-oriented sense.

21.4.1 Object Definition

An *object* can be loosely described as an entity whose behavior is characterized by the actions performed on it, and the actions that it requires of other objects [BOO86]. A formal definition for an object includes the following:

1. An object is an entity that can be abstracted, classified, or categorized by its type, i.e., an object is a member of a class or can be considered an instance of the class. A class can be anonymous.

2. The class of an object has associated with it a set of operations that are allowed on the objects belonging to that class.

3. An object has certain states, e.g., a task can be running, ready, or blocked, and data can be initialized or uninitialized.

4. An object is denoted by a name.

5. An object can be observed either by its specification or its implementation.

21.4.2 Objects and Classes in Ada

Examples of objects in Ada include:

1. Constants, variables, and data structures
2. Subprograms
3. Packages
4. Tasks
5. Generic instantiations of subprograms and packages

Examples of classes in Ada include:

1. Type specifications
2. Generic subprogram specifications
3. Generic package specifications
4. Task type specifications
5. Finite state machine concept (anonymous class)
6. Abstract data types

21.4.3 Object-Oriented Design Approach

We use the objects and classes as abstract building blocks to manage complexity. We identify classes to promote several instances of objects throughout the design and implementation of our program. Our methodology is based on the concepts of creating objects in layers of abstraction, information hiding, and stepwise refinement (deferring of design decisions).

21.4.3.1 Functional and Data Abstraction. From the requirement specifications we draw data flow diagrams (DFDs) to identify the major functional transforms and the data flows between them. A DFD is considered an anonymous class, and the transforms represent abstract functional objects. The data flows and control logic illustrate the interfaces between the objects shown on the DFD.

21.4.3.2 Process Abstraction. Using the DFDs and a set of heuristics we identify abstract *concurrent objects*. These objects are virtual parallel machines that represent the modeling of the problem into a set of concurrent processes and their interfaces. A process can here be considered an anonymous class, and the concurrent processes we identify in our solution model are the objects (instances of the process class) that will later be implemented as Ada packages, subprograms, and tasks.

21.4.3.3 Tasks and Task Coupling. From the context diagram and the process structure chart we determine the Ada tasks that will implement our concurrent solution model. We introduce intermediary tasks for the proper level of coupling between producer and consumer tasks. The intermediary tasks are usually instantiations (objects) of generic specifications (classes) for buffers, relays, and transporters. Identical application tasks are implemented as task objects declared using a task type specification (class).

21.4.3.4 Packaging . The package classification shown in the taxonomy chart (see Chapter 10) represents classes (some of them anonymous) for the various ways we can construct package objects in Ada. We can, for example, implement an open or a closed package (object) as an ADT (class), or we may choose a resource instead. Some of these packages are created as instantiations (objects) of generic specifications (classes).

21.4.3.5 Implementation. We transform the graphical, abstract design into Ada code using a PDL. The package objects are implemented with various levels of information hiding by specifying private or limited private types (classes) or by placing the types in a package body. We also delay the importation of elements that reside in library packages by deferring the context clauses (*with*ing) to package and subprogram bodies, and to subunits. Stepwise refinement (deferring of design decisions) is promoted by using the *separate* statement for the top-level PDL. The bodies (implementation) are supplied as subunits during the detailed design and coding phases. This supports the layered virtual machine concept, where objects can be replaced or modified without disturbing the overall architecture.

We have shown in this chapter how our entire design methodology is object oriented in the general sense, i.e., with the global definition of classes and objects given above. Our primary concern with objects in this book, however, is in the narrow sense that was described in

Chapters 5 and 12. We use the LVM/OOD approach to create objects to support layered virtual machines as we decompose large Ada tasks.

Ada Design Methodology

This chapter describes the various steps of the real-time design methodology, using a robot controller as a model real-time system to illustrate the methodology. Complete case studies using this methodology are included as Appendixes A, D, and E.

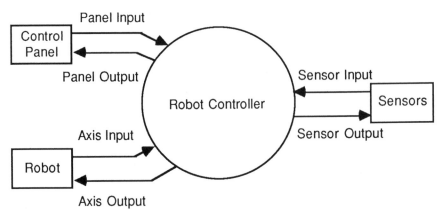

Figure 22-1. Context diagram.

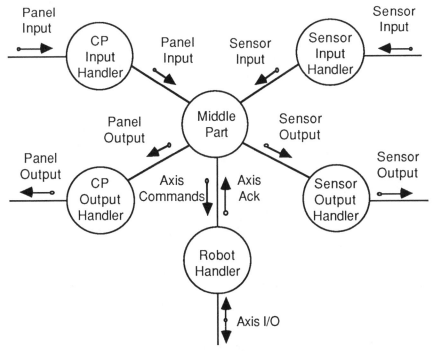

Figure 22-2. Preliminary concurrent process graph.

Our methodology has emerged by taking the parts of MASCOT and DARTS that apply to real-time systems, and complementing them with elements from structured design and object-oriented design. The integrated Ada design approach consists of the following steps to be performed in sequence:

1. *Determine hardware interfaces.* Draw a context diagram to illustrate the interfaces between the software system we are designing and the various hardware devices. An example of a context diagram is shown in Figure 22-1 for a robot controller [GOM84, GRO86]. The hardware devices in this system consist of the operator control panel, the robot itself, and the sensors that control the movements of the robot arms. The circle represents the functionality of the system we are designing, i.e., the program that will control the hardware devices and perform the required functional operations.

2. *Assign processes to the edge functions.* Using the first rule of the process selection rules in Chapter 9, we assign a separate process to each of the hardware devices as shown in Figure 22-2. We have now transformed the context diagram into a

preliminary concurrent process graph that consists of the processes that interface with the hardware devices and a large Middle Part. The processes will be implemented as Ada tasks encapsulated in library packages. The Middle Part can be viewed as a large non-primitive process that must be decomposed into a set of primitive (single-thread) processes.

3. *Decompose the Middle Part.* We use DFDs to decompose the system described in the requirements specification. For a large system we include leveled DFDs as described in Chapter 7. A decomposition of the robot controller is shown in Figure 22-3. This DFD will form the basis for determining the concurrent parts of the system.

4. *Determine concurrency.* We use the functionality displayed on the DFD and the process selection rules of Chapter 9 to combine the transforms of the middle part into processes, as shown in Figure 22-4. This figure depicts all the robot controller processes, represented as rectangles and squares, including the three for the external devices. The rationale for this particular selection is described in detail in the case study in Appendix E.

5. *Determine process interfaces.* The edge processes and the processes of the middle part and their interfaces are represented in a process structure chart as shown in Figure 22-5. This figure depicts a set of communicating sequential processes and shows the level of coupling that we have decided should exist between them. How we made these decisions is discussed in detail in Appendix E.

6. *Introduce intermediary processes.* This step includes the translation of the process structure shown in Figure 22-5 into Ada tasks and the introduction of the necessary intermediary processes, as described in Chapter 15. The addition of intermediary processes results in the Ada task graph shown in Figure 22-6. The procedure we have used to create this structure, including the caller/called decisions, is further discussed below. The result of having completed the caller/called decisions is shown in Figure 22-7.

7. *Encapsulate tasks in Ada packages.* Ada tasks cannot exist as library units; they must be encapsulated in subprograms or packages. We must make appropriate decisions for how this packaging should be performed. The result for the robot controller is shown in Figure 22-8, and the guidelines we used for these decisions are described below.

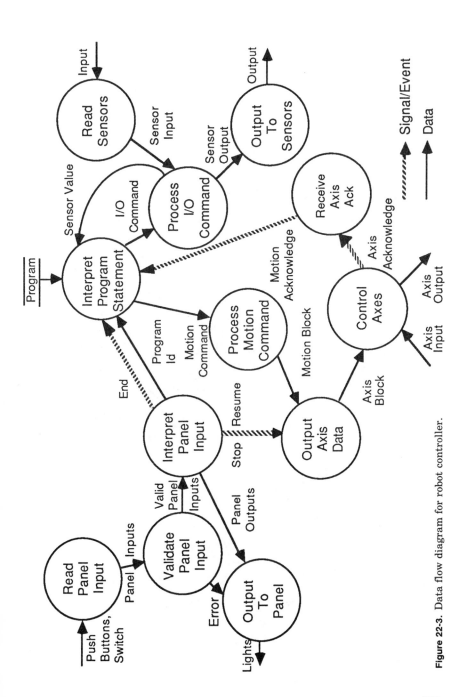

Figure 22-3. Data flow diagram for robot controller.

213

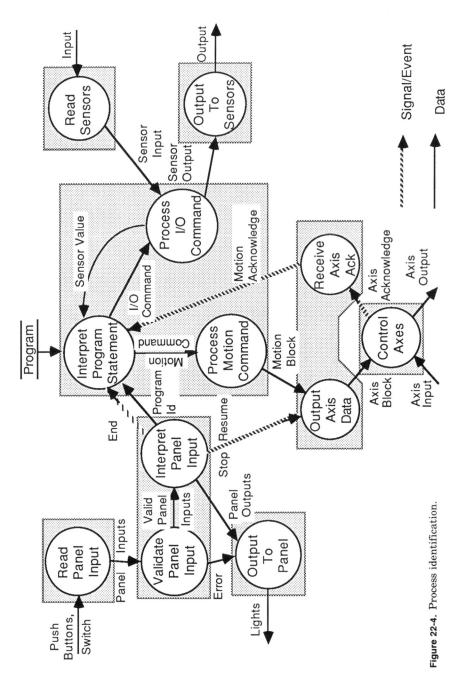

Figure 22-4. Process identification.

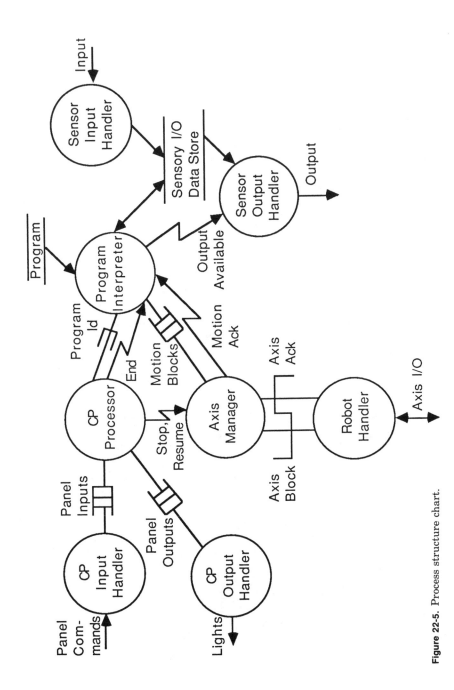

Figure 22-5. Process structure chart.

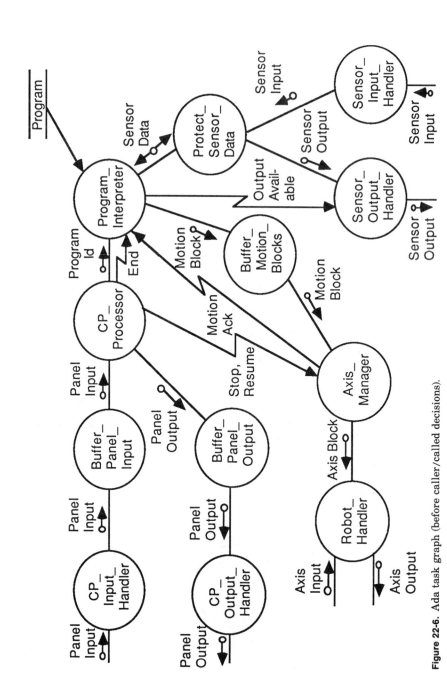

Figure 22-6. Ada task graph (before caller/called decisions).

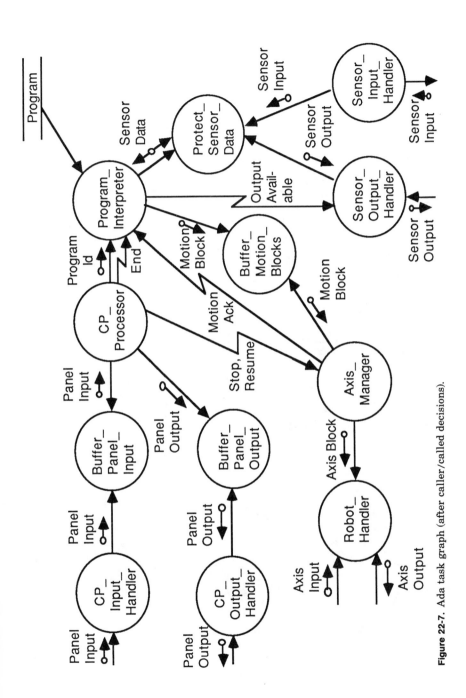

Figure 22-7. Ada task graph (after caller/called decisions).

217

218

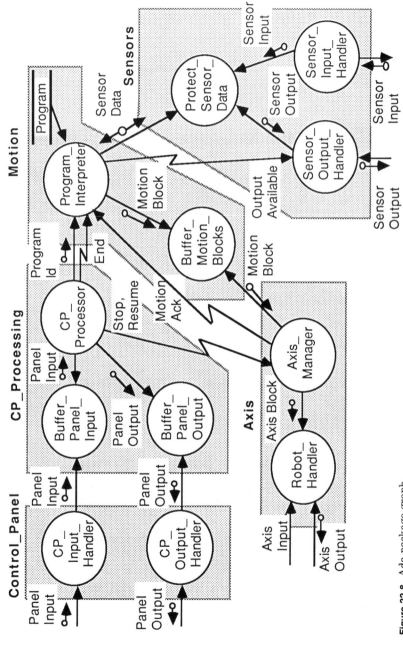

Figure 22-8. Ada package graph.

8. *Translate design into Ada PDL.* The first step toward creating a program that can be implemented on a given machine is to translate the design from graphical and written representations into programming constructs. The general use of an Ada PDL was described in Chapter 7. Chapter 23 presents an outline of the top-level and detailed design for the robot controller. The complete design is included in Appendix E.

9. *Decompose large tasks.* Tasks that are determined to be too large to be implemented in a single task body are further decomposed using the layered virtual machine/object–oriented design approach specified in Chapter 12.

10. *Conduct design reviews.* Informal and formal design reviews should be considered part of the design methodology. Informal reviews should be held throughout the design and coding phases. The first formal design review is held at the completion of the top-level design. The second is held at the completion of the detailed design. Other formal reviews (e.g., to determine if the complete system is ready for validation testing) may be required contractually.

Each step of the methodology described above (except for conducting design reviews) represents a layer of abstraction, with the creation of a set of virtual machines as the product of the step. Every virtual machine in our design represents an abstraction of a portion of the problem specification and provides a clear cross reference between the requirements specification and the problem solution. This greatly facilitates the evaluation of the correctness of the design.

We now examine the various steps in detail. Ada as a PDL is discussed in a separate chapter.

22.1 Decomposing the Middle Part

Decomposing the system is accomplished by first identifying the major transforms and data flows from the requirements specification, and illustrating them graphically with DFDs. We then use the process selection rules given in Chapter 9 to combine transforms into concurrent processes. These processes will be implemented as Ada tasks with, possibly, additional intermediary tasks.

It would be ideal if we could simply use the process selection rules to determine the decomposition of the system. The number of processes created from the transforms in the DFDs (plus the intermediaries) is, however, dependent upon how much tasking overhead we can tolerate for the executing system. When the Ada tasks are competing for the use of a processor, context switches are usually performed to get a new task image ready for execution. Each context switch is associated with a certain amount of overhead that can take microseconds or milliseconds, depending upon the speed of the processor and how efficiently the run-time support is implemented [BUR87]. Each time Ada tasks communicate via a rendezvous, on the average of two context switches take place. The practical implications of this overhead is that even though we can give a set of process selection rules, we must keep the number of Ada tasks small to minimize the run-time overhead. This design concern is not unique to Ada implementations; we would face similar problems when implementing Pascal and C programs that need primitive tasking services from a real-time executive.

22.2   Process Coupling

A combination of loosely and tightly coupled processes (see Chapter 13) are shown in the process structure chart presented as Figure 22-5. Loosely coupled pairs of processes are CP Input Handler and CP Processor, CP Processor and CP Output Handler, and Program Interpreter and Axis Manager. The loose coupling will allow these processes to operate at their own, natural speed in an asynchronous fashion. CP Input Handler, for example, simply stores panel inputs in a queue without waiting for CP Processor to finish its processing of any of these inputs.

Tight coupling is required between Axis Manager and Robot Handler because the former is waiting for a reply (acknowledgement) from the latter. A less severe form for tight coupling is shown between CP Processor and Program Interpreter where the former is passing a command (Program Id) to the latter. The least restrictive form for tight coupling is where a pair of processes interact via signaling. This is depicted as CP Processor sending a signal, "Stop" or "Resume" to Axis Manager, and "End" to Program Interpreter. Axis Manager sends the signal "Motion Ack" to Program Interpreter.

The processes Program Interpreter, Sensor Input Handler, and Sensor Output Handler are coupled through the use of the shared data Sensory I/O Data Store. This form of coupling requires a careful consideration for providing mutual exclusion for access to the shared data to prevent an erroneous program.

22.3 Intermediary Processes

Intermediary processes (*tasks* for an Ada design) are used to implement the required coupling between producer/consumer pairs. A brief discussion of the intermediaries used for the robot controller example is provided in the following paragraphs. A detailed discussion is included for the case study in Appendix E.

22.3.1 Introducing Intermediary Processes

The effect of having two loosely coupled processes, CP Input Handler and CP Processor, is obtained by introducing a buffer task between them as shown in the Ada task graph (ATG) in Figure 22-6. The same effect has been achieved for the process pairs CP Processor and CP Output Handler, and Program Interpreter and Axis Manager. (The underscores used in Figure 22-6 signify that the names now correspond to actual Ada tasks, rather than the abstract processes shown in Figure 22-5).

The protection of the shared Sensory I/O Data Store is obtained by introducing the task Protect_Sensor_Data. This task will guarantee mutually exclusive access to the shared data and prevent erroneous programming.

The intermediary processes that are added to the system will operate on appropriate buffers and queues and will not only store and retrieve data, but will also manipulate the required pointers for proper insertion and removal. The design details of these data structures can be delayed until the detailed Program Design Language (PDL) statements are written (see Chapter 23 for details).

22.3.2 Caller/Called Decisions

The task control shown in the ATG of Figure 22-7 represents all the caller/called decisions that have been made for the robot controller. For example, the CP_Input_Handler is an interrupt handler that has an entry for the panel input interrupt. When an interrupt is accepted, this task retrieves the panel input (from a hardware buffer), calls an entry in the task Buffer_Panel_Input, and passes the panel input as an *in* parameter. Buffer_Panel_Input also has an entry for providing panel input as an *out* parameter when this entry is called by CP_Processor. The latter task has no entries; it is a caller in relation to both Buffer_Panel_Input and Program_Interpreter. The task Program_Interpreter has three entries. One of these entries accepts a call from CP_Processor with Program Id as an *in* parameter. The other two entries (parameterless) are supplied to accept the signaling events End from CP_Processor and Motion Ack from Axis_Manager.

The caller/called decisions described here and the remaining decisions shown in Figure 22-7 have been made in accordance with the guidelines given in Chapter 16. One thing to keep in mind is that we sometimes must iterate between the choice of an intermediary task and the appropriate caller/called decisions. For example, if we decided that CP_Processor should be called for the delivery of the Panel Input, we would have to replace the buffer task Buffer_Panel_Input with a relay task. Additional details about caller/called decisions for the robot controller are provided in Appendix E.

22.4 Packaging Ada Tasks

Ada tasks cannot be declared as stand-alone units (library units), they must be declared within a subprogram or package. The packaging shown in Figure 22-8 has been made in accordance with the packaging rules given in Chapter 10. The first choice we made was that the tasks should reside within packages and not within subprograms. We could, for instance, have chosen to declare all the tasks within a main procedure. This would have violated the guidelines given in Chapter 10 for recompilation, reusability, and visibility, and is not a viable choice for this system. Generally speaking, the only tasks that should ever be declared within a main procedure are test drivers and tasks that simulate hardware devices.

The combination of tasks into the packages shown in Figure 22-8 is primarily based on their related functionality, which supports the other packaging criteria given in Chapter 10. The package Control_Panel, for example, consists of the two tasks CP_Input_Handler and CP_Output_Handler. Both of these tasks handle interrupts from the control panel.

CP_Processing contains all the tasks that deal with accessing and processing input and output for the control panel. The package Axis contains the highly related tasks Robot_Handler and Axis_Manager. This package could also have contained the three tasks that operate on the motion data, but that would have reduced the possibility for reusability, and increased the amount of recompilation required when changes were made. The two tasks Program_Interpreter and Buffer_Motion_Blocks were instead combined into the package Motion. The final three highly functionally related tasks, Protect_Sensor_Data, Sensor_Output_Handler, and Sensor_Input_Handler, were collected in the package Sensors.

Any additional tasks that may be required to test the system can be declared within the main procedure, or, if there is a high likelihood of reusability, in suitable separate packages.

22.5   Decomposing Large Ada Tasks

When we determine that the functionality of any one of the tasks is too large to be expressed within the prescribed number of lines of code for a task body, we must further decompose this task. The decomposition will be made with virtual machines and objects (see Chapter 12) for the sequential processing that represents the functionality of the task. We do not expect to find additional concurrency within the task; we hope that the concurrency aspects of the real-time system has already been established. If we do find that the task should be decomposed into two or more tasks, we have to perform a redesign which involves redrawing the graphics charts affected and making additional packaging decisions for the additional tasks.

As an example of the decomposition of a large task, we use the task CP_Processor, shown in Figure 22-8 to reside in the application package CP_Processing. The functionality of this task (see Figure 22-4) is to first get the next set of control panel inputs from the buffer. It must then validate the input received from the control panel. If the input is valid, it must interpret the input as a command and pass the command to the appropriate task. It must also prepare output for the operator at the control panel (seen by the operator as panel lights). The decomposition is performed by creating a layered virtual machine as illustrated in Figure 22-9. We have used a structure chart to show the hierarchy of the abstractions (subprograms) used to implement the functionality, and the data flow between the subprograms. Most of the instruction set for this machine consists of operations on an object. The object (data manager) is shown as the Ada package CP_Manager in the OOD diagram in Figure 22-10. The implementation of this package is included in the PDL for the case study in Appendix E.

22.6   Object Orientation

The object-oriented design method described by Booch [BOO83] *begins* with the identification of objects (packages) based on the informal (i.e., tailored) problem specification. We *end* with a set of objects that contain the concurrent elements of the system, based on the formal problem specification. The package graph shown in Figure 22-8 clearly illustrates the objects that comprise the design of

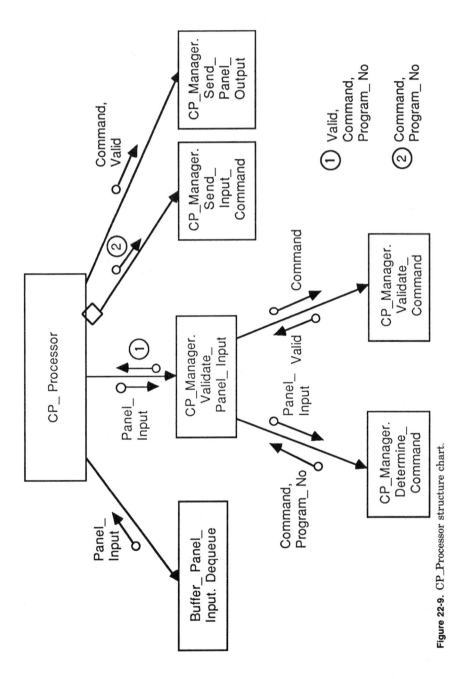

Figure 22-9. CP_Processor structure chart.

CP_Manager

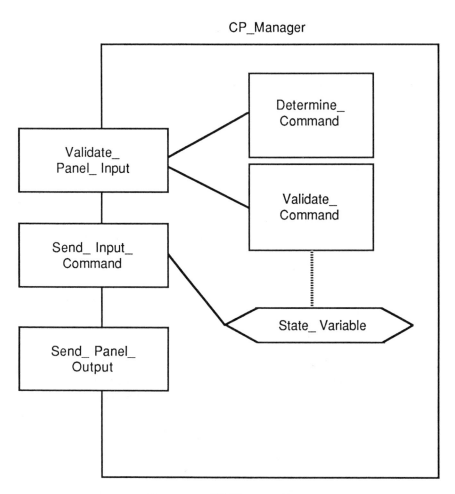

Figure 22-10. CP_Manager object.

the robot controller. Other examples of this object orientation are shown in Appendix A (Figure A-9) for the Remote Temperature Sensor System, and in Appendix D (Figure D-16) for the Air Traffic Control System.

We arrive at objects by a direct consideration of functionality and coupling; by providing guidelines for packaging criteria other than object encapsulation; and (most importantly) by providing explicit consideration of concurrency, including heuristics for task identification and interaction.

22.7   Design Reviews

The purpose of design reviews is to analyze and evaluate the design presented to the reviewers. The primary objective of the reviewers is to uncover flaws in the design. Other objectives include monitoring of progress and determining if adequate documentation is provided with the design. The paragraphs that follow discuss informal and formal design reviews and the documentation that should be provided.

22.7.1   Informal Reviews

Informal design reviews are not held with a specific frequency, but they should be held often, especially during the analysis phase and top-level design phase. The correct interpretation of the requirements specification for a large real-time system is extremely important and should not be performed in isolation by one or two individuals. Data flow diagrams form the basis for the top-level design and should be carefully reviewed by all the senior designers before the top-level design phase starts. During the top-level design phase, the graphics tools used to express the design should be reviewed after each stage. This includes the context diagrams, state-transition diagrams, DFDs, process identification charts, process graphs, process structure charts, Ada task graphs, and Ada package graphs.

During the detailed design phase, the primary review material is the Ada PDL. This should be reviewed for correspondence with the top-level design, adherence to project coding and design standards, and the proper structuring of the top-level design into Ada program units. A set of evaluation guidelines is provided in Chapter 26.

During the coding phase, the primary emphasis is on the correct implementation of the algorithms, the proper usage of design paradigms (e.g., exception handling), and adherence to coding standards.

It is important that software development files (SDFs) be maintained with records kept of all the design decisions made during, or as a result of, the informal reviews. This may be a contractual obligation for large government contracts, but should be used for any large software development project.

22.7.2   Formal Reviews

The formal design reviews conducted for a large real-time system are usually specified by contractual agreements and represent major milestones in the development process. They are conducted as formal presentations by the software developers, and attended by the customers. The first of these takes place after the top-level design is completed (we assume the requirements specification has been reviewed and accepted). This is sometimes referred to as the Preliminary Design Review (PDR), where the customer verifies that the functional specifications have been correctly and completely mapped to the top-level design.

The second formal design review is held at the end of the detailed design phase. This is sometimes called the Critical Design Review (CDR), where the customer verifies that the design decisions deferred during top-level design have now been completed. This includes any redesign that was required as a result of the PDR, and the algorithms necessary to implement the functionality of the system.

For certain government contracts a test readiness review is held at the end of the integration test phase. This is to verify that formal validation and acceptance testing can start. This review is a test of the complete system conducted under laboratory conditions. Simulators may be used for the hardware that is only available under field conditions.

There is currently a tendency within the software engineering community to prefer the use of rapid prototyping, rather than having a CDR for the complete system. If this tendency continues, this may lead to having a PDR of the complete top-level design, and mini-CDRs for the detailed design of each prototype implementation.

22.8 Documentation

Documentation is an integral part of the design methodology. It is necessary to provide adequate documentation for the following reasons:

1. To describe the design to others for their evaluation, or for their understanding as maintainers or users

2. To remind a designer or programmer why certain design decisions or programming steps were made

3. To fulfill contractual obligations

We have emphasized the use of graphical descriptions to represent the design, and for reducing the complexity of a large real-time system. This includes the graphical design tools described in Chapter 7. The other primary design documentation is the Ada PDL with its associated coding standards. It is extremely important that these standards be followed exactly, to provide a uniform format for reading large stacks of PDL listings. Most government contracts for large systems require design documentation with standardized contents and format, e.g., DOD-STD-2167 [DOD85]. This standard specifies a series of documents that are tied to the phases of the software development process. Examples are the Software Top-Level Design Document (STLDD) to be presented at PDR, and the Software Detailed Design Document (SDDD) to be presented at CDR. These documents include the use of graphical illustrations, PDL, and English descriptions.

22.9 Language Dependence

The emphasis throughout this book has been to develop a consistent design methodology for Ada implementations. Implementations in other programming languages may use parts of the methodology described here and tailor the remaining steps to the specific language. Of the steps outlined in the beginning of this chapter, the first five are language independent. The process structure chart presented for the robot controller in Figure 22-5 does not depend on Ada or the Ada tasking model. This structure can be implemented in any other programming language such as C, Pascal, or Fortran by implementing the processes and their interfaces using real-time executive service primitives available for the specific language. The remaining steps of our Ada methodology can be emulated for another language. Ada task graphs, for example, are replaced by concurrent process graphs, and Ada packaging is replaced by appropriate collections into "include" files. The use of an Ada PDL is not recommended for implementations in other languages. Even with a chosen Ada subset to fit the target language, the amount of effort required to change from Ada PDL to the target source code is not cost effective. A PDL in the target language can be used, but the benefits of Ada's strong type checking is lost. An alternative is to use a general purpose PDL that can be tailored to a specific target language, e.g., SDDL [KLE81].

The layered virtual machine approach can be used for sequential processing, but most other languages do not provide the equivalent of an Ada package for the convenient creation of objects. Structure charts for the hierarchical ordering of the layered virtual machines can be used exactly as we have demonstrated. The documentation of the machines is more straightforward than with Ada since the subprograms do not reside in various Ada packages.

23

Ada as Program Design Language

A program design language (PDL) is used to translate the design expressed in graphical terms into programming constructs. Process, procedural, and data abstractions have been made prior to the start of the PDL phase, which is tailored to a specific implementation language. The language in our case is Ada, and we use an automated PDL that has an Ada compiler as a "front end." The programming constructs will be legal Ada as specified in the language reference manual [DOD83], and the compiler will perform type checking of all interfaces between packages, subprograms, and tasks. The automated PDL can be a specialized tool such as Byron [INT85], or an Ada compiler such as DEC's VAX Ada. The rationale for choosing one automated PDL over another is project dependent and is not treated here.

The following paragraphs in this chapter describe the methodology of using an automated PDL for top-level and detailed design. A combination of a bottom-up and top-down approach is illustrated below using the robot controller as an example. A detailed treatment of the same example is included in Appendix E.

```
----------- Global Definitions -----------

package Definitions is
  Max_CP_Chars        : constant := 2;  -- max length of CP command
  Max_CP_Input        : constant := 10; -- max input to be buffered
  Max_CP_Output       : constant := 10; -- max output to be buffered
  Max_Commands        : constant := 36; -- max commands in a program
  Command_Length      : constant := 16; -- length of program command
  Max_Motion_Chars    : constant := 24; -- max length of Motion block
  Max_Axis_Chars      : constant := 12; -- max length of Axis block
  Max_Motion_Blocks   : constant := 10; -- max motion blocks to buffer
  Max_Sensory_Data    : constant := 8;  -- max sensory data to buffer
  Sensor_Data_Length  : constant := 26; -- max length of sensory data
  Sensor_Scan_Period  : constant Duration := 3.0;
                                 -- scan sensors every 3 seconds

    subtype CP_Index        is Positive range 1 .. Max_CP_Chars;
    subtype Motion_Index    is Positive range 1 .. Max_Motion_Chars;
    subtype Axis_Index      is Positive range 1 .. Max_Axis_Chars;
    subtype CP_Input        is String (CP_Index);
    subtype CP_Output       is Integer range 1 .. 9;
    subtype Motion_Command  is String (1 .. Command_Length);
    subtype Axis_Command    is String (1 .. Command_Length);
    subtype Motion_Block    is String (Motion_Index);
    subtype Axis_Block      is String (Axis_Index);
    subtype Sensory_Data    is String (1 .. Sensor_Data_Length);
    subtype Program_Command is String (1 .. Command_Length);
    subtype Program_Id      is Character;
    subtype Command_Index   is Positive range 1 .. Max_Commands;

    type Command_Type is
      record
        Index   : Positive;
        Command : Program_Command;
      end record;

    type CP_Command   is (Run_Start, Stop, End_Program, Run_Resume);
    type State_Type   is (Manual, Running, Suspended);
    type CP_Input_Code is ('S', 'H', 'E', 'R');
                    -- S: Start;  H: Stop;  E: End;  R: Run;
```

Figure 23-1. Definitions (package specification).

```
type CP_Output_Code is (R_On_M_Off, T_On_M_On, S_Off_R_On,
                        R_Off_S_On, Invalid_On);

    -- R_On_M_Off : Running on, Manual off
    -- T_On_M_On  : Terminating on, Manual on
    -- S_Off_R_On : Suspended off, Running on
    -- R_Off_S_On : Running off, Suspended on
    -- Invalid_On : Invalid on
for CP_Output_Code use (1, 2, 3, 4, 9);

end Definitions;
```

Figure 23-1 *(continued)*. Definitions (package specification).

23.1 Bottom-Up Approach

The bottom-up approach is utilized to create a set of packages and subprograms that are *with*ed by other packages, subprograms, or tasks to implement the overall design structure. The packages and subprograms that are created first include those used in a "server" role. They were identified in our package taxonomy (see Chapter 10) as Helper packages and include global type and constant definitions, adaptation parameters, and machine dependencies. They also include generic Communication packages.

The modules described below for the robot controller (see Figure 22-8 for the application packages) include the package Definitions that contains constants and type definitions; the package Robot_HDP that contains absolute addresses for hardware interrupts and buffers, and a generic buffer package that contains the functions required to create and manipulate a buffer.

23.1.1 Definitions

Global definitions that are available to other program units are contained in the package Definitions, as shown in Figure 23-1. This package contains constants such as the maximum length of a control panel command (Max_CP_Chars) and subtypes such as the character string for a motion block (Motion_Block). This package will be *with*ed by any other package, subprogram, or task that needs one or more of the constants or type definitions.

```
---------- Hardware Dependent Constants ----------

package Robot_HDP is

    CP_In_Int_Address        : constant := 16#00A0#; -- interrupt loc
    CP_In_Buff_Address       : constant := 16#00A4#; -- h/w buffer loc

    CP_Out_Int_Address       : constant := 16#00B0#;
    CP_Out_Buff_Address      : constant := 16#00B4#;

    Axis_In_Int_Address      : constant := 16#00C0#;
    Axis_In_Buff_Address     : constant := 16#00C4#;

    Axis_Out_Int_Address     : constant := 16#00D0#;
    Axis_Out_Buff_Address    : constant := 16#00D4#;

    Sensor_In_Int_Address    : constant := 16#00E0#;
    Sensor_In_Buff_Address   : constant := 16#00E4#;

    Sensor_Out_Int_Address   : constant := 16#00E8#;
    Sensor_Out_Buff_Address  : constant := 16#00F0#;
end Robot_HDP;
```

Figure 23-2. Robot_HDP (package specification).

23.1.2 Hardware Dependencies

All hardware dependencies are collected in the package Robot_HDP as shown in Figure 23-2. Absolute addresses have been assigned as constants to be associated with their respective hardware interrupt or buffer. For example, the address of hex 00A0 is associated with the interrupt for the control panel input (CP_In_Int_Address). Any other hardware dependencies (e.g., channel numbers or status registers) will also be included in this package (or separate packages for a given device if a single package becomes too large and unmanageable). This package will be *with*ed only by the device handlers for the various hardware units.

23.1.3 Generic Units

The generic buffer package shown in Figure 23-3 contains a buffer task. The user of this package instantiates it with actual generic parameters for the buffer size and the type of items to be buffered.

```
generic
  Size : in Natural := 20;
  type Item is private;

package Buffer_Overwrite is
  procedure Enqueue (I : in Item);
  procedure Dequeue (I : out Item);
  pragma Inline (Enqueue, Dequeue);
end Buffer_Overwrite;

package body Buffer_Overwrite is
  task Buffer is
    entry Enqueue (I : in Item);
    entry Dequeue (I : out Item);
  end Buffer;

  task body Buffer is separate;

  procedure Enqueue (I : in Item) is
  begin
    Buffer.Enqueue (I);
  end Enqueue;

  procedure Dequeue (I : out Item) is
  begin
    Buffer.Dequeue (I);
  end Dequeue;

end Buffer_Overwrite;
```

Figure 23-3. Buffer_Overwrite (package specification and body).

23.2 Top-Level Design

The top-level design for the application packages identified in Figure 22-8 proceeds in a top-down fashion as soon as the required "server" packages and subprograms have been compiled and placed in the Ada library (a large program could have several Ada libraries). The general approach is to use the graphical description provided in the Ada package graph (see Figure 22-8 above) and create appropriate Ada constructs for the tasks, packages, and interfaces between the various modules. The Ada package graph shows all the application packages required, the tasks that reside within each package, and the data flow between the tasks. Interfaces between tasks residing in different packages will require the addition of

```
package Axis is

  procedure Stop;
  procedure Resume;

  -- Calls
    -- Motion.Motion_Ack
    -- Motion.Dequeue_Motion_Block
end Axis;

with Definitions;  use Definitions;
with Robot_HDP;    use Robot_HDP;
package body Axis is

  procedure Prepare_Axis_Block (M : in Motion_Block;
                                A : out Axis_Block) is separate;
  task Robot_Handler is
    entry Take_Block (B : in Axis_Block);

    entry Axis_In_Interrupt;
    for Axis_In_Interrupt use at Axis_In_Int_Address;

    entry Axis_Out_Interrupt;
    for Axis_Out_Interrupt use at Axis_Out_Int_Address;
  end Robot_Handler;

  task Axis_Manager is
    entry Stop;
    entry Resume;

    -- Calls
      -- Motion.Motion_Ack
      -- Motion.Dequeue_Motion_Block
  end Axis_Manager;

  task body Robot_Handler is separate;
  task body Axis_Manager  is separate;

  procedure Stop is
  begin
    Axis_Manager.Stop;
  end Stop;
```

Figure 23-4. Axis (package specification and body).

```
procedure Resume is
begin
  Axis_Manager.Resume;
end Resume;

end Axis;
```

Figure 23-4 *(continued)*. Axis (package specification and body).

entrance procedures to control task access. The steps described below use the packaging shown in Figure 22-8 to create a complete top-level PDL.

23.2.1 Package Construction

The PDL statements shown in Figure 23-4 represent the package Axis. The package specification includes entrance procedures for the signals Stop and Resume and comments that show that calls will be made to the entrance procedures Motion_Ack and Dequeue_Motion_Block in the package Motion. The package body contains the declarations of the procedure Prepare_Axis_Block and the two tasks Robot_Handler and Axis_Manager. The first task has an entry for receiving Axis blocks (Take_Block) and two interrupt entries (Axis_In_Interrupt and Axis_Out_Interrupt). This task is a pure server and makes no calls. The second task has entries for the signals Stop and Resume and makes calls to Motion_Ack and Dequeue_Motion_Block in the package Motion. Address constants (Axis_In_Int_Address and Axis_Out_Int_Address) associated with the interrupt entries have been imported from the package Robot_HDP. The details of the task bodies and the procedure are deferred until the detailed design phase by using the *separate* construct.

It is important to note the use of the "entrance" procedures Stop and Resume for the corresponding task entries in Axis_Manager. We have protected this task by declaring it in the package body. It cannot be inadvertently aborted by another task, and its entries can only be accessed via calls to the entrance procedures visible in the package specification. The bodies of the entrance procedures are shown to make the calls to their respective task entries. This is also used to control conditional and timed entry calls. The calls of this type are placed in the entrance procedures if they are required, rather than being made directly from outside the package. The use of entrance procedures is highly recommended as a means of controlling communication between tasks that reside in different packages.

```
with Definitions;  use Definitions;

package CP_Processing is

  procedure Take_CP_Input (T : in CP_Input);
  procedure Provide_CP_Output (CP_Out : out CP_Output_Code);

  -- Calls
    -- Motion.Start_Program
    -- Motion.End_Event
    -- Axis.Stop
    -- Axis.Resume

end CP_Processing;



with Buffer_Overwrite;
package body CP_Processing is

    task CP_Processor is
    -- Calls
      -- Buffer_Panel_Input.Dequeue
      -- Validate_Panel_Input
      -- Send_Input_Command
      -- Send_Panel_Output
    end CP_Processor;

-- Instantiate buffer task for CP input

    package Buffer_Panel_Input is new Buffer_Overwrite
       (Size    => Max_CP_Input,
        Item    => CP_Input);


  -- Instantiate buffer task for CP output

    package Buffer_Panel_Output is new Buffer_Overwrite
        (Size    => Max_CP_Output,
         Item    => CP_Output_Code);
```

Figure 23-5. CP_Processing (package specification and body).

```
package CP_Manager is

   procedure Validate_Panel_Input (Panel_Input : in      CP_Input;
                                   Valid       : out     Boolean;
                                   Command     : in out  CP_Command;
                                   Program_No  : out     Program_Id);

   procedure Send_Input_Command (Command : in out CP_Command;
                                 Id      : in     Program_Id);

   procedure Send_Panel_Output (Command : in out CP_Command;
                                Valid   : in     Boolean);
end CP_Manager;


package body CP_Manager is separate;

task body CP_Processor is separate;

procedure Take_CP_Input (T : in CP_Input) is
begin
   Buffer_Panel_Input.Enqueue (T);
end Take_CP_Input;

procedure Provide_CP_Output (CP_Out : out CP_Output_Code) is
begin
   Buffer_Panel_Output.Dequeue (CP_Out);
end Provide_CP_Output;

end CP_Processing;
```

Figure 23-5 *(continued).* CP_Processing (package specification and body).

We have used comments to document the calls made to tasks that reside in other packages. This has the drawback that the comments must be changed manually when the design is altered. This extra effort is considered worthwhile for the value of (correctly!) documenting the interfaces to other packages in the design.

One of the important parts of our design methodology is the deferring of design decisions. During top-level design we concentrate our efforts on the structure of the design and not on algorithmic details. This is illustrated in Figure 23-4 with the use of the *separate* clause for the procedure Prepare_Axis_Block and the two tasks Robot_Handler and Axis_Manager. We are not concerned at this stage of the design with the algorithmic details of these three bodies; we are deferring those details until the detailed design phase.

The PDL statements for the other application packages shown in Figure 22-8 are supplied for the case study in Appendix E.

23.2.2 Using Library Units

Library units have been employed by the top-level package Axis shown in Figure 23-4. The package body is *with*ing the package Definitions for types needed by the formal parameters in the procedure and entry calls. It is also *with*ing the package Robot_HDP for the address associations of the interrupt entries in the task Robot_Handler. Another example of the use of a library unit is shown in Figure 23-5, where the package body CP_Processing is *with*ing the generic package Buffer_Overwrite needed for the instantiations of the packages containing the buffer tasks for panel input and output.

23.2.3 Positioning of Context Clauses

The general rule for positioning of context clauses is that the *with*ing of packages and subprograms should be done as closely as possible to the unit that uses the imported items. The basic rationale for this positioning rule is to minimize the amount of recompilation that will be required when changes are made. This is illustrated in Figure 23-5 for CP_Processing. The package specification only includes a context clause for the library package Definitions for the importation of the types CP_Input and CP_Output_Code. The package body has a context clause for the generic package Buffer_Overwrite. If changes are required in the latter package, only the package body of CP_Processing needs to be recompiled, not the package specification. It is noted in the "Calls" comments that the task Control_Panel_Processor makes calls to entrance procedures in the packages Motion and Axis. Context clauses for these packages are not included in the package body for CP_Processing; they are deferred until the specification of the task body of the task CP_Processor (the details of the latter are deferred by using the *separate* facility).

23.2.4 Creating Stubs

The creation of stubs is used to defer the implementation of details during the design process. Ada provides the *separate* facility for this purpose. As was noted in the paragraph above, the details of the task body CP_Processor are deferred in the package body CP_Processing (see Figure 23-5). This prevents the designer from having to consider details of task implementation during the top-level design and, by careful positioning of context clauses, may contribute to reducing the amount of recompilation necessary when changes are made to higher level units.

```
with Control_Panel;

procedure Robot_Controller is
begin
  null;
end Robot_Controller;
```

Figure 23-6. Robot_Controller (Main procedure).

23.2.5 Main Procedure

The main procedure for the robot controller is shown in Figure 23-6. This almost trivial procedure simply contains a context clause for the package Control_Panel and a *null* statement for the executable part. The context clause starts the elaboration of the other packages and the activation of the tasks. The *null* statement is included only to satisfy the Ada syntax rules. Note that there are no executive service calls for the activation of the tasks; the elaboration process includes an implicit task activation (see Reference DOD83, BAR84, or SHU88 for details of the elaboration and activation process).

23.2.6 Type Checking of Interfaces

The top-level design for the robot controller has been done by incrementally adding new packages to the Ada library. The Ada compiler performs type checking of interfaces before a new module is added to the library. An example of this type checking is the use of the type mark CP_Input in the specification of the procedure Take_CP_Input in the package specification for CP_Processing (see Figure 23-5). CP_Input is specified as a string in package Definitions (see Figure 23-1), and this package must be available in the library before the package CP_Processing can *with* the former and use the types or constants specified there. Another example of the kind of type checking that the compiler performs is the instantiation of the generic package Buffer_Overwrite in package body CP_Processing (see Figure 23-5). The actual (generic) parameters for

Size and Item are checked against the formal generic parameters specified in the package Buffer_Overwrite (see Figure 23-3). Any type or object used in the instantiation must be available (i.e., visible) to the compiler at the point of the instantiation for a successful compilation. Any time an error message of the form "undeclared < Ada name >" appears, there is a high likelihood that the compiler has performed type checking (ignoring missing local declarations here), and has detected a missing type or object definition. The remedy is to *with* the intended package or subprogram, or to create the missing elements and include them in the library. The type checking performed by the Ada compiler is extremely valuable in ensuring correct interfaces for the top-level and detailed design.

All the specifications and bodies for the application packages must be completed before the top-level design is finished. A careful review must be performed of the top-level PDL and associated graphics material before the detailed design phase can start.

23.3   Detailed Design

The detailed design phase consists of supplying the design decisions that were deferred during top-level design. This includes the algorithms of the tasks and subprograms deferred with the *separate* clause, and the decomposition of any task that needs virtual machines and data managers for its implementation.

The paragraphs that follow describe the detailed design effort, in terms of what should be furnished during the detailed design phase and what can be delayed until the coding phase.

23.3.1   Generic Subunits

Generally speaking, subunits can be furnished in any order, but some implementations may impose certain restrictions. For example, some Ada implementations may require that generic subunits be available in the library before an instantiation can take place. The generic subunit required for the robot controller is shown in Figure 23-7 (note the differences between this implementation and the one presented in Figure 10-12). The parent of this subunit is Buffer_Overwrite as shown in Figure 23-3. The task Buffer operates as an object manager and guarantees mutual exclusion for buffer insertion and removal.

```ada
separate (Buffer_Overwrite)

task body Buffer is
  subtype Index_Type is Positive range 1 .. Size;
  subtype Count_Type is Natural  range 0 .. Size;

  Buf : array (Index_Type) of Item;
  Insert : Index_Type := 1;
  Remove : Index_Type := 1;
  Count  : Count_Type := 0;
begin
  loop
    select
      accept Enqueue (I : in Item) do
        Buf (Insert) := I;
      end Enqueue;
      Insert := (Insert mod Buf'Last) + 1;

      if (Insert = Remove) then
        Remove := (Remove mod Buf'Last) + 1;
      else
        Count  := Count + 1;
      end if;
        -- If (Insert = Remove), the buffer is full.
        -- We will put the new element on
        -- top of the oldest.  We advance the Remove
        -- pointer to prevent the element just inserted
        -- from being removed next.  We do not
        -- increment Count.
    or
      when Count > 0 =>
        accept Dequeue (I : out Item) do
          I := Buf (Remove);
        end Dequeue;
        Remove := (Remove mod Buf'Last) + 1;
        Count  := Count - 1;
    or
      terminate;
    end select;
  end loop;
end Buffer;
```

Figure 23-7. Buffer (task body).

```
with Motion;
separate (Axis)

task body Axis_Manager is
  Stop_Flag   : Boolean := False;
  Axis_Motion : Motion_Block;
  Axis_Output : Axis_Block;
begin
  loop
    select
      accept Stop;
      Stop_Flag := True;
    else
      if Stop_Flag then
        accept Resume;
        Stop_Flag := False;
      end if;

      Motion.Dequeue_Motion_Block (Axis_Motion);
      Prepare_Axis_Block (Axis_Motion, Axis_Output);

      Robot_Handler.Take_Block (Axis_Output);
      -- Task waits here for block completion
        Motion.Motion_Ack;
    end select;
  end loop;
end Axis_Manager;
```

Figure 23-8. Axis_Manager (task body).

23.3.2 Other Subunits

All subunits for which implementation details have been deferred must be placed in the library prior to program execution, but not necessarily during the detailed design phase. The complete algorithms are provided during the detailed design phase, typically with a combination of Ada code and comments. Examples of Ada code include loops, select statements, and calls to known task entries and subprograms. The final implementation details can be deferred until the coding phase. The example shown in Figure 23-8 illustrates the inclusion of the subunit Axis_Manager, who's parent is Axis. This subunit needs to interface with package Motion, and the latter is *with*ed here rather than in the parent. Local objects are specified in the declarative part, and the algorithm is implemented with a select statement in the task body. All the details of the implementation are not known at this point, and a call is made to the procedure Prepare_Axis_Block which was specified in the package body of Axis. The details of this procedure can be deferred until the coding phase, but the outline of the algorithm is specified with comment statements during the detailed design phase.

23.3.3 Implementation Detail

The amount of implementation detail to be furnished during the detailed design phase can be divided into three categories:

1. *Completely coded.* The Ada code for the implementation is complete; no additional coding is required.

2. *Partially coded.* The implementation is a mixture of the Ada code required for a successful compilation and additional commented statements in pseudocode format.

3. *Implementation omitted.* The unit has been specified, but the subunit is not furnished.

If the details of an implementation are known, they can be included during the detailed design phase. The danger of including code during this phase is that the emphasis may shift from design to coding, and that is not desirable for a large, complex system. If too much coding is done before the design has been completed, the possibility for redesign increases drastically because the emphasis is on coding rather than design.

The other extreme is to specify the detailed design down to the unit level, and to omit all the Ada subunits. This has the advantage that the design phase and coding phase are not intermingled, but it may turn out later that the tasks identified are quite large and may have to be redesigned into more tasks, virtual machines, and data managers. The redesign may require a revision of the top-level design document.

The most desirable approach is the second category listed above, where all the units are defined, and their implementations are included as subunits with a combination of legal code that shows a skeletal view (and which is required for a compilable PDL) and commented pseudocode. This will ensure that the design is complete to the unit level, and that a minimum of redesign will occur.

The examples included above for the robot controller illustrate the use of all three categories. The task body Buffer and Axis_Manager shown in Figures 23-7 and 23-8, respectively, are completely coded Ada subunits that require no further coding details. The procedure Prepare_Axis_Block shown in Figure 23-9 has a combination of Ada

```
separate (Axis)

procedure Prepare_Axis_Block (M : in Motion_Block;
                              A : out Axis_Block) is
begin
  -- while not end of motion block loop
    -- determine axis
    -- determine motion for this axis
    -- prepare output for this axis
  -- end loop
  null;  --\
end Prepare_Axis_Block;
```

Figure 23-9. Prepare_Axis_Block (procedure body).

code to ensure successful compilation and commented pseudocode. The details of the pseudocode will be furnished during the coding phase, but we must be reasonably well assured that the commented statements will not expand into additional tasks, virtual machines, or objects (data managers) before we consider ourselves finished with the detailed design. The third category is illustrated by omission. In Figure 23-4, for example, we notice that the task body Robot_Handler is stubbed with a *separate* statement, and we have not furnished any details about its implementation. This can be acceptable for a simple task, but we may have some unpleasant surprises for a complicated task, with resulting redesign.

Summary

Our Ada real-time design methodology is an integration of elements of MASCOT, DARTS, Structured Design, Object-Oriented Design, and Layered Virtual Machines. Chapter 21 provides the background description of these different approaches. Our methodology supports widely used design paradigms such as information hiding, stepwise refinement, and deferring of design decisions. Chapter 22 describes the various steps of our methodology as follows:

1. Determine hardware interfaces
2. Assign processes to edge functions
3. Decompose the middle part
4. Determine concurrency
5. Determine process interfaces
6. Introduce intermediary processes
7. Encapsulate tasks in Ada packages
8. Translate design into Ada PDL
9. Decompose large tasks

10. Conduct design reviews

Even though our methodology is very Ada specific, several of the steps are language independent. The remaining steps can be tailored for an implementation in a programming language other than Ada.

The use of Ada PDL is an integral part of the methodology. Chapter 23 describes how an Ada PDL is used for the top-level and detailed design phases. A bottom-up approach is used to first provide the helper and communication packages required by the application packages. The top-level design of the application packages then proceed top-down, *with*ing the packages previously placed in the Ada library during the bottom-up phase. Design decisions are deferred using the *separate* clause. The positioning of context clauses are deferred to the subunits, if possible. Subunits and their algorithms are supplied during detailed design. The algorithms can be expressed completely as Ada code, or as a combination of Ada code and commented pseudocode.

Evaluating an Ada Real-Time Design

An important part of the design process is the evaluation of the real-time design and the correction of deficiencies. It is not sufficient only to verify that the requirements have been implemented correctly and to validate the system performance; we must also ensure that the design is amenable to implementation of future enhancements and to correct deficiencies detected during the maintenance phase.

To fully evaluate a design, it is important that proper tools be used to create and express the design. The primary design tools that we use in our evaluation include data flow diagrams, process structure charts, Ada package graphs, Ada structure graphs, structure charts, OOD diagrams, and PDL.

Design evaluation should be a continuous process and should not only be carried out at the conclusion of the design phase. As outlined in Chapter 22, informal design reviews are held throughout the complete design phase, with formal reviews at the conclusion of the preliminary design and the detailed design.

In the chapters that follow, we first describe briefly the formal verification and validation procedures, and then we present a set of practical design evaluation guidelines. These guidelines are intended to aid the reviewers in recognizing the characteristics of an effective Ada design. They also highlight aspects of a design that should raise the reviewers' suspicions as to the quality of the design. The structures and rules of the guidelines are by no means absolute. Violations of these rules, however, should be noted, and appropriate justification should be provided by the designers for the rationale of the questionable design features chosen.

Verification and Validation

Software verification and validation are formal activities performed during the software development cycle. *Verification* is the process of evaluating the correctness and completeness of the implementation of the functional requirements. *Validation* is the process of determining the correct implementation of the performance requirements. Verification takes place throughout the software development phases. Some of the validation activity can be performed with estimating techniques and simulation of code size and execution timing, but the primary validation activity can only be performed when executable code has been produced. Verification includes the determination of compliance with stated design and programming standards and practices.

25.1 Design Verification

We assume that the requirements documents have been verified to ensure completeness, consistency, and lack of ambiguity, and are only concerned here with verification during the design phase. Formal design reviews are conducted at the conclusion of the preliminary design and the detailed design. The purpose of the preliminary design review is to establish that the functional requirements have been mapped correctly and completely into a set of suitable software components and their interfaces, and that the proposed model solution has a high correspondence to the stated requirements. Software design and coding standards and procedures are also reviewed at this time. This includes, for example, the use of a compilable PDL for documenting the design decisions and code.

In the detailed design review, the design decisions deferred during the top-level design phase are evaluated for correctness and completeness. This includes all the algorithms that will perform the functions specified by the requirements. The algorithms are either coded completely at this stage, or as a combination of code and pseudocode. If pseudocode is included, it should be complete enough to enable the reviewers to ascertain that the algorithms are completely understood by the designers. A reference to a specific algorithm in a widely available publication (e.g., Communications of the ACM, or Knuth's Fundamental Algorithms) is acceptable in lieu of specifying all the steps of the algorithm. The test plans are also verified during this review to ensure that adequate test cases and procedures have been identified.

The reviewers of the preliminary and detailed design reviews should analyze carefully the aspects of the real-time design that affect maintenance of the operational system. The maintenance phase is the longest and most costly of most large software systems, and entails isolating and correcting software errors. A portion of this phase is also spent on implementing enhancements and modifications to the existing system. The better the original design to promote a reliable system, the lower the potential cost of the maintenance phase.

25.2 Designing for Ease of Maintenance

Specific design approaches that will aid the maintenance of real-time systems include the following:

1. *Modularity.* The proper decomposition of a large system is to create a set of cohesive modules that comprise a single function. This makes it easier for the maintainers to understand the functionality of the module in which they have located a bug, and to implement the correction.

2. *Coupling and cohesion.* The proper use of the coupling and cohesion concepts we have expanded from traditional structured design (see Chapter 13) will make it easier to prevent a rippling effect of bugs when the code is corrected.

3. *Data abstraction.* The proper construction of data managers, in terms of abstract data types and resources (see Chapter 10), will make it easier to correct bugs that are linked to data structures.

4. *Program structure.* A properly structured program in terms of Ada packages, tasks, and subprograms will make it easier for the maintainers to understand the real-time aspects of the system.

5. *Design documentation.* The most important tool for the maintenance programmers is the software documentation. This may be limited to simply code listings. Proper design documentation for ease of maintenance should include the graphical tools used during the design phase, English descriptions of program structure and algorithms, and code listings and PDL.

The evaluation guidelines presented in Chapter 26 address these design concerns explicitly.

25.3 Code Verification

The code produced to implement the design solution is inspected for potential problems and for non-compliance with the design and coding standards. Bugs are not expected to be found by inspecting compiled code listings from an Ada compiler. The type checking performed by the compiler will uncover any syntax errors, inconsistencies in parameter usage in calls to subprograms and task entries, and importation of data, types, and program units using context clauses. The real verification of the code is performed during unit and integration testing. Unit testing is performed to verify that individual program units perform as expected by the software requirements specification. Unit testing can proceed either bottom-up or top-down as specified in the test plan. A combination of the two approaches can be used that will minimize the amount of special drivers that will have to be written. Integration testing is performed to verify that proper interfaces have been established between the various program units. Integration testing can proceed top-down using the program units already tested during the unit test phase.

It is important that test cases and test results be kept in a software development file for each unit tested, as well as for the integration of the complete system. The information in these files will be used by the maintenance programmers during retesting as they are correcting a problem or modifying the system.

25.4 System Validation

The conclusion of the integration test phase can be considered as the starting point for system validation. This involves testing the complete system to determine if it satisfies the specified performance requirements. In a formal software development process, such as for the U.S. Department of Defense, a test readiness review is held to decide if the system validation test can start. This test is usually attended by the customer, including the personnel that will operate the system. A major problem with the validation of a real-time system is that the hardware that our software is intended to control is not available. This may require the design and implementation of complex software to simulate the hardware. The operation of these simulators will never be identical to the actual hardware devices, and the final system validation may have to be postponed until the system is actually field tested.

Ada Design Evaluation Guidelines

The previous chapter discussed the formal aspects of verification and validation in general. This chapter provides a practical guideline for how to evaluate an Ada real-time design. Specific areas covered include the design methodology employed, the degree of correspondence between the system requirements specification and the solution, the simplicity or complexity of the solution, system performance characteristics, the process design using Ada tasks, coupling and cohesion, the tasking overhead associated with the Ada task paradigms used, reusable components, caller/called decisions made for the task interfaces, the design structure, the use of exceptions, and the portability of the solution.

26.1 Design Methodology

The overall design approach must be examined to determine if it is commensurate with Ada. If, for example, the design has not made any use of Ada packages, we would suspect that the designers do not fully understand the design capabilities of Ada, and that the design is less than adequate. We would require redesign of the system to take advantage of Ada's excellent design features such as packages. The following specific areas should be examined:

1. *Recommended design approach.* The design methodology should be evaluated to determine if it is based on the approach specified in the Software Development Plan (SDP). This is particularly important for large government projects where the methodology is subject to audits. If a government contractor fails an audit, it may prevent that contractor from receiving future contracts.

2. *Use of graphics.* Graphical illustrations represent the best medium for documenting and describing the design of a large system and are used in the evaluation of the design. The following graphics is recommended for expressing the design of a large real-time Ada system (see Chapter 7):

   a. Data flow diagrams (DFDs)

   b. Process identification charts (superimposed on DFDs)

   c. Process structure charts

   d. Ada task graphs (ATGs)

   e. Ada package graphs (superimposed on ATGs)

   f. Structure charts (sequential processing within a single task)

   g. Ada structure graphs (Buhr diagrams; isomorphic to PDL)

   h. OOD diagrams

   i. State-transition diagrams

3. *Packages.* Packages represent the primary encapsulation mechanism in Ada and should be used liberally in a large system. If packages are not found as the major building blocks of the system solution, we would suspect that the designers do not have a proper Ada mind set, and that a significant amount of redesign would have to be performed.

4. *Generics.* The generic capability in Ada was introduced to promote software reusability. If no generics is found in the design of a large Ada system, it is quite possible that functional areas have been overlooked for the creation or use of reusable components. The contents of the Ada Software Repository [CON87] should be examined to see if components are already available for reuse. Examples of what is found in the Ada Repository include a Virtual Terminal, the Graphics Kernel System (GKS), and metrics tools. Some of the software in the Repository is not in the form of generic units and may have to be adapted for a given system.

5. *Exception handling.* Exceptions in Ada should be used as a means to promote fault tolerant real-time systems. If exceptions

have not been used as part of the overall design methodology, the system should probably be redesigned to take advantage of this advanced Ada feature. If the designers deliberately avoided the use of exceptions because they were found to be associated with too much run time overhead, the fault tolerant aspects of the system should be carefully evaluated.

6. *Tasking model.* If the Ada tasks used in the design are made to interface with a real-time executive (the executive could be written in Ada or assembly language) rather than using the features of the Ada tasking model, we would suspect that the designers do not fully understand the Ada tasking capabilities. It is, of course, possible that the designers have been forced to interface with an executive because the Ada run time support imposes an overhead that is unacceptable from a performance point of view. If, during a design review, the latter explanation is found to be justified, the design could be acceptable. Otherwise, the system should be redesigned using the Ada tasking model without any interfaces to a real-time executive external to the Ada run time support.

7. *Data abstraction.* If the design is created from a strictly functional decomposition with a set of highly nested subprograms, we would suspect that the designers have not made adequate use of data managers. The system should be redesigned using a combination of data structuring (hiding of design decisions) and functional decomposition. Such a design would take advantage of the encapsulation capabilities in Ada of data types and their operations (see Chapter 10).

8. *Deferring of design decisions.* A liberal use of the *separate* construct should be evidence that the designers have deferred design decisions, rather than get bogged down in the details of how to implement the algorithms. If this important design feature has not been used, the possibility exists that a redesign should be performed to properly structure the system in terms of objects and layered virtual machines (see Chapters 5 and 12).

26.2 Correspondence

The overall software solution will be evaluated to determine how closely the solution matches the problem specification. A high degree of correspondence will make it easier to implement a correct solution, and to anticipate future adaptations and modifications. The following areas should be examined for proper correspondence:

1. *Concurrency.* An inherently concurrent system should be modeled as a solution with an appropriate set of Ada tasks, packages, and subprograms. A strictly sequential system should be designed with Ada packages and subprograms. Ada tasks may be used to speed up processing of certain functions, e.g., input/output, but a strictly sequential system should not be modeled as a concurrent system.

2. *Data structures.* The data structures implied or stated in the requirements specification should be implemented accordingly, with the simplest structure possible.

3. *Non-determinism.* The areas for non-determinism implied or stated in the requirements specification include:

   a. Task scheduling (including preemption)

   b. Interrupts

   c. Asynchronism

   d. Task prioritization

   The real-time design should be analyzed carefully to determine the degree of correspondence in these areas.

4. *Hardware interfaces.* The device drivers must be implemented properly to account for devices that are interrupt driven and those that are polling devices.

If a software solution is found to have low correspondence in any of the areas listed above, a redesign may be required to increase the correspondence, and hence, the chance for a better solution.

26.3 Simplicity

The software solution should be implemented with the highest degree of simplicity possible. Simplicity promotes easier unit and integration testing, higher system reliability, and easier maintenance. The attempt to achieve a simple design is particularly important because of the inherent complexity of real-time systems.

No specific metric is available for measuring the simplicity of a real-time design, but areas for scrutiny include:

1. *Modularity.* A highly modular design will reduce the complexity of a real-time design compared with a monolithic design. The layered virtual machine approach supports this principle.

2. *Levels of entry calls.* Entry calls within a rendezvous would be suspect. This would represent an extremely tight coupling of (at least) three tasks that are locked in (at least) two separate rendezvous. Although this is sometimes necessary, it is more frequently desirable to redesign such that the accept body making the entry call to the third task be a separate task, and the tasks be uncoupled by introducing intermediaries.

3. *Nested tasks.* Tasks declared within tasks would make debugging and maintenance very difficult. Such tasks should generally be made siblings of a common master, rather than having a nested relationship.

4. *Shared data.* Shared data not protected by a monitor would be suspect. The possibility for an erroneous program is very high, and every effort should be made to protect shared data with an appropriate monitor.

5. *Race conditions.* If the possibility (no matter how remote) of race conditions can be detected, a redesign is required. This can occur if the attribute Count is used, and delayed or conditional entry calls are allowed directly (without the use of entrance procedures) from another task.

6. *Complexity of selective wait.* If several accept bodies are included in a single, or nested, select statement with complicated logic, the task body should be broken down into two or more tasks to simplify the logic.

7. *Complexity of task body.* If the task body is long and complex (independent of a select statement), it should be decomposed into a set of subprograms (or packages) to reduce the complexity. This is accomplished using the LVM/OOD approach described in Chapter 12.

8. *Non-deterministic scheduling.* If correspondence to the problem space is not violated, a deterministic scheduling can be imposed to simplify the scheduling process (e.g., pragma Time_Slice in DEC Ada). This would prevent a potential starvation condition for blocked tasks by ensuring that they would regain access to the processor after a certain multiple of time slices. It can also be an aid in debugging a system with several tasks.

9. *Timing problems.* If timing problems can be predicted from the use of delay statements to affect task synchronization, the pragma Priority can be used (in a preemptive scheduling system) to force synchronization and avoid timing problems. The normal effect of a delay statement in an Ada task (without the use of the pragma Priority) is that the task will be blocked for *at least*

the amount specified. There is no guarantee that the task will ever get control of the processor again, and a starvation condition could exist for the task. The introduction of the pragma will, however, introduce a non-portable condition into the solution.

26.4 Performance

It is difficult to predict how a system will perform based only on a top-level or detailed design. It is possible, however, to get a measure of performance characteristics by modeling the design using a simulation program. If the simulation program indicates performance problems, the system should be redesigned to satisfy the performance specifications. Another way of obtaining an indication of how well or how poorly a system will behave is by performing a set of benchmarking experiments. The real-time parameters to be modeled for an Ada design, or measured via benchmarking, include:

1. Task activation and termination
2. Total number of tasks used in the solution
3. Rendezvous synchronization (context switching)
4. Exception propagation
5. Polling
6. Timed and conditional entry calls
7. Tasking paradigms (number of intermediaries)
8. Task scheduling
9. Interrupt handling

26.5 Process Design

The following characteristics are evaluated to determine if the composition of processes (Ada tasks) has been properly accomplished:

1. *Number of processes.* The use of Ada tasks incurs a certain amount of overhead for each task in the system. The more tasks introduced (e.g., by the use of intermediaries), the higher the overhead. The system should be scrutinized to determine if the number of tasks representing the solution is acceptable, based on the associated run time overhead.

2. *Process interactions.* Process interactions are evaluated in terms of appropriate caller/called decisions (Chapter 16) and the passing of parameters in entry calls.

3. *Tasking paradigms and overhead.* The use of buffers, transporters, and relays are evaluated regarding the appropriate decoupling between tasks, and the associated overhead [BUR87].

4. *Cyclic process dependencies.* The Ada tasking model is inherently asynchronous, and any cyclic process dependencies would have been created by the designers. If this is in correspondence with the problem specification, and the solution is correct, the design will be acceptable. Otherwise, a redesign will have to be performed using the scheduling capabilities available with the run-time support.

5. *Polling.* If polling is associated with "busy wait" [GEH84] it is probably not acceptable in the design and will have to be redesigned. This is especially true for rendezvous polling (see Chapter 17).

6. *Shared data and mutual exclusion.* Shared data is allowed in Ada, but mutual exclusion is not guaranteed and will have to be supplied by the designers. If the pragma Shared is used, the designers will have to justify its use, since it is implementation dependent and restricted to scalar and access types. Data shared between Ada tasks should preferably be protected by a monitor task where the mutual exclusion is implemented with accept bodies in a selective wait statement.

7. *Rendezvous and blocking.* Since the caller is blocked during the rendezvous, the rendezvous (accept body) should be as short as possible. The only possible exception to this rule is in a system that uses an optimization scheme to reduce the number of context switches by replacing the entry call with a procedure call.

26.6 Coupling and Cohesion

A good software design encompasses highly cohesive modules that are loosely coupled. This is also true for a real-time design that consists of a set of concurrent processes (Ada tasks). Special evaluation methods have to be applied to the coupling of Ada tasks and the cohesion of Ada task bodies that include accept bodies in a selective wait statement, and to the coupling of modules that use Ada packages. The extensions of the traditional coupling and cohesion rules to include Ada packages and tasks were discussed in Chapter 13. Coupling and cohesion rules used to evaluate an Ada real-time design are described below.

26.6.1 Coupling Rules

The following coupling rules apply to Ada real-time designs:

1. *Package coupling.* Ada program units use different entities encapsulated in the package, but do not share any of the entities. Examples of this type of acceptable coupling include the use of mathematics libraries and graphics utilities.

2. *Definition coupling.* Ada programs share entities encapsulated by the package. An example of this type of acceptable coupling includes the use of a Definitions package containing global constants, types, and adaptation parameters.

3. *Concurrency coupling.* The "liveness" property of a set of Ada tasks is satisfied with the following conditions:

   a. All the caller/called decisions have been properly made.
   b. No cyclic dependencies are detected.
   c. The polling used is necessary and has a minimum of busy wait.
   d. All the accept bodies are small.
   e. Proper modes have been used for entry call parameters.
   f. Shared data is protected by appropriate monitors.

   The "safety" property of a pair of Ada tasks is satisfied when:

   a. Signals are implemented as parameterless entry calls.
   b. The modes *in* or *out* are used whenever possible.
   c. The use of the modes *in out* or the combination *in* and *out* (the tightest possible coupling between two Ada tasks) is necessary.

4. *Traditional coupling.* The traditional coupling concepts for subprograms, rated from good to bad, are the same as used in Structured Design [PAG80]:

   a. *Data coupling.* Data is transferred by parameter passing only.

b. *Stamp coupling.* Data structures are passed as parameters, even though a subprogram may only need a component of the structure.

c. *Control coupling.* The internal logic of a subprogram is controlled by the passing of a flag.

d. *Common coupling.* Subprograms share common data. This is acceptable in Ada if the data areas are properly protected.

e. *Content (pathological) coupling.* Statements within a subprogram are altered by another subprogram.

26.6.2 Cohesion

The traditional cohesion rules used in Structured Design [PAG80] apply equally well to Ada subprograms, and to task bodies without any selective wait statements:

1. *Functional cohesion.* The program unit implements a single function.

2. *Sequential cohesion.* Output data from one activity (set of instructions) serves as input data to the next activity.

3. *Communicational cohesion.* Various activities within the program unit use the same data structure.

4. *Procedural cohesion.* The program unit consists of different and possibly unrelated activities, in which *control* flows from one activity to the next.

5. *Temporal cohesion.* The program unit contains several activities that are time related.

6. *Logical cohesion.* The program unit contains several activities of the same general kind. The selection of an activity from the "grab bag" is made from outside the unit.

7. *Coincidental cohesion.* The program unit contains several unrelated activities.

We use these guidelines for Ada subprograms and task bodies without selective wait statements, i.e., functional cohesion is preferred and logical and coincidental cohesion are not acceptable. Temporal cohesion may sometimes be acceptable as a means of localizing temporal conditions into one program unit, e.g., for initialization or termination.

We introduced a new term (see Chapter 13) that applies to Ada task bodies with selective wait or delay statements: timed sequential cohesion. This accounts for a code section that is executed when a particular event takes place, e.g., a rendezvous or the expiration of a delay, and represents a break in the normal, sequential flow of execution. This is used in Ada to have the effect of periodicity, or to model cyclic events, and is quite acceptable. It may also be acceptable to have procedural, temporal, and logical cohesion at the task level with selective waits, provided that each accept body within the selective wait exhibits functional, sequential, or communicational cohesion.

26.7 Tasking Overhead

For each task we introduce into our design, there is a run time overhead associated with it. The more tasks in our design, the higher the overhead. To evaluate an Ada real-time system, we must examine the use of tasks in terms of this overhead. Specific areas to investigate include:

1. *Use of intermediaries.* We introduce intermediaries to create the desired coupling between each producer/consumer pair. The amount of overhead introduced into our system depends upon the specific paradigm we have chosen (see Chapter 15). To have the effect of loose coupling we may have selected the PTBTC paradigm, thus introducing three extra tasks into our design. It may be possible that a PBC combination could have sufficient coupling, and we could eliminate two tasks from the design. Each producer/consumer pair and their associated intermediaries should be scrutinized to determine if the proper trade-off between desired coupling and acceptable run time overhead has been achieved.

2. *Conditional and timed entry calls.* Conditional and timed entry calls are used to control the rendezvous between Ada tasks. Conditional entry calls have the potential for introducing run time overhead with possible associated busy wait. Timed entry calls introduce overhead via the delay statement by invoking the scheduling and dispatching functions. Both conditional and timed entry calls should be evaluated to determine if they have been used properly and have not introduced unnecessary run time overhead.

3. *Terminate option.* The terminate option is used to ensure proper termination of a task after it completes [SHU88]. It does introduce a run time overhead, however, and should be evaluated (see table 15-1).

4. *Exception handling.* The use of exception handling in Ada tasks may introduce a significant amount of run time overhead. This is especially true for exceptions raised in an accept body, where the exception is propagated both to the caller and within the task containing the accept body. Exception handling in Ada tasks should be carefully evaluated to determine if it is required for the implementation of fault tolerance, or is simply a convenience for the programmers.

A general guideline for the evaluation of tasking overhead in Ada is to first isolate the tasks that have critical timing requirements. These are the tasks that the above rules should be applied to, with suggestions for redesign, if necessary. For non-critical tasks the run time overhead is less important, and redesigning is usually not required.

During a design review, the system is not yet available for execution, and the overhead associated with the tasks cannot be measured directly. Estimates can be made, however, from benchmarking results obtained with task modeling on a specific target system [BUR87]. Benchmark test cases tailored specifically for measuring the efficacy of the Ada run time support are available [CON87], and can be run to obtain estimates of Ada tasking overheads for a given target. These benchmarks should be rerun for each new target, or for a new version of the Ada run time support for the same target.

26.8 Reusable Components

An Ada real-time design should be evaluated for its employment of reusable components. This applies to the creation of generic units that can be shared by the various program units, as well as "lifts" from other projects within the company and from collection points such as the Ada Software Repository [CON87].

For a real-time design, the immediate area for creating reusable components is for intermediary tasks. Buffer, transporter, and relay tasks should be encapsulated inside generic packages and instantiated as required throughout the program. Other functional areas that lend themselves to the creation of generic units include device drivers, sorting and merging, finding roots of mathematical functions, input/output for different data types (e.g., Text_IO), and the handling of different message types. The determination of functional areas for creation of generic units should be accomplished as part of the top-level design review.

The most readily available collection of Ada reusable components is the Ada Software Repository (ASR). The following is a list of categories of software that is collected in the ASR [CON87, p. 113]:

1. ASR-specific information and programs
2. Artificial intelligence
3. Benchmarks
4. Communications
5. Reusable software components
6. Data base management
7. Documentation
8. Graphics
9. Project management
10. Ada software development tools
11. Other tools
12. The WIS (World Wide Military Command and Control System *Information System*) Ada tool set

A different use of reusable software is to interface to a library of subprograms written in a different programming language such as Fortran. The pragma Interface (or a particular vendor implementation of an equivalent pragma) can be used to call the subprograms in the library from Ada program units. The evaluation of this type of reuse should focus on the cost-effectiveness of using the existing library versus creating new units in Ada, and on the long term maintenance effects of the Ada program with a mixture of languages.

Generic program units should be evaluated during the detailed design review for the following characteristics:

1. *Structure.* Whether the generic units have been constructed as stand-alone subprograms or encapsulated in Ada packages.

2. *Generic parameters.* The appropriateness of objects, types, or subprograms as generic parameters.

3. *Completeness.* Whether or not the operations allowed cover all expected uses of the generic unit.

4. *Understandability.* How easy it is to understand the use of the unit in terms of what it does and how it can be instantiated, and the functionality of the unit from the view of a maintainer. The most important part of a generic program unit is the documentation that accompanies it.

5. *Efficiency.* A program unit that might be used in several instances within a program, and with the possible reuse by other projects, should be implemented as efficiently as possible. The evaluation will include individual algorithms within each subprogram, as well as the set of operations encapsulated inside a package.

26.9 Caller/Called Decisions

The caller/called decisions of Ada tasks should be evaluated using the guidelines given in Chapter 16:

1. *Intermediaries.* The caller/called relations of intermediary tasks are established by convention, e.g., buffer tasks are pure servers and transporter tasks are pure callers.

2. *Hybrids.* The use of hybrid tasks is acceptable. We do not require that tasks be strictly callers or strictly servers.

3. *Service tasks.* Tasks with functions that are similar to executive services should be pure servers.

4. *Device drivers.* The caller/called relations of device drivers depend on the devices they interface with. Drivers for polling devices are most likely pure callers: caller relative to the device (polling mode), and caller relative to the task that is the recipient of the data received by the driver from the device.

   Drivers for interrupt driven *input* devices are most likely hybrids: server relative to the interrupt driven device, and caller relative to the task that is to receive the input data. Drivers for interrupt driven *output* devices are most likely pure servers: server relative to the task from which it receives the data to be sent to the device, and server relative to the interrupt driven device.

5. *Busy tasks.* Busy tasks that control several rendezvous are called.

6. *Algorithmically complex tasks.* Complex tasks are callers to reduce complexity by employing an abstraction in place of a complex function.

26.10 Design Structure

The overall structure (aside from the task structure) of a large Ada real-time design is evaluated in terms of the way it is packaged, the level of nesting, visibility, and the use of data managers.

26.10.1 Packaging

The packaging of a large Ada program should follow the guidelines given in Chapter 10. The following characteristics of the packaging should be evaluated:

1. *Taxonomy.* The taxonomy for Ada packages provided in Chapter 10 should be followed in the creation of application, communication, and helper packages:

   a. Application

   b. Communication

   c. Helper

      i. Definitions

      ii. Services

      iii. Data manager

         (1) Type manager (ADT)—open and closed

         (2) Object manager

2. *Nesting.* The level of nesting should not be too deep, in order to prevent a potential visibility problem and to minimize the amount of recompilation required when changes are made. Data managers created should be encapsulated in separate Ada packages and should not be nested within other packages. If they are nested, many more modules have to be recompiled when changes are made than if they are separate packages. We do not expect to have a completely "flat" design with only library units, but the level of nesting should be restricted to three or four levels. It is difficult to write down a specific guideline here because the accepted level of nesting is dependent on the size of the system to be developed.

26.10.2 Use of Data Managers

Data managers are created as part of the design process and represent the primary tool in Ada of having the effect of hiding major design decisions (aside from hiding implementations of algorithms with the *separate* clause). The first step in the evaluation process is to determine if the data manager has appropriately been made an abstract data type (type manager) or a resource (object manager). The ADT is suitable in a design where each user of the package creates an object to be manipulated by the operations in the ADT.

There will thus be multiple objects of the same type existing during program execution. The object is passed as a parameter to the subprograms that operate on it. The data structure should be hidden, if possible, using a private type declaration (i.e., using a closed ADT).

A resource should be used when only a single object (ignoring multiple instantiations of a generic resource) of the given type is required for the entire program. That object is allocated inside the resource and is not passed as a parameter to the subprograms that operate on it.

The implementation of the algorithms should be driven by the composition of the data structure, and the data structure should reflect a high correspondence to the requirements specification.

26.11 Use of Exceptions

The proper use of exceptions should be evaluated in terms of the exception taxonomy presented in Chapter 18. The general usage of exception handling will typically be specified during top-level design and evaluated during detailed design. The following uses are accepted:

1. *Anticipated conditions.* Applies to conditions that are expected to occur during the normal execution of the program.

2. *General purpose software.* Exceptions are raised to protect general purpose software from misuse.

3. *Hardware failures.* Exceptions are used to implement a fault tolerant system.

4. *Invalid input data.* Exceptions are raised if invalid input data is detected.

5. *Unanticipated errors.* The *others* clause is used to handle software bugs.

The evaluators should make sure that exceptions have not been used for program control, and that unnecessary exceptions have been eliminated.

26.12 Portability

The portability of a design is evaluated by listing all the non-portable items discovered and their method of documentation. Specific items to look for in a real-time design include:

1. *Use of pragmas.* The use of pragmas fall into two categories:

   a. *Predefined pragmas.* These are implementation dependent and may differ from one system to another (e.g., pragma Shared or Priority).

   b. *Vendor-supplied pragmas.* These are unique for a given implementation and may not exist in another system (e.g. pragma Time_Slice in VAX Ada).

2. *Use of representation clauses.* The use of representation clauses includes the specification of word size, layout of records, enumeration representation, and absolute address association of interrupts and hardware buffers.

3. *Use of predefined types.* The use of predefined types such as Integer, Float, Long_Float, etc., represent non-portable instances in the design since these types are implementation dependent.

4. *Device drivers.* Device drivers should be clearly identified to make the required changes from one system to another as easy as possible.

5. *Timing considerations.* Any fine tuning required of the tasks for a given target by use of, for example, delay statements, should be clearly identified. Adaptation parameters should be used for this and collected in one or more Ada packages.

The portability of a system should be planned early in the design phase, and appropriate standards should be written to simplify the changes that have to be made as a complete system is moved from one machine to another. Appendix F supplied with the Ada Language Reference Manual for a given system should be scrutinized for differences in vendor implementations.

Summary

In this part we have briefly described the formal verification and validation process, and have provided practical guidance for evaluating Ada real-time designs. Chapter 25 describes the verification process of ensuring that the functional requirements have been correctly and completely expressed in the design. Suggestions for specific design approaches that will aid the maintenance of real-time systems include:

1. Modularity
2. Coupling
3. Data abstraction
4. Program structure
5. Design documentation

Verification of the code is described in terms of code reviews, unit testing, and integration testing. The importance of maintaining software development files on program units is emphasized. A brief description is given of the validation of the system performance requirements. We note that software simulators may be used as part of the validation process, with the final validation postponed until field testing.

In Chapter 26 we present a number of practical guidelines for evaluating Ada real-time designs. The guidelines apply to the following evaluation areas:

1. Design methodology
2. Correspondence
3. Simplicity
4. Performance
5. Process design
6. Coupling and cohesion
7. Tasking overhead
8. Reusable components
9. Caller/called decisions
10. Design structure
11. Portability

Case Study 1: Remote Temperature Sensor

The recommended Ada design methodology is illustrated below with a problem adapted from the Remote Data Acquisition System suggested by Young [YOU82]. The application presented in the case study is a remote temperature sensor (RTS) that obtains temperature readings from a digital thermometer and reports the values back to a host computer. The specification and design of this application are given below.

A.1 Problem Specification

The function of the RTS is to query a digital thermometer for the temperature of a specified furnace. The temperature values are transmitted to a remote host computer. The remote host computer specifies the time interval between temperature readings for each furnace. A furnace thus becomes activated. The host can deactivate a furnace by specifying a special value (outside the allowable range for activation) for the time interval.

The specific tasks performed by the RTS are:

1. Receives and stores orders (control packets) from the host computer. The control packets contain:

    a. Sequence number

    b. Furnace number

    c. Time interval between temperature readings of a given furnace

2. Keeps track of time.

3. Queries the digital thermometer and stores temperatures.

4. Transmits furnace number and temperature (data packets) to the host computer.

5. Handles the message protocol with the host computer.

The characteristics of the host computer are:

1. It is remote from the RTS and digital thermometer.

2. It transmits control packets to control the time interval for reading the temperature of each furnace.

3. It receives messages in a simple format. The messages contain:

    a. Furnace number and temperature of a given furnace; or

    b. CP sequence number and CP ACK/NAK.

4. It implements the message protocol with the RTS.

The digital thermometer accepts an input as a furnace number in the range 0 to 15 and provides an output of the temperature of the furnace in the range 0 to 1000°C. It generates an interrupt to the RTS after it has placed the temperature in a designated hardware buffer.

The RTS and host computer exchange messages. The host computer sends control packets (CPs) to the RTS, and the RTS sends data packets (DPs) to the host computer. The message formats and the message exchange protocol are highly simplified for the purposes of this case study. The formats are:

1. CP FORMAT: (STX) (SN) (FF) (SS) (ETX)

2. DP FORMAT: (STX) (FF) (TTTT) (ETX)

where SN = 1-digit sequence number

FF = furnace number in range 0–15

SS = seconds between temperature measurements (minimum time between readings) in range 10–99; a special value of 0 is used to designate that the given furnace should no longer be monitored

TTTT = temperature in range 0–1000°C

STX = start of text

ETX = end of text

The transmit and receive protocols are similar for the RTS and the host computer:

1. *Transmit.* Transmit the message, and wait for one of three events:

   a. Receive acknowledgement (ACK) => send next message.

   b. Receive negative acknowledgement (NAK) => retransmit message.

   c. Timeout (2-second delay) => retransmit message (oldest message for the host).

   For the host, steps (a)–(c) above are all accomplished for each specific message, based on the CP sequence number.

2. *Receive.* Receive a message and check for validity.

   a. If valid, send acknowledgement (ACK).

   b. If invalid, send negative acknowledgement (NAK).

The criteria for validity are that the message must have an STX, and the fields of the message must contain numbers in the correct range. The messages are transmitted as a continuous sequence of ASCII characters.

Figure A-1 shows the interfaces between RTS and the various system devices. CP_ACK represents either an acknowledgement or negative acknowledgement (i.e., an ACK or NAK) of a control packet sent from the host to RTS. Similarly, DP_ACK represents an ACK or NAK of a data packet sent from RTS to the host.

The processing for the RTS is required to be as follows:

1. At any time, receive control packets from the host. Buffer up to six control packets at a time. When the buffer is full, ignore additional incoming messages. Generate ACK or NAK for incoming control packets from the host computer.

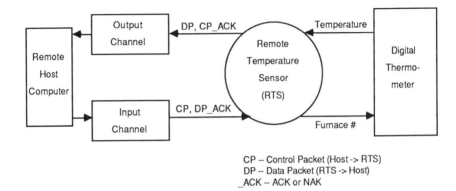

CP -- Control Packet (Host -> RTS)
DP -- Data Packet (RTS -> Host)
_ACK -- ACK or NAK

Figure A-1. Context diagram.

2. At any time, receive ACKs and NAKs of data packets.

3. Build and maintain a control table containing the time interval for temperature readings of each furnace. This control table is queried periodically (the period is specified with an adaptation parameter) for active furnaces.

4. Read the temperature of each furnace in accordance with its specified time interval. Query the digital thermometer to determine the temperature of the furnace. Store the necessary information for a data packet in a buffer.

5. Provide a buffer for the data packet information. Buffer up to 100 furnace/temperature readings, overwriting the oldest information when necessary. The queue discipline is first-in–first-out (FIFO). In order to store the information as compactly as possible, the buffer is to contain information in numeric, rather than ASCII, format. The furnace number and temperature value in such a form is called an Internal Data Packet (IDP).

6. Whenever there is information in the buffer, build data packets and transmit them to the host computer in accordance with the communication protocol. Transmit ACK or NAK for the control packets from the host computer.

   The processing described above is dependent upon three adaptation parameters (system parameters) that must be easy to modify. The parameters should be highly visible in the code. The only changes necessary to modify the parameters are a change in one location and a recompilation of the code. These parameters and default values are:

1. Timeout before retransmit of a data packet: 2 seconds.

2. Periodicity of querying the control table for active furnaces: 5 seconds.

3. Size of the input buffer for control packets: 6 messages.

A.2 External Interfaces

The context diagram shown in Figure A-1 illustrates the interfaces between the RTS and the external devices. Control packets (CP) and acknowledgements of data packets (DP_ACK) are received from the host computer. Positive or negative acknowledgement of the control packets (CP_ACK) and their associated sequence numbers are returned to the host. A furnace number, representing the furnace for which the temperature is to be read, is sent from RTS to the digital thermometer. A temperature reading for the given furnace is received from the digital thermometer. A data packet (DP) is constructed and sent to the host computer.

A.3 Edges-In Approach

The Edges-In approach is employed by first determining the processes required to interface with the external devices. Figure A-2 represents a process graph that shows three processes interfacing with the external devices. We have used the first rule of the process selection rules (see Section 9.1) and assigned a process to each external device. The remaining functionality of RTS is contained in the "Middle Part" and will be decomposed later. The three edge processes are:

1. *Receive Host Message* (RX_Host_Msg). This process receives either a control packet (CP) or an acknowledgement (ACK or NAK) of a data packet. It determines whether a CP or ACK/NAK is received and passes the CP (STX and ETX are stripped off) or ACK/NAK (single character) to the RTS Middle Part for further processing.

2. *Transmit Host Message* (TX_Host_Msg). This process transmits either a data packet or an acknowledgement (ACK or NAK) of a control packet.

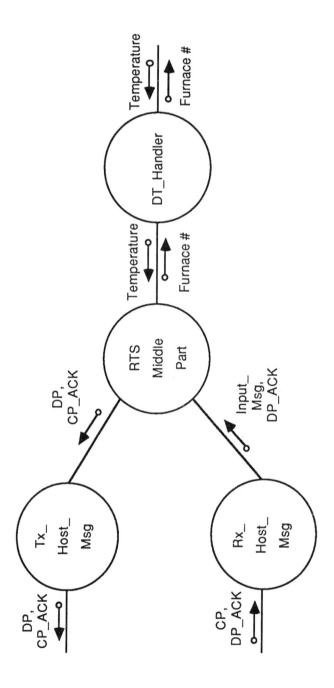

Figure A-2. Processes for edge functions.

3. *Digital Thermometer Handler* (DT_Handler). This process sends a furnace number to the digital thermometer and receives from it the corresponding temperature value.

A.4   Decomposing The Middle Part

To decompose a large and complicated middle part, it is necessary to use data flow diagrams (DFDs) and a set of heuristics (Process Selection Rules, Section 9.1) to determine a suitable set of processes. The DFD for RTS is shown in Figure A-3 and represents a functional restatement of the problem specification (including the edge functions). We use the functional cohesion rule to combine the transforms of the middle part into processes, as shown in Figure A-4. This figure depicts all the RTS processes, including the three for the external devices. The process structure chart in Figure A-5 shows all the concurrent processes and their interfaces. The processes for the middle part shown in Figure A-6 have been separated from the edge processes and are described as follows:

1. Analyze_Host_Input. This process analyzes the input that comes from the host computer and passes it on as follows:

   a. An input message is analyzed for validity, and a CP_ACK (ACK for valid message, or NAK for invalid message) is sent to another process (not shown in Figure A-6) for transmission back to the host.

   b. A valid input message is converted from ASCII to decimal values and passed on to the process Manage_Temperature_Reading. The converted entity is called an "Internal Control Packet," or ICP.

   c. An invalid input message is discarded.

2. Manage_Temperature_Reading. This process manages the table of time intervals for reading the various furnaces and determines the time and order for the reading of temperatures. The furnace number and time for next temperature reading is passed to the process Create_IDP.

3. *Create Internal Data Packet* (Create_IDP). This process sends the furnace number received to the DT_Handler at the appropriate time and waits for a return of the respective temperature value. An IDP containing decimal values of the furnace number and corresponding temperature is created and sent to the next process.

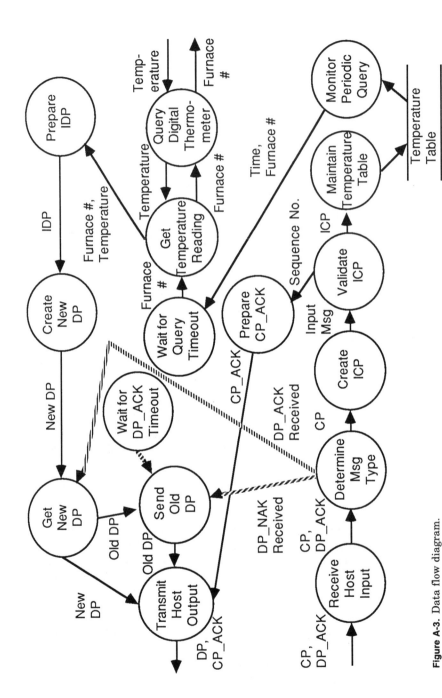

Figure A-3. Data flow diagram.

278

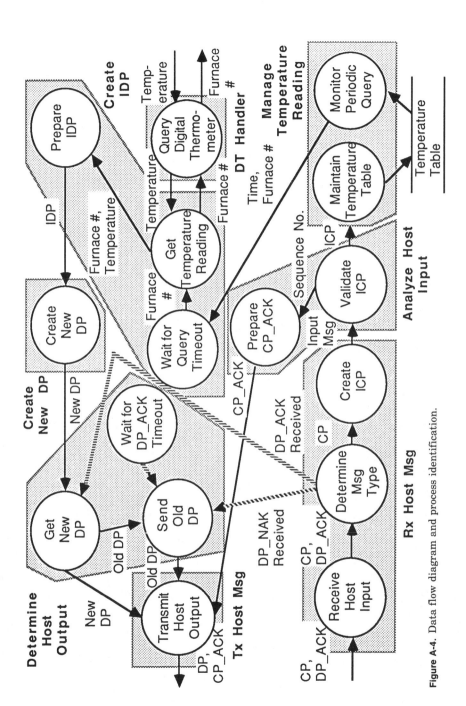

Figure A-4. Data flow diagram and process identification.

279

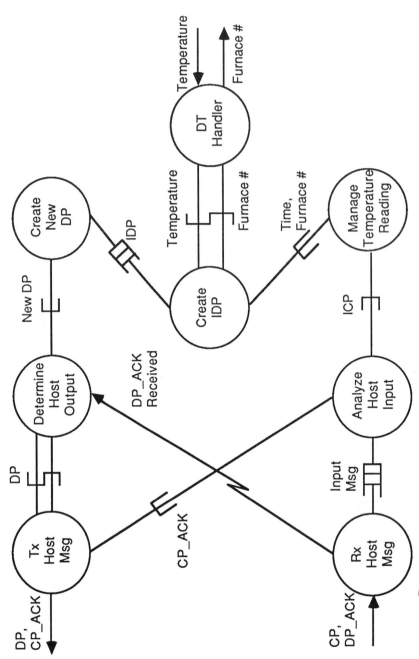

Figure A-5. Process structure chart.

280

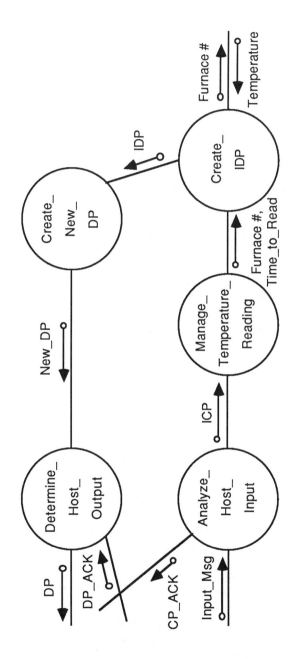

Figure A-6. Decomposition of middle part.

4. *Create New Data Packet* (Create_New_DP). This process gets the next IDP and converts the furnace number and corresponding temperature to ASCII. These ASCII characters are preceded by STX and followed by an ETX to create the proper format for a new data packet (DP).

5. Determine_Host_Output. This process determines whether to retransmit the same message or to transmit the next message. After initiating transmission of a DP, it waits for either a DP_ACK or a timeout. (This satisfies the transmit protocol described in the problem specification.) This process receives a data packet acknowledgement (DP_ACK) from Rx_Host_Msg. If the acknowledgement is positive, this process fetches a new data packet (New_DP) from Create_New_DP and passes it to the process that will send it to the host. If the acknowledgement is negative, it sends out the old DP for retransmission. The latter action is also taken if no DP_ACK is received within the specified timeout interval.

A.5   Introducing Intermediary Processes

The proper decoupling of processes (see Figure A-5 for process interfaces) is accomplished by introducing intermediary processes as shown in Figure A-7. The intermediaries are:

1. Buffer_Input_Msgs

2. Relay_DP_ACK

3. Buffer_IDPs

The input messages from the host are stored in FIFO order in ASCII format using the process Buffer_Input_Msgs. When the buffer is full, additional input messages are ignored. A relay is added between Rx_Host_Msg and Determine_Host_Output to ensure asynchronous behavior for these two processes. If this was not done, incoming characters from the host could be lost while Rx_Host_Msg was waiting for a rendezvous. (Determine_Host_Output could be busy interacting with other processes.)

The processes Create_IDP and Create_New_DP have been decoupled by introducing the buffer process Buffer_IDPs between them. This allows temperature readings to be continued to be made even if positive ACKs are not received for the DPs sent. When the IDP buffer is full, the oldest IDPs are overwritten, rather than ignoring the latest data (as with the host input messages).

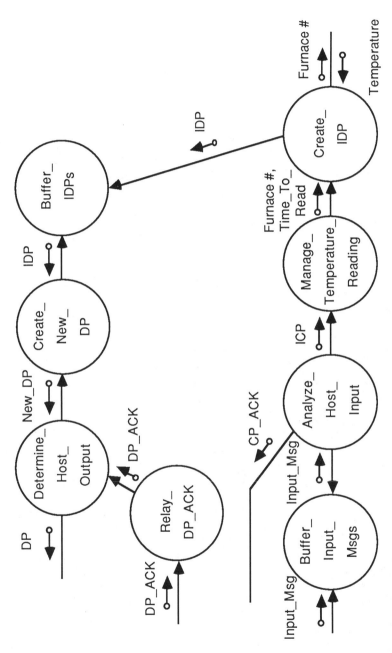

Figure A-7. Introduction of intermediaries.

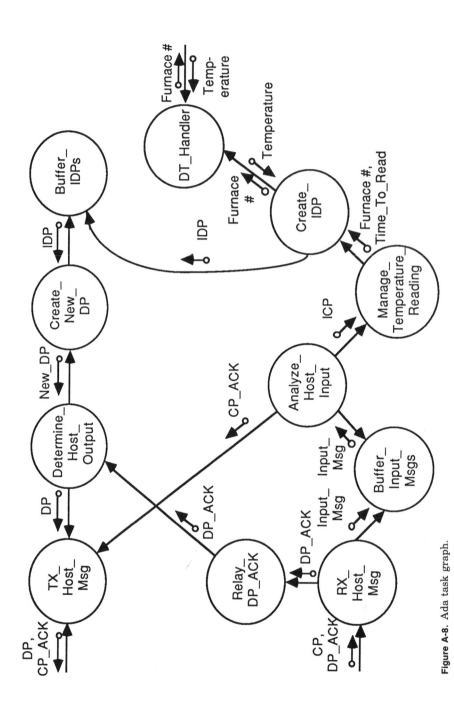

Figure A-8. Ada task graph.

284

A.6   Caller/Called Decisions

The introduction of intermediaries allows us to complete the caller/called decisions of the Middle Part, as shown in Figure A-7. The composition of all the RTS processes is shown in Figure A-8.

Relay processes accept input from a producer and pass the same input to a consumer. This makes Rx_Host_Msg (the producer) a caller relative to Relay_DP_ACK, and Relay_DP_ACK a caller relative to Determine_Host_Output (the consumer).

Buffer processes are always pure servers. This makes Rx_Host_Msg and Analyze_Host_Input callers with respect to Buffer_Input_Msgs. Similarly, Create_IDP and Create_New_DP are callers relative to Buffer_IDPs.

Tx_Host_Msg receives either a CP_ACK from Analyze_Host_Input or a DP from Determine_Host_Output, and is considered a pure server. It does not make sense to have Tx_Host_Msg call either of the other two processes as this would severely restrict it as a simple device handler.

Manage_Temperature_Reading receives an ICP (request to update the table for temperature readings) and scans the table when a time-out has expired. This process must not be waiting for a rendezvous with Analyze_Host_Input when the timeout expires, and the reception of the ICP will be implemented with a guarded accept in Manage_Temperature_Reading. When the temperature table is scanned, this process determines the next temperature reading. The process Create_IDP should not be tied up during this scanning and is thus made the called process.

The process DT_Handler is a simple device handler for the digital thermometer and is therefore called by Create_IDP.

Determine_Host_Output makes a decision whether to send an old DP or if it needs to fetch a new DP from Create_New_DP. This decision process makes it natural for Determine_Host_Output to call Create_New_DP.

A.7   Ada Packaging

The processes shown in Figure A-8 have been encapsulated in Ada packages as shown in Figure A-9. Packaging decisions have been made based on functionality and minimization of coupling (see Chapter 13). Up to this point we have used the phrase "process" to describe a general concurrent process and have avoided the phrase "task." From now on we will use "task" to describe the specific Ada construct for a concurrent process, and "process" when we don't know yet how a concurrent process will be implemented in Ada. For

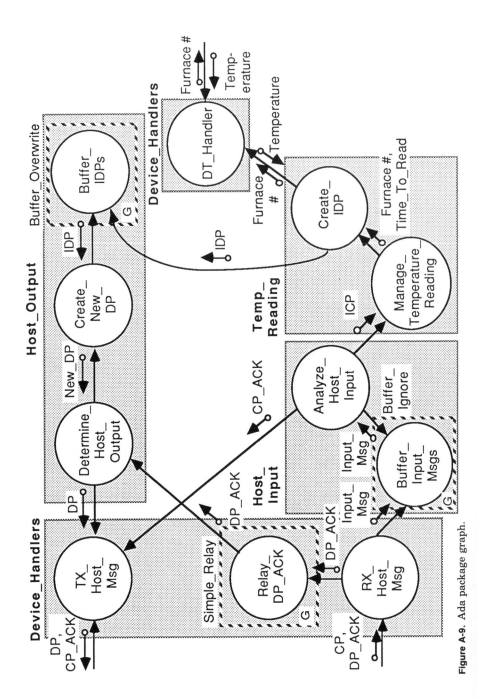

Figure A-9. Ada package graph.

example, the process Buffer_Input_Msgs shown in Figure A-8 will be implemented as an instantiated Ada package with a task Buffer hidden inside its (generic) package body. The implication of this is that there is not necessarily a complete isomorphism between the processes shown in Figure A-8 and the top-level PDL.

The rationale for the Ada packaging decisions is as follows:

1. Device_Handlers. This package contains all the tasks that interface directly with the hardware devices (Rx_Host_Msg, Tx_Host_Msg, and DT_Handler). These device drivers are treated as a group, similar to a collection of mathematical subprograms or a graphics package. This represents "package coupling" as defined in Chapter 13. The generic relay process (Relay_DP_ACK) is instantiated inside the task body of Rx_Host_Msg.

2. Host_Input. This package contains the task Analyze_ Host_Input. The generic buffer process (Buffer_Input_ Msgs) is instantiated inside the package body of Host_Input. Analyze_Host_Input is a fairly extensive task and does not have any functionality in common with the other tasks. It is, therefore, the only task (aside from the buffer process) in this package.

3. Temp_Reading. This package contains the two functionally related tasks Manage_Temperature_Reading and Create_IDP.

4. Host_Output. This package contains the two functionally related tasks Determine_Host_Output and Create_New_DP. The generic buffer process (Buffer_IDPs) is instantiated inside the package body of Host_Output.

5. Other packages. The packages shown in Figure A-9 use "helper" packages, of the form "definitions," that have been prepared in advance. These library packages are withed as required. These packages are:

   a. *Global definitions* (Definitions). This package contains all the constants, adaptation parameters, and types required by the other packages. This collection represents definition coupling as described in Chapter 13.

   b. *Hardware-dependent entities* (HDP). This package contains all the hardware-specific entities such as addresses of hardware interrupts and buffers. This collection represents package coupling, since the various Ada modules will only use the entities that correspond to a given hardware device. DT_Handler, for example, will use the address of the hardware buffer for the digital thermometer in a "for-use-at" clause.

The four application packages described above are also *objects* of the sort discussed in Chapters 5 and 12. This can be seen by a comparison of Figures A-1 and A-9. The Input Channel becomes the Host_Input object, the Output Channel becomes the Host_Output object, and the Digital Thermometer becomes the Temp_Reading object. This object encapsulation is in accordance with the guidelines of Section 10.4.

A.8 Program Design Language (PDL)

The PDL phase consists of transforming the design described in Figure A-9 into a programming structure using Ada constructs. The top-level design illustrates the overall structure; it contains a main procedure, package specifications, and package bodies. The package bodies contain subprogram and task declarations, and entrance procedures for communication between tasks that reside in different packages. An entrance procedure allows a task specification to be hidden in the package body rather than be visible in the package specification. This is good design practice, and Burns recommends that a "procedural interface" be used for "all tasks" [BUR85, p. 113]. Details of task and subprogram algorithms are deferred to the detailed design phase by using Ada's *separate* construct. The compiler used to process the RTS PDL was the DEC VAX Ada compiler. A description of the top-level design phase is given below, followed by the detailed design.

A.8.1 Top-Level Design

The package specifications listed for the top level design only include the information that is required to be visible to users of these packages. This includes entrance procedures, generic formal parameters (for generic packages), comments that specify calls to entrance procedures in other packages, and the pragma Inline where appropriate. All other information that is not necessary to be disclosed to the users of the package is hidden in the package body. The RTS top-level design is as follows:

1. *Helper packages.* Helper packages must be prepared in a bottom-up fashion before we start the top-level design of the application packages in a top-down fashion. The following components are used by the application packages:

```
--  Global definitions  ----

with Calendar;
package Definitions is

   Max_CP_Chars       : constant := 7; -- includes STX and ETX
   Max_DP_Chars       : constant := 8; -- includes STX and ETX
   Max_Furnace        : constant := 15;
   Max_Temp           : constant := 1000;
   Max_CP_Msgs        : constant := 6;
   Max_IDP            : constant := 100;
   Max_Input_String   : constant := 5; -- STX and ETX stripped off
   Max_Sequence_No    : constant := 9;

   Re_Tx_Delay        : constant Duration := 2.0;
   Read_Temp_Period   : constant Duration := 5.0;
   Inactive_Indicator : constant Duration := 0.0;

   subtype CP_Format    is String (1 .. Max_Input_String);
   subtype CP_ACK_NAK   is String (1 .. 4); -- includes seq number
   subtype DP_Format    is String (1 .. Max_DP_Chars);
   subtype Furnace_Type is Natural range 0 .. Max_Furnace;
   subtype Read_Time    is Calendar.Time;
   subtype Temp_Type    is Natural range 0 .. Max_Temp;

   type IDP_Format is
     record
       Furnace_No  : Furnace_Type;
       Temperature : Temp_Type;
     end record;

   type ICP_Type is
     record
       Furnace_No : Furnace_Type;
       Interval   : Duration;
     end record;

   type Temp_Elements is
     record
       Active       : Boolean        := False;
       Time_To_Read : Calendar.Time := Calendar.Clock;
       Interval     : Duration;
     end record;

end Definitions;
```

Figure A-10. Definitions (package specification).

```
-- Hardware dependencies --

package HDP is
   Output_Channel_Adr      : constant := 16#00A0#;
   Output_Buffer_Adr       : constant := 16#00A2#;
   Input_Channel_Adr       : constant := 16#00A4#;
   Input_Buffer_Adr        : constant := 16#00A6#;
   DT_Interrupt_Adr        : constant := 16#00B0#;
   DT_Buffer_Furnace_Adr   : constant := 16#00B2#;
   DT_Buffer_Temp_Adr      : constant := 16#00B4#;
end HDP;
```

Figure A-11. HDP (package specification).

a. Definitions. This package contains constants, adaptation parameters, and types. It imports the package Calendar (supplied with the standard environment). The Ada code is shown in Figure A-10.

b. HDP. This package contains absolute addresses for hardware interrupts and buffers for the host input and output channels, and for the digital thermometer. The Ada code is shown in Figure A-11.

c. Buffer_Ignore. The generic parameters include the size of the buffer and the type of the elements to be buffered. The package body contains the declaration of the task Buffer, and the bodies of the entrance procedures. The conditional entry call in Enqueue ensures that Rx_Host_Msg does not wait for a rendezvous with Buffer_Input_Msgs if the buffer is full. If the call were unconditional, input characters from the host could be lost while Rx_Host_Msg was tied up waiting for the buffer to become not full. The details of the implementation of the task Buffer have been deferred by using the *separate* clause. The Ada code is shown in Figure A-12.

d. Simple_Relay. The generic parameters include the type of the item to be relayed and the procedure name of the consumer. The package contains the declaration and body of the task Relay, and the body of the entrance procedure. The Ada code is shown in Figure A-13.

e. Buffer_Overwrite. The generic parameters are the size of the buffer and the type of the elements to be buffered. The package body contains the task declaration and bodies of the entrance procedures. The only difference between this

```
generic
  Size : in Natural := 20;
  type Item is private;

package Buffer_Ignore is
  procedure Enqueue (I : in Item);
  procedure Dequeue (I : out Item);
  pragma Inline (Enqueue, Dequeue);
end Buffer_Ignore;

package body Buffer_Ignore is
  task Buffer is
    entry Enqueue (I : in Item);
    entry Dequeue (I : out Item);
  end Buffer;

  task body Buffer is separate;

  procedure Enqueue (I : in Item) is
  begin
    select
      Buffer.Enqueue (I);
    else
      null;  -- Request ignored
    end select;
  end Enqueue;

  procedure Dequeue (I : out Item) is
  begin
    Buffer.Dequeue (I);
  end Dequeue;

end Buffer_Ignore;
```

Figure A-12. Buffer_Ignore (package specification and body).

generic buffer package and Buffer_Ignore is that the
entrance procedure Enqueue here does not make a conditional call to the buffer process (Buffer_IDPs). If the buffer
is full, the new element is stored on top of the oldest. (This
is not shown in the top-level design by using the *separate*
clause for the task body Buffer.) The Ada code is shown in
Figure A-14.

```
generic
  type Item is private;
  with procedure Consumer (C : in Item);

package Simple_Relay is
  procedure Relay_Item (I : in Item);
  pragma Inline (Relay_Item);
end Simple_Relay;

package body Simple_Relay is
  task Relay is
    entry Relay_Item (I : in Item);
  end Relay;

  task body Relay is
    X : Item;
  begin
    loop
      accept Relay_Item (I : in Item) do
        X := I;
      end Relay_Item;
      Consumer (X);
    end loop;
  end Relay;

  procedure Relay_Item (I : in Item) is
  begin
    Relay.Relay_Item (I);
  end Relay_Item;

end Simple_Relay;
```

Figure A-13. Simple_Relay (package specification and body).

f. ASCII_Conversions. The package specification include the interfaces to the two functions ASCII_To_Integer and Integer_To_ASCII, and the exception that is raised in the respective function. The details of the function bodies are deferred by using the *separate* clause in the package body. The Ada code is shown in Figure A-15.

2. *Application packages.* The following application packages were prepared for the RTS top-level design:

```
generic
  Size : in Natural := 20;
  type Item is private;

package Buffer_Overwrite is
  procedure Enqueue (I : in Item);
  procedure Dequeue (I : out Item);
  pragma Inline (Enqueue, Dequeue);
end Buffer_Overwrite;

package body Buffer_Overwrite is
  task Buffer is
    entry Enqueue (I : in Item);
    entry Dequeue (I : out Item);
  end Buffer;

  task body Buffer is separate;

  procedure Enqueue (I : in Item) is
  begin
    Buffer.Enqueue (I);
  end Enqueue;

  procedure Dequeue (I : out Item) is
  begin
    Buffer.Dequeue (I);
  end Dequeue;

end Buffer_Overwrite;
```

Figure A-14. Buffer_Overwrite (package specification and body).

a. Device_Handlers. The package Definitions is imported, and various type specifications are used as type marks for subprogram parameters. The comments indicate that modules in this package interface with modules in the packages Host_Input and Host_Output. Task declarations for the various device handlers (Tx_Host_Msg, Rx_Host_Msg, and DT_Handler) are made in the package body. Entities in the package HDP are imported by the package body for the use of "for-use-at" clauses for the interrupt entries. The Ada code is shown in Figure A-16.

b. Host_Input. The package Definitions is imported and used as described for Device_Handlers. The package body

```
package ASCII_Conversions is
   function ASCII_To_Integer (A : String) return Integer;
   function Integer_To_ASCII (I : Integer) return String;
   Invalid_Message : exception;
   Invalid_Integer : exception;
end ASCII_Conversions;

package body ASCII_Conversions is
   function ASCII_To_Integer (A : String) return Integer is separate;
   function Integer_To_ASCII (I : Integer) return String is separate;
end ASCII_Conversions;
```

Figure A-15. ASCII_Conversions (package specification and body).

imports the generic package Buffer_Ignore and instantiates it for a size of Max_CP_Msgs and type CP_Format. Note that the instantiated package name is Buffer_Input_Msgs to match the buffer process described previously in Figures A-7 through A-9. The task Analyze_Host_Input is declared in the package body, with comments indicating calls to other units. This task is a pure caller and has no entries. The Ada code is shown in Figure A-17.

c. Temp_Reading. The package Definitions is imported and used as described above. The tasks Manage_Temperature_Reading and Create_IDP are declared in the package body, with their bodies declared as separate. The Ada code is shown in Figure A-18.

d. Host_Output. The package Definitions is imported and used as described above. The package body imports the generic package Buffer_Overwrite and instantiates it for a size of Max_IDP and type IDP_Format. The name of the instantiated package is Buffer_IDPs to match the buffer process described earlier (see Figures A-7 through A-9). Task declarations are included for Determine_Host_Output and Create_New_DP, with details deferred using the separate construct. The Ada code is shown in Figure A-19.

3. *Main procedure.* Ada requires a main program to start the elaboration process of packages and their objects, subprograms, and tasks. This main procedure is called RTS_Main and is shown in Figure A-20. This procedure simply imports the package Host_Input and has a *null* body. This is sufficient to start the elaboration of the other packages (which contain their own *with* clauses) and the activation of tasks encapsulated within these

```
with Definitions;  use Definitions;


package Device_Handlers is
  procedure Transmit_DP      (DP : in DP_Format);
  procedure Transmit_CP_ACK (ACK_NAK : in CP_ACK_NAK);
  procedure Read_Temp        (F : in Furnace_Type;
                              T : out Temp_Type);
  pragma Inline (Transmit_DP, Transmit_CP_ACK, Read_Temp);
  No_Response_From_DT : exception;  -- raised in Read_Temp
  -- Calls
    -- Host_Output.Acknowledge_DP
    -- Host_Input.Store_Input_Msg
end Device_Handlers;


with HDP;  use HDP;
package body Device_Handlers is
  task Tx_Host_Msg is
    entry Output_Channel;
    for Output_Channel use at Output_Channel_Adr;

    entry Transmit_DP      (DP : in DP_Format);
    entry Transmit_CP_ACK (ACK_NAK : in CP_ACK_NAK);
  end Tx_Host_Msg;


  task Rx_Host_Msg is
    entry Input_Channel;
    for Input_Channel use at Input_Channel_Adr;
    -- Calls
      -- Relay_DP_ACK.Relay_Item
  end Rx_Host_Msg;


  task DT_Handler is
    entry DT_Interrupt;
    for DT_Interrupt use at DT_Interrupt_Adr;

    entry Read_Temp (F : in Furnace_Type;
                     T : out Temp_Type);
    -- raises No_Response_From_DT
  end DT_Handler;
```

Figure A-16. Device_Handlers (package specification and body).

```
task body Tx_Host_Msg is separate;
task body Rx_Host_Msg is separate;
task body DT_Handler  is separate;

procedure Transmit_DP (DP : in DP_Format) is
begin
  Tx_Host_Msg.Transmit_DP (DP);
end Transmit_DP;

procedure Transmit_CP_ACK (ACK_NAK : in CP_ACK_NAK) is
begin
  Tx_Host_Msg.Transmit_CP_ACK (ACK_NAK);
end Transmit_CP_ACK;

procedure Read_Temp (F : in Furnace_Type;
                     T : out Temp_Type)  is
begin
  DT_Handler.Read_Temp (F, T);
end Read_Temp;

end Device_Handlers;
```

Figure A-16 *(Continued)*. Device_Handlers (package specification and body).

packages. Code to be used during the testing phase could be placed in this driver: declarations of simulation tasks and subprograms, test data, and so on.

This completes the top-level design phase. The remaining part of the design process is to supply the Ada subunits that contain the details of the RTS implementation.

A.8.2 Detailed Design

The detailed design consists of supplying all the subunits, and having the Ada compiler check interfaces and proper importation of required entities. These entities should be imported by having the subunits *with* the necessary packages and subprograms, if possible. This will reduce the amount of recompilation required if the imported library units are changed.

If the functionality of a given subunit is too complex for completion of actual code, comments are supplied to outline the algorithm(s) and only an executable statement necessary to satisfy the compiler is supplied, e.g., a *null* for task bodies and procedures,

```
with Definitions;  use Definitions;

package Host_Input is
  procedure Store_Input_Msg (C : in CP_Format);
  pragma Inline (Store_Input_Msg);
  -- Calls
    -- Device_Handlers.Transmit_CP_ACK
    -- Temp_Reading.Use_ICP
end Host_Input;

with Buffer_Ignore;
package body Host_Input is
  -- Instantiate buffer for host input messages

      package Buffer_Input_Msgs is new Buffer_Ignore
                 (Size => Max_CP_Msgs,
                  Item => CP_Format);

  task Analyze_Host_Input is
    -- Calls
      -- Buffer_Input_Msgs.Dequeue
      -- Device_Handlers.Transmit_CP_ACK
      -- Temp_Reading.Use_ICP
  end Analyze_Host_Input;

  task body Analyze_Host_Input is separate;

  procedure Store_Input_Msg (C : in CP_Format) is
  begin
    Buffer_Input_Msgs.Enqueue (C);
  end Store_Input_Msg;

end Host_Input;
```

Figure A-17. Host_Input (package specification and body).

and appropriate *return* for a function. The executable statements for the algorithm(s) are supplied during the coding phase.

It should be noted that generic subunits may be expected by some implementations (e.g., DEC's VAX Ada) to be available in the Ada library before instantiations can be made during the top-level design. If the generic units are available as reusable components, this presents no problem since the templates are already there. If, however, the generic units are being developed as part of the

```
with Definitions;  use Definitions;

package Temp_Reading is
  procedure Use_ICP (I : in ICP_Type);
  pragma Inline (Use_ICP);
  -- Calls
    -- Host_Output.Enqueue_IDP
    -- Device_Handlers.Read_Temp
end Temp_Reading;

package body Temp_Reading is
  task Manage_Temperature_Reading is
    entry Use_ICP (I : in ICP_Type);
    -- Calls
      -- Create_IDP.Take_Temp_Info
  end Manage_Temperature_Reading;

  task Create_IDP is
    entry Take_Temp_Info (F : in Furnace_Type;
                          T : in Read_Time);
    -- Calls
      -- Device_Handler.Read_Temp
      -- Host_Output.Enqueue_IDP
  end Create_IDP;

  task body Manage_Temperature_Reading is separate;
  task body Create_IDP                  is separate;

  procedure Use_ICP (I : in ICP_Type) is
  begin
    Manage_Temperature_Reading.Use_ICP (I);
  end Use_ICP;

end Temp_Reading;
```

Figure A-18. Temp_Reading (package specification and body).

current design, there are two approaches that can be taken:

1. *Dummy subunits.* The bodies contain only the required statements that will lead to a successful compilation.

2. *Complete subunits.* The details of the subunit bodies are supplied as part of the bottom-up phase before the design of the application packages is started (the top-down phase).

```
with Definitions;  use Definitions;

package Host_Output is
  procedure Acknowledge_DP (D : in Character);
  procedure Enqueue_IDP    (I : in IDP_Format);
  pragma Inline (Acknowledge_DP, Enqueue_IDP);
  -- Calls
    --  Device_Handlers.Transmit_DP
end Host_Output;


with Buffer_Overwrite;
package body Host_Output is

  -- Instantiate buffer for IDPs
    package Buffer_IDPs is new Buffer_Overwrite
                 (Size => Max_IDP,
                  Item => IDP_Format);

  task Determine_Host_Output is
    entry Acknowledge_DP (D : in Character);
    -- Calls
      --  Device_Handlers.Transmit_DP
      --  Create_New_DP.Provide_DP
  end Determine_Host_Output;

  task Create_New_DP is
    -- Calls
      --  Buffer_IDPs.Dequeue

    entry Provide_DP (D : out DP_Format);
  end Create_New_DP;

  task body Determine_Host_Output is separate;
  task body Create_New_DP        is separate;

  procedure Acknowledge_DP (D : in Character) is
  begin
    Determine_Host_Output.Acknowledge_DP (D);
  end Acknowledge_DP;

  procedure Enqueue_IDP (I : in IDP_Format) is
  begin
    Buffer_IDPs.Enqueue (I);
  end Enqueue_IDP;
end Host_Output;
```

Figure A-19. Host_Output (package specification and body).

```
with Host_Input;
procedure RTS_Main is
  -- may want to declare simulation tasks here
begin
  null;
end RTS_Main;
```

Figure A-20. RTS_Main (main procedure).

The interfaces between the various subprograms and tasks in the application packages are depicted in the structure graph in Figure A-21. The names and structures shown in this figure are isomorphic with the Ada PDL, and the program architecture has been derived from the PDL. The paragraphs that follow describe the subunits for the helper packages and application packages specified during the top-level design phase.

1. *Helper packages*

   a. Buffer_Ignore

      ▪ *Buffer* (task body). The code for this subunit is shown in Figure A-22. Subtypes and objects are declared for the manipulation of the buffer, and exclusive access is implemented with the select statement. The Enqueue entry is not guarded, and an item is enqueued if the buffer is not full (Count < Size). Otherwise the request is ignored. The Dequeue entry is guarded, and a dequeue request is only honored when Count > 0. The FIFO nature of this buffer ("circular queue") is implemented using the *mod* function to cause the appropriate wraparound effect. This type of buffer represents an "object manager" since storage space for the buffer is declared within the task body, and only the elements in the buffer (not the buffer itself) are passed to and from this task.

   b. Buffer_Overwrite

      ▪ *Buffer* (task body). The code for this subunit is shown in Figure A-23. The parent (Buffer_Overwrite) of the subunit is named in the separate clause. There is no conflict by having the same subunit name as in the previous case since the two parents are unique (Buffer_Ignore and Buffer_Overwrite). This particular buffer task implements the specification that a new element is replacing the oldest element when the buffer is full. The entry call

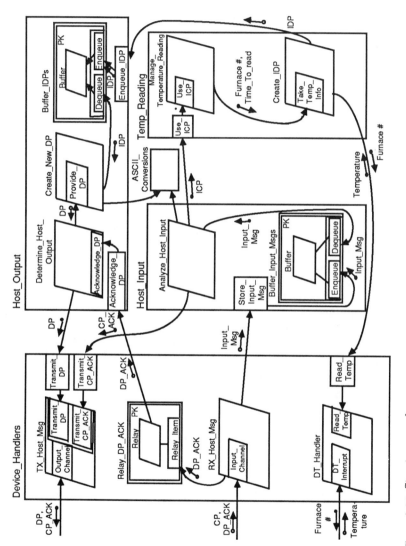

Figure A-21. Structure graph.

```
separate (Buffer_Ignore)

task body Buffer is
  subtype Index_Type is Positive range 1 .. Size;
  subtype Count_Type is Natural  range 0 .. Size;

  Buf : array (Index_Type) of Item;
  Insert : Index_Type := 1;
  Remove : Index_Type := 1;
  Count  : Count_Type := 0;
begin
  loop
    select
      accept Enqueue (I : in Item) do
        if Count < Size then  -- check if request ignored
          Buf (Insert) := I;
          Insert := (Insert mod Buf'Last) + 1;
          Count  := Count + 1;
        end if;
      end Enqueue;
    or
      when Count > 0 =>
        accept Dequeue (I : out Item) do
          I := Buf (Remove);
        end Dequeue;
        Remove := (Remove mod Buf'Last) + 1;
        Count  := Count - 1;
    or
      terminate;
    end select;
  end loop;
end Buffer;
```

Figure A-22. Buffer (task body).

to Enqueue is not guarded, and when the "full" condition is detected, the Remove pointer is advanced to the next oldest element. Count is not incremented for this condition since an exception (Constraint_Error) would occur.

2. *Application packages*

   a.   Device_Handlers

```
separate (Buffer_Overwrite)

task body Buffer is
  subtype Index_Type is Positive range 1 .. Size;
  subtype Count_Type is Natural  range 0 .. Size;

  Buf : array (Index_Type) of Item;
  Insert : Index_Type := 1;
  Remove : Index_Type := 1;
  Count  : Count_Type := 0;
begin
  loop
    select
      accept Enqueue (I : in Item) do
        Buf (Insert) := I;
      end Enqueue;
      Insert := (Insert mod Buf'Last) + 1;

      if (Insert = Remove) then
        Remove := (Remove mod Buf'Last) + 1;
      else
        Count  := Count + 1;
      end if;
        -- If (Insert = Remove), the buffer is full.
        -- We will put the new element on
        -- top of the oldest.  We advance the Remove
        -- pointer to prevent the element just inserted
        -- from being removed next.  We do not
        -- increment Count.
    or
      when Count > 0 =>
        accept Dequeue (I : out Item) do
          I := Buf (Remove);
        end Dequeue;
        Remove := (Remove mod Buf'Last) + 1;
        Count  := Count - 1;
    or
      terminate;
    end select;
  end loop;
end Buffer;
```

Figure A-23. Buffer (task body).

- Rx_Host_Msg (task body). The declarative part includes local declarations for a character associated with a hardware location, a string to hold the input message, an exception for the detection of a protocol error, and an instantiation of a relay task. The name of the instantiated package (Relay_DP_ACK) matches the relay process shown in Figures A-7 through A-9.

  The algorithm, including an exception handler, is implemented within an infinite loop. The interrupt is accepted, and a character is taken from the input buffer. If the character is an ACK or a NAK, it is passed directly to the relay task. If the character is an STX, a message is expected and is collected in Input_Msg. The task is knowledgeable about the protocol for a valid message and ignores both the STX and ETX. If a protocol error is detected, the exception Protocol_Error is raised. A local exception handler is provided inside the loop to prevent the task from terminating. The code for Rx_Host_Msg is shown in Figure A-24.

- Tx_Host_Msg (task body). A local character is declared and associated with an output buffer location. The algorithm is implemented with a select statement within an infinite loop. Guards are not used for the two accept statements to signify that neither is favored over the other. When an entry call to Transmit_DP is accepted, the task puts a character in the output buffer and waits for an interrupt before it puts the next character in. DP'Range determines how many characters should be sent to the output buffer. When an entry call to Transmit_CP_ACK is accepted, a message containing a CP sequence number and a CP ACK or NAK is sent to the host in the same manner as just described for a data packet message. The code for Tx_Host_Msg is shown in Figure A-25.

- DT_Handler (task body). The declarative part includes local buffer declarations and associated hardware locations for a furnace number and a temperature value. The algorithm is implemented inside an infinite loop. When the entry call to Read_Temp is accepted, the furnace number received as a parameter is placed in the digital thermometer buffer. The task waits for an interrupt from the digital thermometer, gets the temperature from the respective buffer location, and passes the temperature

```
with Text_IO;  use Text_IO;
with Simple_Relay;
with Host_Output;
with Host_Input;

separate (Device_Handlers)

task body Rx_Host_Msg is
  X            : Character;
  Input_Buffer : Character;
  for Input_Buffer use at Input_Buffer_Adr;

  Input_Msg : String (1 .. Max_Input_String);
  Protocol_Error : exception;
  -- Instantiate Relay task
      package Relay_DP_ACK is new Simple_Relay
                        (Item    => Character,
                         Consumer => Host_Output.Acknowledge_DP);
begin
  loop
    accept Input_Channel;
    X := Input_Buffer;
    Handle_Protocol_Error :
    begin
      if ((X = ASCII.ACK) or (X = ASCII.NAK)) then
        Relay_DP_ACK.Relay_Item (X);
      elsif (X = ASCII.STX) then
        for I in 1 .. Max_Input_String loop -- ignore STX and ETX
          accept Input_Channel;
          Input_Msg (I) := Input_Buffer;
        end loop;
        accept Input_Channel;   -- get rid of trailing ETX
        Host_Input.Store_Input_Msg (Input_Msg);
      else
        raise Protocol_Error;
      end if;

    -- Inner frame exception handler; we want to stay
    -- within loop:
    exception
      when Protocol_Error =>
        Put ("Protocol_Error or line noise in Rx_Host_Msg");
    end Handle_Protocol_Error;

  end loop;
end Rx_Host_Msg;
```

Figure A-24. Rx_Host_Msg (task body).

```
separate (Device_Handlers)

task body Tx_Host_Msg is
  Output_Buffer : Character;
  for Output_Buffer use at Output_Buffer_Adr;
  Local_ACK_NAK : CP_ACK_NAK;
begin
  loop
    select
      accept Transmit_DP (DP : in DP_Format) do
        for I in DP'Range loop
          Output_Buffer := DP (I);
          accept Output_Channel;
        end loop;
      end Transmit_DP;
    or
      accept Transmit_CP_ACK (ACK_NAK : in CP_ACK_NAK) do
        Local_ACK_NAK := ACK_NAK;
      end Transmit_CP_ACK;

      for I in Local_ACK_NAK'Range loop
        Output_Buffer := Local_ACK_NAK (I);
        accept Output_Channel;
      end loop;
    or
      terminate;
    end select;
  end loop;
end Tx_Host_Msg;
```

Figure A-25. Tx_Host_Msg (task body).

value back to the caller via the *out* parameter. If a response is not received within Max_DT_Response_Time, an exception is raised. This exception is propagated back to the caller, and is also handled within the task loop to allow the task to continue execution. The code for DT_Handler is shown in Figure A-26.

b. Host_Input

    ■ Analyze_Host_Input (task body). Local declarations are made for an input message in control packet format (received from the host), for an internal control packet (converted from ASCII to integer), and for a CP

```
separate (Device_Handlers)

task body DT_Handler is
  DT_Buffer_Furnace : Furnace_Type;
  for DT_Buffer_Furnace use at DT_Buffer_Furnace_Adr;

  DT_Buffer_Temp : Temp_Type;
  for DT_Buffer_Temp use at DT_Buffer_Temp_Adr;

  Max_DT_Response_Time : constant Duration := 3.0;
begin
  loop
    Handle_No_Response :
    begin
      accept Read_Temp (F : in Furnace_Type;
                        T : out Temp_Type) do
        DT_Buffer_Furnace := F;

        select
          accept DT_Interrupt;
        or
          delay Max_DT_Response_Time;
          raise No_Response_From_DT;
        end select;

        T := DT_Buffer_Temp;
      end Read_Temp;

    exception
      when No_Response_From_DT =>
        null;  -- continue task execution
    end Handle_No_Response;
  end loop;
end DT_Handler;
```

Figure A-26. DT_Handler (task body).

ACK/NAK message. Within the infinite loop, the task
gets an input message from the queue and converts it
from ASCII to integer values. The furnace number and
time interval for temperature readings are stored locally
as an ICP. If no exceptions occur during the assignments,
the ICP is passed on for further processing, and an ACK
with the associated CP sequence number is created and

passed to another task for transmission to the host. The exception handler for a possible invalid message is handled within the loop to prevent the task from terminating. The code for Analyze_Host_Input is shown in Figure A-27.

c. Temp_Reading

- Manage_Temperature_Reading (task body). The declarative part includes storage for an ICP, the temperature table (Temp_Read_Table) that is periodically scanned, an index (Index) used to access the temperature table, a time (Time) that specifies the next time the temperature for a given furnace should be read, a time (Check_Temp_Time) used to determine if the timeout has expired, and a counter (Number_Active) used to determine if any of the furnaces have been activated.

  The algorithm is implemented in a select statement with a guarded accept and a delay. The entry call is accepted if the timeout has not expired, and a new ICP is stored locally. The furnace number (first component of the new ICP) is used to index the temperature table, and the time interval (second component of the new ICP) is used to calculate the next time the furnace temperature should be read. If the value of the time interval for the specified furnace indicates that the furnace should be turned off, the active flag is set to FALSE, and the number of active furnaces is reduced by one. Otherwise, the time to read is calculated and the time interval value is saved. If the furnace is inactive, the active flag is set to TRUE and the number of active furnaces is increased by one.

  The delay statement is used to control the timeout. When the timeout expires and there are active furnaces, the temperature table is scanned to determine the next furnace that requires a temperature reading. When a furnace is found, the furnace number and the time the temperature should be read are passed to another task for transmission to the digital thermometer. The next time this furnace should be read is updated by using the time interval stored in the table element. The next timeout is also calculated, using the period (Read_Temp_Period) specified in package Definitions. The code for Manage_Temperature_Reading is shown in Figure A-28.

```
with Temp_Reading;
with Device_Handlers;
with ASCII_Conversions; use ASCII_Conversions;
with Text_IO;           use Text_IO;

separate (Host_Input)


task body Analyze_Host_Input is
  Input_Msg  : CP_Format;
  ICP        : ICP_Type;
  ACK_NAK    : CP_ACK_NAK := (1 => ASCII.STX, 2 .. 3 => ' ',

begin
  loop
    Buffer_Input_Msgs.Dequeue (Input_Msg);
    Handle_Invalid_Message :
    begin
      ICP.Furnace_No := ASCII_To_Integer (Input_Msg (2 .. 3));
                        -- Invalid_Message exception may be raised
      ICP.Interval   := Duration(
                        ASCII_To_Integer (Input_Msg (4 .. 5)));
                        -- Invalid_Message exception may be raised
      Temp_Reading.Use_ICP (ICP);
      -- prepare CP ACK
        ACK_NAK (2) := Input_Msg (1); -- sequence number
        ACK_NAK (3) := ASCII.ACK;
        Device_Handlers.Transmit_CP_ACK (ACK_NAK);


    exception
      when Invalid_Message =>
        Put ("Invalid Input Msg detected in Analyze_Host_Input");
        -- prepare NAK
          ACK_NAK (2) := Input_Msg (1); -- sequence number
          ACK_NAK (3) := ASCII.NAK;
          Device_Handlers.Transmit_CP_ACK (ACK_NAK);
    end Handle_Invalid_Message;

  end loop;
end Analyze_Host_Input;
```

Figure A-27. Analyze_Host_Input (task body).

```
with Calendar;  use Calendar;
separate (Temp_Reading)

task body Manage_Temperature_Reading is
  ICP              : ICP_Type;
  Temp_Read_Table : array (Furnace_Type) of Temp_Elements;
  Index            : Furnace_Type;
  Check_Temp_Time : Read_Time := Clock + Read_Temp_Period;
  Number_Active    : Natural   := 0;
begin
  loop
    select
      -- Check if timeout not expired
        when ((Check_Temp_Time - Clock) > 0.0) =>
          accept Use_ICP (I : in ICP_Type) do
            ICP := I;
          end Use_ICP;

      Index := ICP.Furnace_No;

      -- Check if active furnace should be turned off (inactive)
      -- or have its values changed, or if an inactive furnace
      -- should be activated (turned on):
      if ICP.Interval = Inactive_Indicator then
        if Temp_Read_Table (Index).Active = True then
          Temp_Read_Table (Index).Active := False;  -- turn it off
          Number_Active := Number_Active - 1;
        end if;
      else
        Temp_Read_Table (Index).Time_To_Read := Clock + ICP.Interval;
        Temp_Read_Table (Index).Interval := ICP.Interval;

        if Temp_Read_Table (Index).Active = False then
          Temp_Read_Table (Index).Active := True;  -- turn it on
          Number_Active := Number_Active + 1;
        end if;
      end if;
    or
      delay (Check_Temp_Time - Clock);
      -- When timeout expires, scan the temperature table
      -- for active entries, and check if temperatures should
      -- be read, if any of the furnaces are active:
```

Figure A-28. Manage_Temperature_Reading (task body).

```
    if Number_Active > 0 then
      for I in Temp_Read_Table'Range loop
        if ((Temp_Read_Table (I).Active) and then
            (Temp_Read_Table (I).Time_To_Read - Clock)
                      < Read_Temp_Period) then
          Create_IDP.Take_Temp_Info (I,
                    Temp_Read_Table (I).Time_To_Read);
          -- Calculate next time to read
            Temp_Read_Table (I).Time_To_Read :=
                    Temp_Read_Table (I).Time_To_Read +
                    Temp_Read_Table (I).Interval;
        end if;
      end loop;
    end if;

    -- Update for next timeout
    Check_Temp_Time := Check_Temp_Time + Read_Temp_Period;
  end select;
 end loop;
end Manage_Temperature_Reading;
```

Figure A-28 *(continued).* Manage_Temperature_Reading (task body).

- Create_IDP (task body). Task declarations include a furnace number (Furnace_No), a time (Time_To_Read), and a temperature (Temperature). The task waits for an entry call at the accept statement within the infinite loop. When a call is accepted, the furnace number and the time for the temperature reading are stored in the corresponding local objects. The task is delayed until the time to read has expired. A call is then made to the Device_Handler, requesting that the temperature be read for the given furnace. The task waits for the temperature value to be returned, and passes the new IDP (an aggregate consisting of Furnace_No and Temperature) to Host_Output for storage in a queue. The code for Create_IDP is shown in Figure A-29.

d. Host_Output

- Create_New_DP (task body). The declarations include local objects for an internal data packet (IDP), and for a data packet in ASCII format (DP). The task obtains an IDP from the queue. The new DP is created with an STX as the first character, the furnace number as the next two

```
with Device_Handlers;
with Host_Output;
with Calendar;  use Calendar;
separate (Temp_Reading)

task body Create_IDP is
  Furnace_No    : Furnace_Type;
  Time_To_Read : Read_Time;
  Temperature   : Temp_Type;
begin
  loop
    accept Take_Temp_Info (F : in Furnace_Type;
                           T : in Read_Time) do
      Furnace_No   := F;
      Time_To_Read := T;
    end Take_Temp_Info;

    -- Let time expire (if any)
    --
      delay (Time_To_Read - Clock);

    -- Get temperature and "create" IDP (we are simply
    -- sending the aggregate to be buffered).
    --
      begin
        Device_Handlers.Read_Temp (Furnace_No, Temperature);
        Host_Output.Enqueue_IDP ((Furnace_No, Temperature));
      exception
        when No_Response_From_DT =>
          null; -- take appropriate action here
      end;

  end loop;
end Create_IDP;
```

Figure A-29. Create_IDP (task body).

characters, the temperature value as the next four characters, and an ETX as the last character in the message. The task waits for a caller before it passes on the newly created DP. An exception handler is provided inside the loop for an invalid integer value detected in the function

```
with Text_IO;            use Text_IO;
with ASCII_Conversions; use ASCII_Conversions;
separate (Host_Output)

task body Create_New_DP is
  IDP : IDP_Format;
  DP  : DP_Format;
begin
  loop
    Buffer_IDPs.Dequeue (IDP);
    DP (1) := ASCII.STX;

    Handle_Invalid_Integer :
    begin
      DP (2 .. 3) := Integer_To_ASCII (IDP.Furnace_No);
                    -- Invalid_Integer exception may be raised
      DP (4 .. 7) := Integer_To_ASCII (IDP.Temperature);
                    -- Invalid_Integer exception may be raised
      DP (8)      := ASCII.ETX;

      accept Provide_DP (D : out DP_Format) do
        D := DP;
      end Provide_DP;

    exception
      when Invalid_Integer =>
        Put_Line ("Invalid integer value detected in Create_New_DP");
    end Handle_Invalid_Integer;
  end loop;
end Create_New_DP;
```

Figure A-30. Create_New_DP (task body).

Integer_To_ASCII. The code for Create_New_DP is shown in Figure A-30.

- Determine_Host_Output (task body). Local objects are declared for a DP and a DP_ACK (single character). The task gets a DP from Create_New_DP and sets DP_ACK to NAK in the outer loop. It sends the DP to Device_Handlers and waits for either a DP_ACK or a timeout within the inner loop. If a positive DP_ACK is received, it exits the inner loop and gets the next DP from Create_New_DP. If a negative DP_ACK is received, or the timeout expires (Re_Tx_Delay seconds), the old DP is

```
with Device_Handlers;
separate (Host_Output)

task body Determine_Host_Output is
  DP      : DP_Format;
  DP_ACK : Character;
begin
  loop
    Create_New_DP.Provide_DP (DP); -- Get a DP
    DP_ACK := ASCII.NAK; -- NAK until positive acknowledgement

    Transmit_The_DP:
      loop
        Device_Handlers.Transmit_DP (DP);

        select
          accept Acknowledge_DP (D : in Character) do
            DP_ACK := D;
          end Acknowledge_DP;
        or
          delay Re_Tx_Delay; -- Wait for timeout
        end select;

        exit Transmit_The_DP when DP_ACK = ASCII.ACK;

      end loop Transmit_The_DP;
  end loop;
end Determine_Host_Output;
```

Figure A-31. Determine_Host_Output (task body).

sent to Device_Handlers for retransmission within the inner loop. The code for Determine_Host_Output is shown in Figure A-31.

The detailed design phase is now completed, and any remaining code (for the functions ASCII_To_Integer and Integer_To_ASCII, and test drivers and simulators) are supplied during the code and unit test phase.

A.9 Exercises

The following exercises are suggested for this case study:

1. Prepare software simulators for the input and output channels of the host computer, and the digital thermometer, and implement the current design.

2. Change the protocol such that RTS is not waiting for an acknowledgement of a single data packet (i.e., add a sequence number to the data packets sent from RTS to the host).

3. Remove the requirement specifications that refer to the management of a "temperature table." Redesign the structure of the components that manage the reading of the temperatures and that create the internal data packets. (*Hint:* Could you use an array of tasks?)

4. Remove the requirement that refers to a periodic reading of temperatures; simply read and process the temperatures of the furnaces at the appropriate interval.

5. Implement the RTS using only strict caller and called tasks. Then lift the restriction slightly to allow tasks called by interrupt entries to be callers.

6. Consider alternate interactions between RX_Host_Msg and Determine_Host_Output. What are the implications of not having an intermediary and having RX_Host_Msg make a conditional call? Could the intermediary be a buffer? How do the additional requirements of exercise number 2 affect the intermediary?

B

Case Study 2:
The Draw__Image Problem

This case study is adapted from a problem described by Dijkstra [DIJ72]. Dijkstra presents a design in textual and narrative format. We will use Ada as our vehicle for presenting the text of the design and will add graphics. We modify his design, and sequence of presentation, to be consistent with Ada. We call this the "Draw_Image" problem. The problem and its solution will illustrate the ideas of layered virtual machines discussed in Chapter 12.

B.1 Problem Specification

The problem involves drawing an image in a certain way, given a restricted set of facilities. The drawing facility (you may think of it as a line printer) has two functions, invoked by two commands:

1. NLCR (*New Line Carriage Return*). This moves the print position to the first position of the next line.

2. Print_Symbol. This prints a symbol, given as an argument, at the current print position and moves the current print position immediately to the right.

The only two permitted print symbols are mark and space, where mark is some visible character (say an asterisk) and space is a blank.

The problem environment also consists of two integer functions of integer arguments that satisfy the conditions:

For $0 \leq I \leq 999$:

$$0 \leq FX(I) \leq 99 \qquad 0 \leq FY(I) \leq 49$$

Given this environment, the problem is to create a program that prints 50 lines per page, numbered from top to bottom by a Y coordinate running from 49 through 0. Each line is numbered from left to right by an X coordinate running from 0 through 99. (The X and Y coordinate numbers are not to be printed; the numbering is relative to the relationship given below.) There are thus 5000 print positions per page.

At the 1000 positions specified by the X and Y coordinates given by:

$$X = FX(I) \qquad Y = FY(I) \qquad \text{for I satisfying } 0 \leq I \leq 999$$

a mark is to be printed; all other positions are to remain blank. In other words, the line printer prints a curve given by the functions of X and Y. We are using the line printer as a digital plotter. The functions of X and Y are not specific to the problem; the solution must be valid for any FX and FY satisfying the relationships given above.

Multiple marks at the same print location are permitted. When we say "1000" marks on the page, we are ignoring overstrikes. Figure B-1 illustrates the problem graphically.

B.2   Analysis of the Problem

Let us consider some important aspects of the problem and how they will affect the solution. Since we must proceed from line to line, never backing up, and since we proceed from character to character (in each line), never backing up, the printing of the curve must be independent of the determination (with FX and FY) of where marks should be printed; FX and FY will return values in arbitrary order, inconsistent with the functioning of a printer. Therefore, we need to construct, in a random access storage, an *image* of what we wish to print.

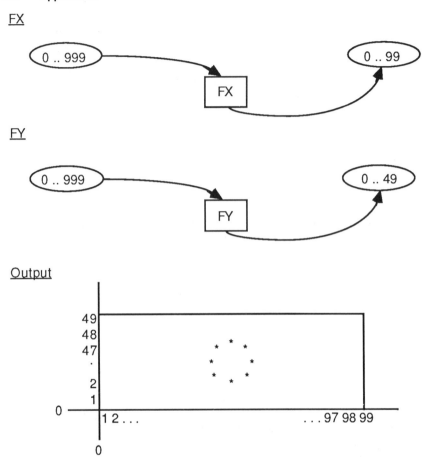

Figure B-1. Draw_Image illustration.

The way in which we store the image is the major decision in this program; it deals with the major data structure and the ways in which that data structure is to be manipulated. We will postpone, or defer, the decision of how to store and (in detail) manipulate the image for as long a time as possible. We will deal with an *abstract* version of the image. This has several beneficial consequences. First, we hope that by dealing with an idealized version of the image we can construct relatively simple, straightforward algorithms. Second, it allows for a separation of concerns; at the first part of program development we deal with the simple algorithms for manipulating the idealized image, while we later confront the details of how to store and manipulate the data structure. Third, the separation of concerns need not result in temporal separation, but rather separation by job assignments to programming teams. Especially in a large programming project, it is advantageous to have several teams working on the same problem, with the interface between the teams being as narrow as possible. In this case, the interface will be merely the methods for the abstract manipulation of the image. Fourth and last, the deferral of details of the data structure makes the part of the program that deals with the abstract image independent of the actual image structure. This eases maintenance (in truth, it also eases program development and testing) in two ways:

1. The mechanisms for manipulating the image data structure may be changed without causing changes in the rest of the program.

2. Any changes to the part of the program that deal with the concrete image are *positively bounded* to that part of the program. We are guaranteed that errors introduced in making changes cannot "ripple" and cause errors in some other part of the program.

It is this deferral of detail that gives rise to the notion of a layered hierarchy of machines.

B.3 Beginning the Design

Our primary abstraction is that of an *image*. We know that drawing the image involves this abstraction; therefore we will develop its package specification before turning our attention to the top-level virtual machine. We know that we must be able to *clear* the image between its separate invocations; we must be able to note which of the positions (indicated by X and Y coordinates) are to have marks—we must be able to *mark positions* that are non-blank; and we must be able to *print* the image. Since there is only one image object in the system, the encapsulation will be of the form object manager (see Chapter 10).

In Ada, the discussion above turns into the following package specification.

```
package Image is
   type X_Coordinate is range 0 .. 99;
   type Y_Coordinate is range 0 .. 49;
```

```
procedure Clear;
procedure Mark_Position (X : in X_Coordinate;
                         (Y : in Y_Coordinate);
procedure Print;
end Image;
```

We have used Ada's ability to define new types to capture some aspects of the problem statement (the range of the X and Y coordinates). This will lead to a more readable program and also provide the advantages of strong typing in preventing inconsistent use of coordinates and other program variables.

Now we turn to the construction of the program that solves the stated problem. Our general approach is to take small (even tiny) steps at each stage of the problem. At every level we defer as much detail as possible in order to make our algorithms simple. By a process of stepwise refinement we will add detail until the problem is solved—building a sequence of virtual machines. The algorithm to draw an image is simple: Build the image, and then print the image. Here is the virtual machine in Ada:

```
with Image;
procedure Draw_Image is
  procedure Build_Image is separate;
begin
  Build_Image;
  Image.Print;
end Draw_Image;
```

We build the image (somehow—the details are deferred) and then use the capabilities of the image abstraction to print the image.

Draw_Image is a virtual machine. Its instruction set is Build_Image and Image.Print. Part of the machine is already available (at least as a specification—we will refine its algorithm later). This is Image.Print. Our next level of refinement will focus on Build_Image.

B.4   Lower Level Machines

The implementation of the Draw_Image machine depends upon the following lower level machines:

1. Build_Image. The implementation of Build_Image is dependent upon a lower-level notion, that of setting marks. Setting marks is an algorithmic function. We will make use of procedural

abstraction to reduce the process of setting marks to the invocation of a machine. Here is its specification:

```
procedure Set_Marks;
```

The function of Set_Marks is to place marks in the image, in accordance with FX and FY. Now we can devise the following algorithm for Build_Image:

```
with Set_Marks;
separate (Draw_Image)
  procedure Build_Image is
  begin
    Image.Clear;
    Set_Marks;
  end Build_Image;
```

Build_Image is a virtual machine. Its instruction set is Image.Clear and Set_Marks. As we develop our algorithm, we clarify the notion of the abstract operations on the image object; we may even discover additional needed operations, emphasizing the interaction and parallel nature of the concern with virtual machines and objects.

2. Set_Marks. This next lower level machine directly supports Build_Image; it can be considered to be an instruction of the Build_Image machine. Setting marks in the image involves two issues. The first is iteration through the 1000 values of the Index given in the problem statement, and the second is adding marks to the image. We will again separate those concerns by envisioning a separate machine instruction for adding marks.

```
procedure Set_Marks is
  type Mark_Range is range 0 .. 999;
  procedure Addmark (Mark : in Mark_Range) is separate;
begin
  for Index in Mark_Range loop
    Addmark (Index);
  end loop;
end Set_Marks;
```

All values of the Index (in the appropriate range as indicated by the typemark) are used to add marks to the image. The "value added" of this procedure is to satisfy the requirement that Index is to iterate over some range, with each value being used one time only to add a mark to the image. *It makes no further commitment!* That is the point of the style of programming that we are illustrating. At each point, we do as little as possible, making as little commitment as possible, and deferring as much as possible.

3. Addmark. The next refinement, that follows from Set_Marks and also minimizes our commitment to a data structure, is to explain the instruction Addmark. The function of Addmark is, for a given value of its input, to compute FX and FY of the input, and to mark the corresponding position in the image:

```
with Image;
separate (Set_Marks)
  procedure Addmark (Mark : in Mark_Range) is

    function FX (Mark : Mark_Range)
                    return Image.X_Coordinate is separate;
    function FY (Mark : Mark_Range)
                    return Image.Y_Coordinate is separate;
  begin
    Image.Mark_Position (FX (Mark), FY (Mark));
  end Addmark;
```

We introduce the functions FX and FY here, deferring their implementation until later. They are yet lower level machines!

There are five levels of machines, with each higher level depending upon the lower level. The machines/levels are:

1. Draw_Image
2. Build_Image
3. Set_Marks
4. Addmark
5. FX and FY

At this point we have essentially completed the program, at a high level of abstraction. Figure B-2 is an OOD diagram as described in Chapter 7. The lines indicate dependency relationships. In the Image object, the ellipses represent type definitions and the small rectangles represent visible subprograms. Figure B-3 is a structure chart of the program so far. It does not show the internals of the image abstraction, treating it as a primitive concept.

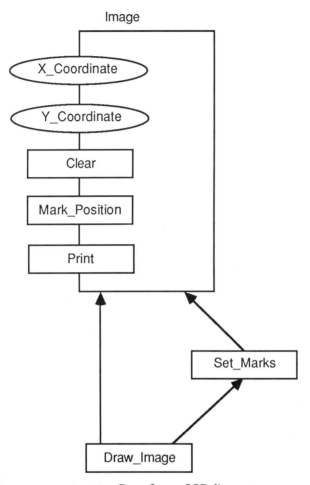

Figure B-2. Draw_Image OOD diagram.

It is of some significance that we have been able to construct so much of the program without being concerned with the details of the image. We have been able to accomplish this by using our powers of abstraction. The image abstraction can be constructed in a number of different (correct) ways, without affecting what we have done so far. By postponing concern for the data structures involved in the image, we have successfully separated concerns and allowed development by refinement in small steps.

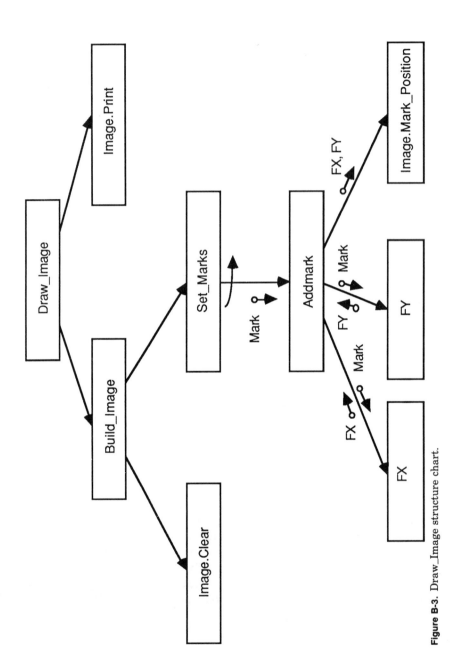

Figure B-3. Draw_Image structure chart.

B.5   Lower Level Objects

We are now ready to begin the design of the image abstraction. We can proceed no further without committing to a specific data structure. However, let's continue to apply the principle of minimal commitment. We will decide that the image is to be made up of an array of lines, but there is no need yet to decide upon the structure of a line.

B.5.1   First Lower Level Object Specification

We will specify an abstraction of the notion of line. We start by making the abstraction generic on lines of any length. Since there may be many lines, created by one or more users of the package, we want a manager of the form *type manager*, with the specific Line to be operated on passed as a parameter to each operation. To accomplish this, we provide an abstract type definition of Lines as *limited private*, restricting the user of the package to only the operations exported by the package. The only possible operations on objects of type Lines are to clear, mark in a specified position, and print. These characteristics of the line manager are captured by the package specification below:

```
generic
   type Line_Length is range <>;
package Line_Manager is
   type Lines is limited private;

   procedure Clear_Line (Line     : in out Lines);
   procedure Mark_Line  (Position : in      Line_Length;
                         Line     : in out Lines);
   procedure Print_Line (Line     : in      Lines);
private
   -- the structure of Lines goes here
end Line_Manager;
```

B.5.2   Higher Level Object Implementation

Now we are ready to develop the image abstraction, based on the Lines abstraction. The first step is to create an instance of the Line_Manger package. This instance is called Line_Mgr. We then use the exported abstract type to create a type Images as an array of abstract lines. The array will be indexed by the Y coordinate of our image, as illustrated in the problem specification. Then we create the actual variable, the object, that is encapsulated and managed by the package. Last, we provide the implementation of the operations exported by the package specification.

```
with Line_Manager;
package body Image is
  package Line_Mgr is new Line_Manager
                          (Line_Length => X_Coordinate);
  type Images is array (Y_Coordinate) of Line_Mgr.Lines;
  Image_Of_Lines : Images; -- this is the object being managed

  procedure Clear is
  begin
    for A_Line in Y_Coordinate loop
      Line_Mgr.Clear_Line (Image_Of_Lines (A_Line));
    end loop;
  end Clear;

  procedure Mark_Position (X : in X_Coordinate;
                           Y : in Y_Coordinate) is
  begin
    Line_Mgr.Mark_Line (X, Image_Of_Lines (Y));
  end Mark_Position;

  procedure Print is
  begin
    for A_Line in reverse Y_Coordinate loop
      Line_Mgr.Print_Line (Image_Of_Lines (A_Line));
    end loop;
  end Print;
end Image;
```

The Image_Of_Lines is the "object" being managed by this package. It is the array of abstract lines.

An important point to recognize is that we still have not committed to a representation for a line. We have deferred that decision in order to focus on the manipulation of the lines in the image. We therefore simplify the manipulation of the image. In addition, we could have a parallel programming effort to implement the Line_Manager, while we are implementing the Image package.

There are some additional observations to be made at this point. Heretofore, we have been refining the *algorithms* used to solve the problem. At this level, we are refining the *data structures* used to solve the problem. This example illustrates most vividly that design involves a parallel or alternating consideration of data structure and algorithms. Another important point is that the definition of data structure does not occur "all at once"; it involves the same sort of refinement as does the development of the algorithms. We have also repeatedly made the point that "modules" (in Ada, packages and subprograms) should be used to hide *design decisions*. The earlier levels were hiding, or abstracting, design decisions about algorithms. The Image package, however, also hides a design decision about a data structure. Therefore, it is also an "object" in the sense of object-oriented design.

B.5.3 Lower Level Object Implementation

We are finally ready to consider implementation of the line abstraction. First we show what the private part of the package Line_Manager might look like. A first attempt might assume an array of lines:

```
-------------------------------------------------------------------
-- this is the private part of the package specification --

  type Print_Symbols is (Mark, Space);
  type Lines is array (Line_Length) of Print_Symbols;
-------------------------------------------------------------------
```

We could implement and use the package with the above private part in an operating Draw_Image solution. An important aspect of the use of abstraction in programming is that the programs are easy to change. For example, suppose we choose to change the representation of a Line. We can change the implementation of the abstract line without causing any change in higher level machines. For example, if we chose to explicitly maintain the position of the last mark in a line (this makes some of the line algorithms more efficient), we could define a line as:

```
-------------------------------------------------------------------
-- this is the private part of the package specification --

  type Print_Symbols is (Mark, Space);
  type Lineimage is array (Line_Length) of Print_Symbols;
  type Lines is
    record
      Last   : Line_Length;
      Symbol : Lineimage;
    end record;
-------------------------------------------------------------------
```

This change, and corresponding changes to the body of the Line_Manager, will have no effect on higher level machines. The system can be rebuilt with the new Line_Manager without causing any changes to the rest of the code.

The implementation of the Line_Manager depends upon yet a lower level object, the printer. The printer object encapsulates the print capabilities described in the problem specification and is needed only by the Print_Line procedure of the Line_Manager. Ada gives us the capability to limit visibility to only that procedure.

B.5.4 Yet Another Lower Level Object

In order to implement the Line_Manager, we need a lower level object, a printer. As usual, we will first provide only the specification of the object, deferring its implementation until later. We will specify an abstract printer suited to our needs, allowing the implementation of the abstract printer to use the problem-specified Print_Symbol and NLCR. Here is the specification of the printer:

```
package Printer is
  procedure Mark;
  procedure Space;
  procedure Next_Line;
end Printer;
```

At this point we can show the complete OOD diagram and structure chart, as Figures B-4 and B-5, respectively.

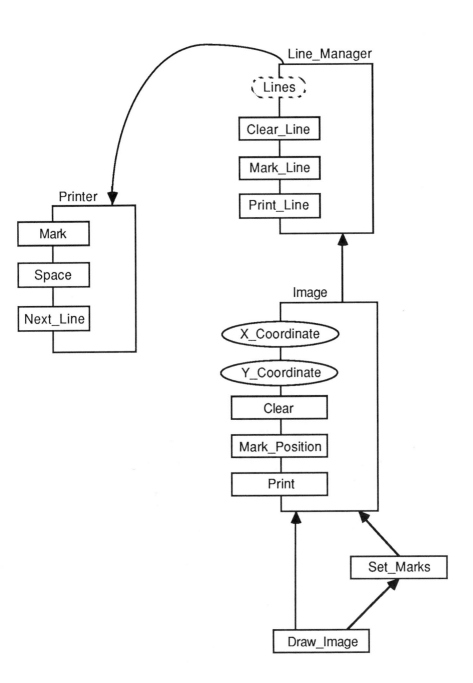

Figure B-4. Complete Draw_Image OOD diagram.

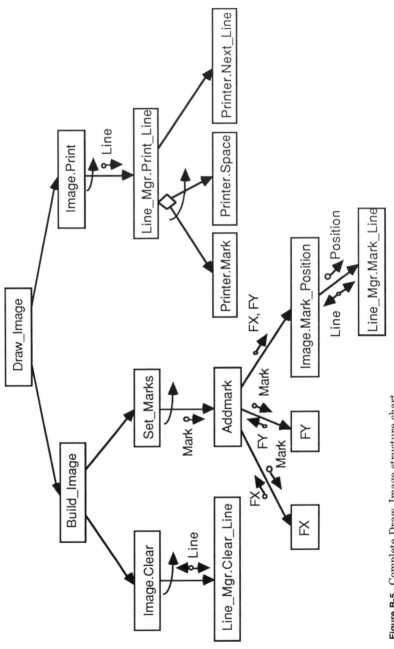

Figure B-5. Complete Draw_Image structure chart.

B.5.5 Intermediate Level Object Implementation

After having specified the Printer object, we can implement the intermediate object that depends upon the Printer—the Line_Manager:

```
package body Line_Manager is
  procedure Print_Line (Line : in Lines) is separate;

  procedure Clear_Line (Line : in out Lines) is
  begin
    Line.Last := Line_Length'First;
    Line.Symbol (Line_Length'First) := Space;
  end Clear_Line;

  procedure Mark_Line  (Position : in     Line_Length;
                        Line     : in out Lines) is
  begin
    while Line.Last < Position loop
      Line.Symbol (Line.Last) := Space;
      Line.Last := Line.Last + 1;
    end loop;

    Line.Symbol (Position) := Mark;
  end Mark_Line;
end Line_Manager;
```

Since we once again deferred detail, using only the stub

```
procedure Print_Line (Line : in Lines) is separate;
```

in the body of the package, we could also have deferred the specification of the Printer package to this point in the program text. Either way is correct. Here is the proper body for Print_Line:

```
with Printer;
separate (Line_Manager)
  procedure Print_Line (Line : in Lines) is
  begin
    for Each_Position in Line_Length'First .. Line.Last loop
      case Line.Symbol (Each_Position) is
        when Mark  => Printer.Mark;
        when Space => Printer.Space;
      end case;
    end loop;

    Printer.Next_Line;
  end Print_Line;
```

B.6 Implementation Details

At this point we fill in the final details with the lowest level machines, including the machines that implement the operations of the objects. This lowest level of machine no longer operates abstractly on programmer-defined lower level machines, but uses the actual instruction set of the implementation high-level language. We should occasionally remind ourselves, however, that a high-level language statement is actually a "machine" that uses yet lower level constructs as a result of compilation. Here is the implementation of the package body Printer:

```
with Text_IO; use Text_IO;
package body Printer is

  A_Mark  : constant Character := '*';
  A_Space : constant Character := ' ';

  -- this printer uses Ada Text_IO
  -- to simulate the Print_Symbol and NLCR

  procedure Mark is
  begin
    -- Print_Symbol (mark)
    Put (A_Mark);
  end Mark;
```

```ada
procedure Space is
begin
  -- Print_Symbol (space)
  Put (A_Space);
end Space;

procedure Next_Line is
begin
  -- NLCR
  New_Line;
end Next_Line;
end Printer;
```

Here is a possible implementation of FX and FY:

```ada
with Image; use Image;
separate (Set_Marks.Addmark)
  function FX (Mark : Mark_Range) return X_Coordinate is
  begin
    return X_Coordinate (Mark mod Mark_Range (X_Coordinate'Last));
  end FX;

with Image; use Image;
separate (Set_Marks.Addmark)
  function FY (Mark : Mark_Range) return Y_Coordinate is
  begin
    return Y_Coordinate (Mark mod Mark_Range (Y_Coordinate'Last));
  end FY;
```

The layered virtual machine/object-oriented design methods presented in this appendix illustrate how abstraction, deferral of detail, and a parallel focus on algorithms and data structures can be the basis for the design of software systems. The method is strongly object oriented, but it uses the virtual machine concept to retain a sense of the *steps* needed to solve the problem. The Ada programming language is well suited for the use of LVM/OOD to design and implement software, using packages to encapsulate design decisions.

B.7   Exercises

The following exercises are suggested for this case study:

1. Implement the design described above, and test the program with the SIN and COS functions.

2. Use the guidelines in Chapter 11 to determine additional areas for generic components. Reimplement your solution.

3. Gather all the type definitions together in one package, and the "environment" (printer, FX and FY) into another package. How does this influence the design of the rest of the system?

4. Make the Image package to be of the style type manager rather than object manager. What does this do to data flow in the top-level machine?

5. Have an Image package that implements most of the functionality of the system, i.e., have it offer two operations on the image object: Image.Build and Image.Print. How does this affect the reusability of the Image design object?

C

Case Study 3:
The Simple Mail System (SMS)

The purpose of this case study is to illustrate the use of Layered Virtual Machine/Object-Oriented Design as presented in Chapter 12.

The case study illustrates the relationship between traditional structured design and the use of packages in Ada. Particular emphasis is on the concept of packaging by the use of "information hiding" and the related use of "abstract data types." It further applies the ideas of layered virtual machines in a sequential problem.

C.1 Problem Specification

The Simple Mail System provides a means for people to leave messages for each other at a single location. The mail system pays attention to one user at a time, allowing that user to send mail or read mail. The system is sort of a "drop point" where people can leave messages for each other. The messages are not sent anywhere else—that is the major simplification of this system. Figure C-1 illustrates the general situation, showing how one person can use

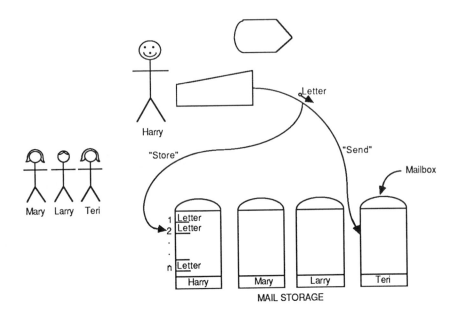

Figure C-1. Simple mail system.

the system to store letters either in that person's own mailbox or to send letters to other users' mailboxes.

Commands available to the user at the top level of the system, after entering the user name, are: send mail, read mail, quit.

Sending mail involves letting the user create a letter and then storing the letter in another user's mailbox. The user can optionally also store the letter in his/her own mailbox. (Creating a letter is very simple; it must be created immediately before being sent. For example, a user cannot resend a stored letter.) Commands available to the user at the sending mail level are: destroy letter, send letter, send and store letter.

Reading mail includes an option to display a summary of all letters in the user's mailbox. The summary is the index number (the index to where the letter is located in the mailbox) and the subject. The user can read the complete text of a letter that is selected by an index number. The user may also discard letters from his/her mailbox, selected by index number. The user performs the various reading mail activities until he/she enters a "quit" command. Commands available to the user at the reading mail level are: display summary, display letter, discard letter, quit.

Figure C-2 summarizes the commands available to the users, and the corresponding states and state transitions of the system.

The letters themselves are very simple, consisting of an originator, an addressee, a subject, and a message. The originator and addressee are the users, and are limited to Harry, Mary, Larry, and Teri. The subjects are limited to Gossip, News, Lesson. The text of the message is limited to Marriage, Divorce, Birth, Death, Scandal. Each user's mailbox is limited to 100 letters. (The above limitations are part of the simplification of the system.)

The system is very simple; it need have little in the way of man-machine niceties and explanation. Each user is expected to be familiar with this specification.

C.2   Overview of Solution

Before presenting the details of the design, we will establish the foundation for the design by presenting a "road map" to the rest of the solution: the top-level virtual machine and the immediately supporting virtual machines at the next lower level.

C.2.1   General Approach

The approach to the solution of the problem is to apply the LVM/OOD methods described in Chapters 5 and 12 and illustrated in the Appendix B. The design, as compilable Ada, will be presented in a legal compilation order. However, in order to provide motivation for the helper packages that must be compiled (at least the specification) before the top-level virtual machine, we will present abstract versions of the machines.

The order of presentation of the material is:

1. *Abstract representation of machines.* The paragraphs immediately following this section introduce very abstract pseudocode (non-compilable) representations of the highest level machines in the system. This is done to motivate the design of the helper packages for those machines.

2. *Top-level design.* This includes package specifications for the helper packages for the top-level machines. One package, called Commands, is a services package (see the taxonomy presented in

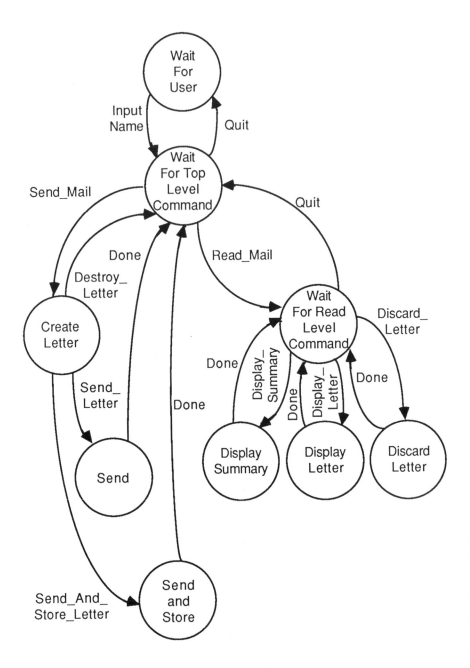

Figure C-2. SMS state diagram.

Chapter 10). The primary data manager (Post_Office) is introduced during this phase and is of the style object manager.

The top- and second-level machines are completely specified in functionally abstract terms. In order to provide a general outline of the package body of the Post_Office, it is necessary to introduce lower level data managers, both of the form type manager. One of them is generic. The private parts of the package specifications of the type managers are abstract; the detail of the data representation is properly part of the detailed design.

This section also includes a discussion of the form of presentation of the top-level design in Ada, and shows how it is consistent with traditional notions of a top-level design.

3. *Detailed design.* This section presents the package body for the Post_Office, the complete private parts and bodies of the type managers, and the package body for Commands. Most of the procedures are presented as stubs.

The detailed design is the place for the explicit definition of algorithms for individual subprograms. Most of the subprograms of the SMS are so simple that no design is necessary; they may be directly implemented in Ada. (This is partly a result of the simplifications made in the SMS, partly a consequence of the LVM/OOD method.) The algorithms for subprograms of one of the packages are more complex, and they are presented as compilable PDL/pseudocode.

4. *Implementation.* This section presents the Ada code for all the subunits.

C.2.2   Abstract Representation of Machines

In order to motivate the need for helper packages, particularly the major data abstraction or design object, we must have an abstract design of the top-level machine, the basic functional abstraction of the SMS. Fundamentally, what must be done is to control the repeated interactions with the various users, control the repeated interaction with each user, and perform the top-level functions specified by the state diagram in the problem statement. Here is the algorithm:

```
loop forever
  establish session with user;
  loop for this session
    get a command for the top level;
    case on the command is
      send_the_mail;
      read_the_mail;
      quit this session;
    end case;
  end loop for this session;
end loop forever;
```

The top-level machine makes use of following two lower level functional abstractions, lower level machines:

1. *Send Mail Machine.* This machine accomplishes the functions associated with sending the mail as stated in the software specification. Here is the algorithm:

```
create a letter;
get a command for the send level;
case on the command is
  send the letter;
  send and store the letter;
  destroy the letter;
end case;
```

2. *Read Mail Machine.* This lower level abstraction is the read mail machine. It accomplishes the functions associated with reading mail as stated in the software specification. Here is the algorithm:

```
read mail loop
  get a command for the read level;
  case on the command is
    display summary;
    discard letter;
    display letter;
    exit the read mail loop;
  end case;
end read mail loop;
```

C.3 Top-Level Design

The top-level design is described using Ada PDL. We first establish the helper packages for the commands and post office abstractions, and then provide the top-level and lower level machines to send and read mail. Additional helper packages are provided to support the post office machines.

The virtual machines we present will not only be complete, compilable PDL, they will actually be fully coded Ada—they will not contain any pseudocode. But do not be fooled into thinking that this is "coding." This expression of the top-level algorithm is truly design work; it is simply taking advantage of Ada's ability to express the design in compilable form.

The following components are developed as part of the top-level design:

1. *Commands.* This package encapsulates the command types and the functionality for interfacing with the users to determine the send and read commands.

2. *Post_Office.* This package represents the fundamental abstraction of the system, and contains all the individual mail boxes.

3. *Simple_Mail_System.* This is the main procedure and is the top-level virtual machine.

4. *Send_Mail.* This subunit of Simple_Mail_System is a lower level machine that contains the instructions for sending mail.

5. *Read_Mail.* This subunit of Simple_Mail_System is a lower level machine that contains the instructions for reading mail.

6. *Letter.* This package encapsulates the type definitions and operations that deal with a single letter.

7. *Storage.* This package encapsulates the type definitions and operations that deal with a single mail box.

C.3.1 Package Specification for Commands

This package contains the set of definitions for the user commands that accomplish state transitions of the system. The functionality encapsulated represents the ability to get the commands from the users. We have grouped all the command-related type definitions and associated functions together in a single package. This is an illustration of a package that is not an object; it is a package of the style "services." It also has a flavor of a "definitions" package. The Ada PDL for Commands is the following:

```
package Commands is
   type Top_Commands  is (Send_Mail, Read_Mail, Quit);

   type Send_Commands is (Send_Letter,
                          Send_And_Store_Letter,
                          Destroy_Letter);

   type Read_Commands is (Display_Summary, Display_Letter,
                          Discard_Letter, Quit);

   function Top_Command  return Top_Commands;
   function Send_Command return Send_Commands;
   function Read_Command return Read_Commands;
   -- inputs the command from the user and returns it to caller
end Commands;
```

The package specification captures much of the information from the problem specification, presenting the commands of the user interface directly in Ada syntax. The package combines the commands with functions that return specific values of the command from the user.

The use of functions to acquire and represent the command means that the function name, such as Top_Command, may be used directly in a place where a command is required. (For example, a subprogram call with *in* mode parameters, or the discriminant in a case statement.) There is no need to separate the notions of first acquiring the command and later using it. The names of the functions reenforce the notion that they directly represent the command; they *are the command*.

C.3.2 Package Specification for Post__Office

We have created an abstraction of the mail storage in the form of an object manager. It provides all the operations on the letters: creating, storing, and so on. It also provides for the initiation of the session with the user since the user name is also a component of a letter (the originator). The Ada PDL is the following:

```
package Post_Office is
  procedure Establish_Session_With_User;
  procedure Create_Letter;
  procedure Send_Letter;
  procedure Store_Letter;
  procedure Destroy_Letter;
  procedure Display_Summary;
  procedure Discard_Letter;
  procedure Display_Letter;
end Post_Office;
```

This is the major data abstraction in the system, the major design object. It provides all the data-related functionality needed for the system. Once again, note how a package specification can be used to capture the problem specification in Ada syntax.

All the detail of the data structure to hold the mail storage for the system is hidden by this package; the decisions are deferred. We can separate concerns of algorithms and data structures by this approach. We will use the visible, but abstract, operations on the data structure for the creation (with stepwise refinement) of the algorithms. A later layer of stepwise refinement will involve the definition of the data structures.

The procedure Establish_Session_With_User is not directly called out in the problem specification but is implicit in the need to interact with different users at different times. It is placed as part of the Post_Office abstraction as a result of a design decision that the Post_Office should always know the name of the user, since the user is also the originator.

Other decisions may have been made on this issue; for example, having the top-level machine pass the name of the user to many of the procedures of the Post_Office, or passing it once as a "set user" function. The design as presented minimizes data flow and simplifies the interface—the principle of parsimony or Occam's razor.

C.3.3   Main Procedure of the Simple Mail System

The following Ada PDL expresses the abstraction of the top-level machine:

```
with Post_Office;
with Commands;
with Text_IO; use Text_IO;
procedure Simple_Mail_System is
```

```
   procedure Send_Mail is separate;
   procedure Read_Mail is separate;
begin
  SMS_Functions:
  loop
    Put_Line ("Welcome to the Simple Mail System.");
    Put_Line ("Program terminates by ""control Z."" ");
    Put_Line ("Enter your name.");
    New_Line;

    Post_Office.Establish_Session_With_User;

    For_This_User:
    loop
      case Commands.Top_Command is
        when Commands.Send_Mail =>
          Send_Mail;
        when Commands.Read_Mail =>
          Read_Mail;
        when Commands.Quit       =>
          exit For_This_User;
      end case;
    end loop For_This_User;
  end loop SMS_Functions;

exception
  when End_Error =>
    Put_Line ("Simple Mail System Completed");
end Simple_Mail_System;
```

The main procedure is quite simple, being based on its two helper packages and on locally defined lower level machines for sending and reading mail. It captures the top-level functioning of the system, especially the notions of looping forever (at least until a control-z raises End_Error), looping for each user, and either sending or reading mail.

The procedure is fully coded Ada, no comments to represent pseudocode. Is this design? Is this *top-level* design? Yes! In other languages or with other design styles we might have had:

```
-- loop for this user
  -- case on the top-level command received
    -- when send the mail command
      -- send the mail;
    -- when read the mail command
      -- read the mail;
    -- when quit command
      -- exit the loop for this user;
  -- end case;
-- end the loop for this user;
```

But the Ada PDL version presented not only will not have to be later "coded," it is also more readable—assuming that the reader of PDL is familiar with the language being used.

The reason why this top-level solution is completely coded is that it takes advantage of powerful abstract machines that are completely represented in Ada syntax. The top-level machine takes advantage of Ada's design-oriented expressive notation. This then is properly PDL, is also full Ada, and is also properly top-level design.

C.3.4 Lower Level Machine for Sending Mail

The following PDL statements represent the abstraction for sending mail:

```
separate (Simple_Mail_System)
  procedure Send_Mail is
  begin
    Post_Office.Create_Letter;

    case Commands.Send_Command is
      when Commands.Send_Letter =>
        Post_office.Send_Letter;
      when Commands.Send_And_Store_Letter =>
        Post_Office.Send_Letter;
        Post_Office.Store_Letter;
      when Commands.Destroy_Letter =>
        Post_Office.Destroy_Letter;
    end case;
  end Send_Mail;
```

In a manner similar to the top-level machine, the Send_Mail machine expresses the next *layer* of the solution. This is also fully coded.

C.3.5 Lower Level Machine for Reading Mail

The following PDL statements represent the abstraction for reading mail:

```
separate (Simple_Mail_System)
  procedure Read_Mail is
  begin
    Reading_Mail:
    loop
      case Commands.Read_Command is
        when Commands.Display_Summary =>
          Post_Office.Display_Summary;
        when Commands.Discard_Letter =>
          Post_Office.Discard_Letter;
        when Commands.Display_Letter =>
          Post_Office.Display_Letter;
        when Commands.Quit =>
          exit Reading_Mail;
      end case;
    end loop Reading_Mail;
  end Read_Mail;
```

Similar to the Send_Mail machine, the Read_Mail machine expresses the next *layer* of the solution. It is fully coded.

At this time we can capture in graphical form the nature of the first phase of the top-level design. Figure C-3 shows the OOD diagram, while Figure C-4 is a structure chart showing the nature of the virtual machines and their use of the Post_Office object. For large systems it is necessary to show the packages associated with a subprogram, as we discussed in Chapter 7. We show Post_Office, abbreviated as PO, and Commands to describe the subprogram package association.

We show the structure chart here after the PDL. Actually, the development of the PDL and the graphics may well proceed partly in parallel and partly in a cyclic manner, the insights gained from the graphics causing modifications to the PDL, and vice versa. The first phase of the top-level design is not complete, however, until *both* the PDL and the graphics are complete. Then the design is ready for review by others. Since this review is an integral part of the design process, it may well cause further iterations of both graphics and PDL.

We may ask ourselves at this point, "Is the top-level design complete?" The answer is "no." Although we have adequately expressed the solution to the problem and would find it easy (at a design

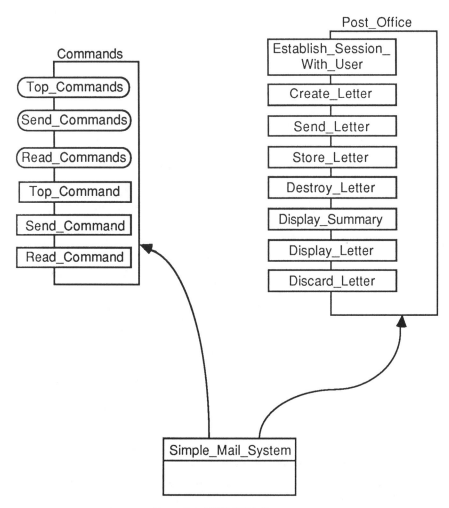

Figure C-3. SMS OOD diagram.

review) to show that the original problem specification was satisfied (since the Ada syntax captured so much of the problem specification directly), we have not arrived at the technical core of the solution.

It is clear that the Post_Office will be quite complex. Not even the most general outline of the data structures, or the methods for manipulating the data structures, have been established. This is properly part of the top-level design. Therefore, we continue to refine the design with the LVM/OOD process.

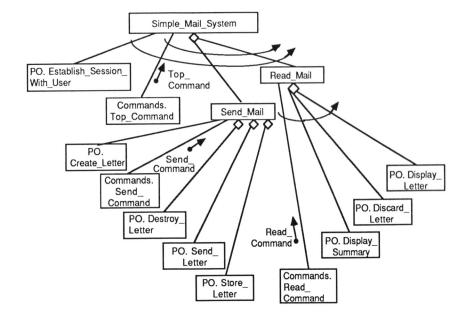

Figure C-4. SMS structure chart.

C.3.6 Refining the Top-Level Design

We need to understand if the package bodies may be implemented in a straightforward manner, primarily with Ada constructs, or if the bodies will make use of lower level abstractions. If the development of the body requires lower level abstractions, we need to specify them. The specifications should be to the *what* level, including package specifications, but not to the *how* level of detail.

The Commands package will be relatively easy to implement with predefined Ada operations and Text_IO. If it does need any helper packages, they will be relatively low level and properly part of detailed design. Therefore, we will not further consider Commands during the top-level design.

The Post_Office package is of considerably greater complexity than the Commands package. At this point, we have neither a strategy for its implementation, nor a specification of the data structures to be used for the storage of mail. The next layer will focus on the general nature of implementation of the Post_Office, and even more so on the specification of required helper packages.

C.3.6.1 Design Issues of the Post_Office. An important consideration for the design of the Post_Office is the data structures. We will first address this issue for the letters, and then for the storage for the letters.

Letters. We should always stop and think at this point in the design to investigate opportunities for deferral of design decisions and for hiding of information. In this case, the Post_Office does not have to know much about the *contents* of the letters, it only has to *move them around.* It certainly does not have to know the details of the data structure used to tie together the various components of a letter.

Since there will be many letters, created, stored, and so on by the Post_Office, the appropriate model of information hiding of details about letters (and the deferral of the design decision about the structure of the letter) is the abstract data type, the type manager form of a data manager (see Chapter 10).

The capabilities needed by the Post_Office in regard to letters are to obtain the name of the current user, to create (for the user) a letter, to output a letter, and (in order to display a summary of all letters for a user) to output the subject.

Although we may not think of it immediately, the Post_Office also needs to know what the address of the letter is, in order to be able to send a letter. If we don't think of this at first (and it is easy to miss), we can deal with the issue by a revision of the top-level design during the detailed design phase. This would be a typical instance of the iterative nature of design, and an example of how the needs of a virtual machine may dictate the nature of a data abstraction. Sometimes the needs of the virtual machine do not become clear until a lower layer of the design is reached.

Storage for the Letters. There are two aspects of the storage of mail. One is the storage for each mailbox, the other is the storage of all the mailboxes. It is useful to think of this as two separate problems. We will make the decision now to use an array of mailboxes, but we do not yet have to commit to the final structure of a mailbox. We will defer the decision about the nature of an individual mailbox, using a data manager called Storage to hide and defer the design decisions. Since there are to be multiple mailboxes, the data manager will be a type manager. We will create it to be specific to this problem about users, mail, and so on, using and depending upon the capabilities of the Letter data manager. One of the exercises listed at the end of this appendix suggests the transformation of the Storage package into a reusable software component.

The capabilities needed to manipulate the mailbox are to insert a letter into a box, display a summary of the contents of a box, discard a letter from a box, and display a letter from a box. If there is no more room in a box, the Storage should raise an exception. Similarly, an exception should be raised if there is no letter to discard. We will make the decision that the query of the user as to which letter to display or discard will be accomplished by the Storage, using the capabilities of Letter.

The specification of the package Storage will be shown after the specification of Letter.

C.3.6.2 Package Specification for Letter. Here is the completed version of the abstract data type Letter:

```
package Letter is
   type Users is (Harry, Mary, Larry, Teri);
   subtype Addresses is Users;

   type Format is private;

   function Name return Users;
   -- inputs the name of current user

   function Create_For (User : Users) return Format;

   function Address_Of (Mail : Format) return Addresses;

   procedure Put_Letter  (Mail : in Format);
   procedure Put_Subject (Mail : in Format);
private
   type Subjects is (Gossip, News, Lesson);
   type Messages is (Marriage, Divorce, Birth, Death, Scandal);
   subtype Originators is Users;
```

```
type Format is
  record
    Originator : Originators;
    Address    : Addresses;
    Subject    : Subjects;
    Message    : Messages;
  end record;
end Letter;
```

Each of the capabilities noted in the previous paragraph is provided by the specification of the package Letter. The package is an object (we say "design object") in the sense of object-oriented design. Since it is of the form abstract data type, the actual objects (the letters, or the mail) are created and stored by the users of the abstract data type. The Letter design object knows the details of the data structure, the letter format, and provides the operations on mail provided as a parameter. The letter object is a *lower level* object, illustrating the layering of the LVM/OOD approach.

The Create_For function is an example of what Liskov and Guttag [LIS86, p. 90] call a "constructor." The Address_Of a letter function is an example of an "observer." We discussed these in Chapter 10.

C.3.6.3 Package Specification for Storage. Here is the Ada PDL for the abstract data type Storage:

```
with Letter;
package Storage is
  type Box is limited private;

  procedure Insert            (This_Box    : in out Box;
                               This_Letter : in Letter.Format);
  No_More_Room : exception;

  procedure Display_Summary (This_Box    : in     Box);

  procedure Discard_Letter  (This_Box    : in out Box);
  No_Letter_To_Discard : exception;

  procedure Display_Letter  (This_Box    : in     Box);
private
  Size_Of_Mailbox : constant := 100;
  type Letter_ID is range 1 .. Size_Of_Mailbox;
```

```
type Letter_Boxes (Has_Mail : Boolean := False) is
  record
    case Has_Mail is
      when True =>
        Mail : Letter.Format;
      when False =>
        null;
    end case;
  end record;

type Box is array (Letter_ID) of Letter_Boxes;
end Storage;
```

The specification provides the capabilities needed for the Post_Office to perform its functions. We have included the structure of the mail box here. If we later decide to change that structure, it will not affect the users of this package, since the type Box was declared to be limited private. (There will, of course, be recompilation of the components that *with* Storage.) Figures C-5 and C-6 provide the graphical view of the design.

The design of the package bodies and the subunits are provided as part of the detailed design.

C.4 Detailed Design

The detailed design includes all information needed for implementation of the program; it is everything but the final coding details. It is in the nature of LVM/OOD that the use of virtual machines brings the presentation down to a relatively low level of detail, completely compilable, using subprogram calls. It is only the lowest level of subprograms that must be implemented in actual Ada code without use of lower level machines.

This lowest level of subprograms frequently consists of *nothing but coding details* and will not be represented at all in the detailed design. There is an occasional need for the use of pseudocode to present complex algorithms, even though they use no lower-level machines. The style for using pseudocode in detailed design is illustrated below.

The Ada PDL presented is:

1. The package body of Post_Office
2. The package Validate (generic enumeration validator)

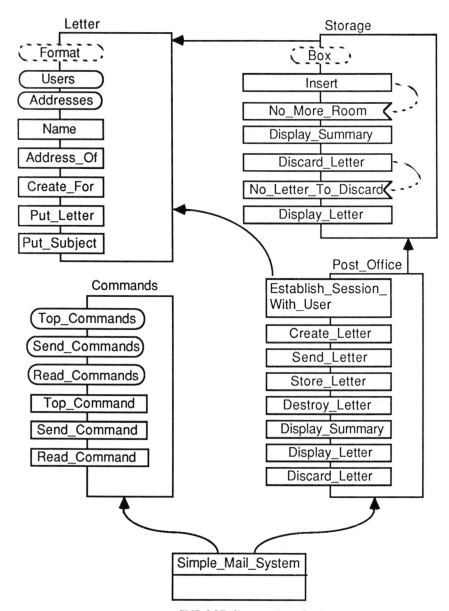

Figure C-5. SMS OOD diagram (complete).

3. The package body of Letter
4. The package body of Storage
5. Subunits of Storage (with pseudocode)

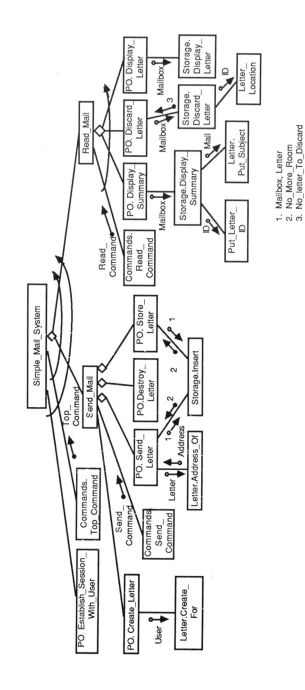

Figure C-6. SMS structure chart (complete).

1. Mailbox, Letter
2. No_More_Room
3. No_letter_To_Discard

354

6.   The package body of Commands

C.4.1   Package Body Post__Office

The Ada PDL for the body of Post_Office is the following:

```
with Storage;
with Letter;
package body Post_Office is
   type Mail_Boxes is array (Letter.Users) of Storage.Box;

   User          : Letter.Users;
   Mail          : Letter.Format;
   Mail_Storage : Mail_Boxes;

   procedure Establish_Session_With_User is
   begin
     User := Letter.Name;
   end Establish_Session_With_User;

   procedure Create_Letter    is separate;
   procedure Send_Letter      is separate;
   procedure Store_Letter     is separate;

   procedure Destroy_Letter  is
   begin
     null; -- don't have to do anything at all
   end Destroy_Letter;

   procedure Display_Summary is separate;
   procedure Discard_Letter  is separate;
   procedure Display_Letter  is separate;
end Post_Office;
```

C.4.2   Package Specification for Generic Enumeration Validator

The PDL for the generic package that validates an enumeration type is the following:

```
with Text_IO; use Text_IO;
generic
  type Enum is (<>);
package Validate is
  function Valid_Enum return Enum;
    -- may raise End_Error
end Validate;
```

C.4.3 Package Body Letter

The PDL for the body of Letter is the following:

```
with Validate;
with Text_IO; use Text_IO;
package body Letter is
  package Valid_Name    is new Validate (Users);
  package Valid_Address is new Validate (Addresses);
  package Valid_Subject is new Validate (Subjects);
  package Valid_Message is new Validate (Messages);

  function Name return Users                        is separate;
  function Create_For (User : Users) return Format  is separate;
  function Address_Of (Mail : Format) return Addresses is separate;
  procedure Put_Letter (Mail : in Format)           is separate;
  procedure Put_Subject (Mail : in Format)          is separate;
end Letter;
```

C.4.4 Package Body Storage

The following statements represent the PDL for the body of Storage:

```
with Text_IO; use Text_IO;
package body Storage is
  package Int_IO is new Integer_IO (Letter_ID); use Int_IO;

  -- local subprograms

  procedure Put_Letter_ID (ID : in Letter_ID) is separate;
  function Letter_Location return Letter_ID   is separate;
```

```
-- procedures in specification

procedure Insert            (This_Box    : in out Box;
                            This_Letter : in Letter.Format)
                                                    is separate;
procedure Display_Summary (This_Box    : in      Box) is separate;
procedure Discard_Letter  (This_Box    : in out Box) is separate;
procedure Display_Letter  (This_Box    : in      Box) is separate;
end Storage;
```

C.4.5 Subunits of Storage

These are the only procedures in the system that are complex
enough to merit detailed design of the algorithms. As usual, we use
pseudocode for compilable PDL.

```
-- procedures in specification

separate (Storage)
  procedure Insert (This_Box    : in out Box;
                    This_Letter : in Letter.Format) is
  begin
    for Box_Index in This_Box'Range loop
      -- if the letter box does not have mail then
        -- insert this letter in the mailbox;
        -- indicate that the letter box has mail;
        return;
      -- end if;
    end loop;

    raise No_More_Room;
  end Insert;
```

```
separate (Storage)
  procedure Display_Summary (This_Box : in Box) is
  begin
    for Box_Index in This_Box'Range loop
      -- if the letter box has mail then
        -- output the box index of the letter box;
        -- output the subject of the letter in the letter box;
      -- end if;
      null; --\
    end loop;
  end Display_Summary;

separate (Storage)
  procedure Discard_Letter  (This_Box : in out Box) is
    Location : Letter_ID := Letter_Location;
  begin
    -- if the letter box at the Location does not have mail then
      raise No_Letter_To_Discard;
    -- end if;

    -- make the letter box not contain mail
  end Discard_Letter;

separate (Storage)
  procedure Display_Letter (This_Box : in Box) is
    Location : Letter_ID := Letter_Location;
  begin
    -- if the letter box at the Location has mail then

      -- display the letter;

    -- end if;
    null; --\
  end Display_Letter;
```

C.4.6 Package Body Commands

The package body Commands includes the following PDL statements:

```
with Validate;
with Text_IO; use Text_IO;
package body Commands is
```

```
package Valid_Top_Command  is new Validate (Top_Commands);
package Valid_Send_Command is new Validate (Send_Commands);
package Valid_Read_Command is new Validate (Read_Commands);

function Top_Command return Top_Commands  is separate;
function Send_Command return Send_Commands is separate;
function Read_Command return Read_Commands is separate;
end Commands;
```

C.5 Implementation

This section presents the complete code, the final PDL, for the solution to the problem.

The Ada PDL presented is:

1. Subunits of Post_Office
2. Subunits of Storage
3. Package body Validate
4. Subunits of Commands
5. Subunits of Letter

C.5.1 Subunits of Post__Office

The complete Ada code is provided for the following subunits of Post_Office:

1. Create_Letter

```
separate (Post_Office)
  procedure Create_Letter is
  begin
    Mail := Letter.Create_For (User);
  end Create_Letter;
```

2. Store_Letter

```
with Storage;
with Text_IO; use Text_IO;
separate (Post_Office)
  procedure Store_Letter is
  begin
    Storage.Insert (Mail_Storage (User), Mail);
```

```
    exception
      when Storage.No_More_Room =>
        Put_Line ("There is no more room in your mail box.");
    end Store_Letter;
```

3. Send_Letter

```
with Storage;
with Text_IO; use Text_IO;
separate (Post_Office)
  procedure Send_Letter is
    Address  : Letter.Addresses;
  begin
    Address  := Letter.Address_Of (Mail);
    Storage.Insert (Mail_Storage (Address), Mail);

    exception
      when Storage.No_More_Room =>
        Put_Line ("There is no more room in the addressed
                                              mail box.");

    end Send_Letter;
```

4. Display_Summary

```
with Storage;
separate (Post_Office)
  procedure Display_Summary is
  begin
    Storage.Display_Summary (Mail_Storage (User));
  end Display_Summary;
```

5. Display_Letter

```
with Storage;
separate (Post_Office)
  procedure Display_Letter is
  begin
    Storage.Display_Letter (Mail_Storage (User));
  end Display_Letter;
```

6. Discard_Letter

```
with Storage;
with Text_IO; use Text_IO;
separate (Post_Office)
  procedure Discard_Letter is
  begin
    Storage.Discard_Letter (Mail_Storage (User));

  exception
    when Storage.No_Letter_To_Discard =>
      Put_Line ("There is no such letter to discard.");
  end Discard_Letter;
```

C.5.2 Subunits of Storage

We would normally follow the sequence of the package specifications and bodies in showing the implementation. However, we will deviate from that general principle here since the implementation of Storage is quite interesting, while the implementation of the Letter procedures is a very low-level detail best left until the end of the discussion. We start with the procedures that are visible in the package specification:

1. Insert

```
separate (Storage)
  procedure Insert (This_Box    : in out Box;
                    This_Letter : in Letter.Format) is
  begin
    for Box_Index in This_Box'Range loop
      if not This_Box (Box_Index).Has_Mail then
        This_Box (Box_Index) := (Has_Mail => True,
                                 Mail     => This_Letter);
        return;

      end if;
    end loop;

    raise No_More_Room;
  end Insert;
```

2. Display_Summary

```
separate (Storage)
  procedure Display_Summary (This_Box : in Box) is
  begin
    for Box_Index in This_Box'Range loop
      if This_Box (Box_Index).Has_Mail then

        Put_Letter_ID (Box_Index);
        Letter.Put_Subject (This_Box (Box_Index).Mail);

      end if;
    end loop;
  end Display_Summary;
```

3. Discard_Letter

```
separate (Storage)
  procedure Discard_Letter  (This_Box : in out Box) is
    Location : Letter_ID := Letter_Location;
  begin
    if not This_Box (Location).Has_Mail then
      raise No_Letter_To_Discard;
    end if;

    This_Box (Location) := (Has_Mail => False);
  end Discard_Letter;
```

4. Display_Letter

```
separate (Storage)
  procedure Display_Letter  (This_Box : in Box) is
    Location : Letter_ID := Letter_Location;
  begin
    if This_Box (Location).Has_Mail then
      Letter.Put_Letter (This_Box (Location).Mail);
    end if;
  end Display_Letter;
```

We now continue with the subprograms that are local to the package body:

1. Put_Letter_ID

```
separate (Storage)
  procedure Put_Letter_ID (ID : in Letter_ID) is
  begin
    Put ("Letter Id is:  "); Put (ID); New_Line;
  end Put_Letter_ID;
```

2. Letter_Location

```
separate (Storage)
  function Letter_Location return Letter_ID is
    ID : Letter_ID;
  begin
    Put ("Enter Letter ID:  "); Get (ID); New_Line;
    return ID;
  end Letter_Location;
```

C.5.3 Package Body Validate

The following Ada code is provided for package body Validate. It is an example of an implementation of a generic validator that handles the interface with the operator. It provides the choices (of the enumerated type) to the operator, validates the input, and reminds the operator of legal choices upon detecting incorrect input.

```
with Text_IO; use Text_IO;
package body Validate is
  package Valid_Enumeration_IO is new Enumeration_IO (Enum);

  function Valid_Enum return Enum is
    Data : Enum;
  begin
    Put_Line ("Enter choice of: ");

    for Element in Enum'First .. Enum'Last loop
      Valid_Enumeration_IO.Put (Element);
      New_Line;
    end loop;
```

```
    loop
      begin
        Valid_Enumeration_IO.Get (Data);
        return Data;
      exception
        when Data_Error => -- raised by Get on invalid input
          Put_Line ("Illegal entry");
          Put_Line ("Enter choice of: ");
          for Element in Enum'First .. Enum'Last loop
            Valid_Enumeration_IO.Put (Element);
            New_Line;
          end loop;
      end;
    end loop;
  end Valid_Enum;
end Validate;
```

C.5.4 Subunits of Commands

In the detailed design we showed the procedures of Commands as
being separate. However, we decided not to use separate after all,
since the procedures were so simple. The important aspect of the
use of separate during detailed design was the *conceptual* separation
of design and implementation. The new package body of Commands, with the details provided in the subprograms, is the following:

```
with Validate;
with Text_IO; use Text_IO;
package body Commands is
  package Valid_Top_Command  is new Validate (Top_Commands);
  package Valid_Send_Command is new Validate (Send_Commands);
  package Valid_Read_Command is new Validate (Read_Commands);

  function Top_Command return Top_Commands is
  begin
    return Valid_Top_Command.Valid_Enum;
  end Top_Command;

  function Send_Command return Send_Commands is
  begin
    return Valid_Send_Command.Valid_Enum;
  end Send_Command;
```

```
   function Read_Command return Read_Commands is
   begin
      return Valid_Read_Command.Valid_Enum;
   end Read_Command;
end Commands;
```

C.5.5   Subunits of Letter

We also show an alternate implementation for the package Letter, with the details of the subprograms provided, rather than using the separate clauses. The code is as follows:

```
with Validate;
with Text_IO; use Text_IO;
package body Letter is
   package Valid_Name    is new Validate (Users);
   package Valid_Address is new Validate (Addresses);
   package Valid_Subject is new Validate (Subjects);
   package Valid_Message is new Validate (Messages);


   function Name return Users is
   begin
      return Valid_Name.Valid_Enum;
   end Name;


   function Create_For (User : Users) return Format is
      Mail : Format;
   begin
      Mail.Originator := User;
      Mail.Address := Valid_Address.Valid_Enum;
      Mail.Subject := Valid_Subject.Valid_Enum;
      Mail.Message := Valid_Message.Valid_Enum;

      return Mail;
   end Create_For;


   function Address_Of (Mail : Format) return Addresses is
   begin
      return Mail.Address;
   end Address_Of;
```

```
procedure Put_Letter (Mail : in Format) is
begin
  Put ("Originator is:  ");
  Put_Line (Originators'Image (Mail.Originator));
  Put ("Address is:  ");
  Put_Line (Addresses'Image (Mail.Address));
  Put ("Subject is:  ");
  Put_Line (Subjects'Image (Mail.Subject));
  Put ("Message is:  ");
  Put_Line (Messages'Image (Mail.Message));
end Put_Letter;

procedure Put_Subject (Mail : in Format) is
begin
  Put ("Subject is:  ");
  Put_Line (Subjects'Image (Mail.Subject));
end Put_Subject;
end Letter;
```

The designers must decide on the approach regarding the consistent use of the separate clause, or providing the details of the subprograms inside the package bodies. The tradeoff between the two approaches is that the consistent use of the separate clause supports the concepts of stepwise refinement, deferral of design decisions, and minimal commitment. It also, however, creates lots of files in a file oriented system, since we will need a separate file for each subunit. This can become a configuration management problem for a large system. The other approach—providing the details of the subprograms within the package bodies—may shift the emphasis of design to an emphasis of providing implementation details. This may not yield as flexible a design as the other approach, but we will end up with fewer files to manage.

C.6 Exercises

The following exercises are suggested for this case study:

1. Reimplement the Storage package as a generic package with the contents of a mailbox, and an index type to indicate the size of the mailbox as generic parameters. This makes the Storage design object a generic, reusable component. It must not have any knowledge of the mail system problem embedded within it. Does it become more complex, or simpler? How about the user

of Storage? *Hint:* An instantiation of the generic storage package could be of the form:

```
package Storage is new Generic_Storage
                  (Contents_Of_Box => Letter.Format,
                   Box_Index       => Letter_ID);
```

2. Change the implementation of Storage. For example, use a linked list. Do you have to change the Post_Office?

3. Don't use a layered object—eliminate the Storage package. What does this do to the complexity of the Post_Office? What are the implications of changing the implementation of the data structure, for example, from a two-dimensional array to an array of pointers to linked lists?

4. Make the following changes and discuss their effect on other parts of the program. Make subject and message to be text strings. Add some users. Don't allow Harry to receive mail from other users.

5. Implement the system without private types and discuss the potential consequences of the changes noted above.

6. Distribute the type definitions and the functions of the Commands package as close to where they are needed as possible. Is this a significant change? What are the tradeoffs of the two approaches?

7. Do not implement the operation Establish_Session_With_User in the Post_Office. Next, do not have the Post_Office retain knowledge of the current user. How do such design choices affect data flow?

8. For the design presented in the case study, change the data structures of the letter and an individual mailbox (i.e., Letter.Format and Storage.Box), and discuss how this affects the overall design of the system.

Case Study 4:
Air Traffic
Control System (ATCS)

This case study is designed to provide a model of a large real-time system that illustrates our design methodology, with special emphasis on the use of the Ada package taxonomy described in Chapter 10.

The following sections present a problem specification, the environment for the ATCS software development, the edges-in approach followed by decomposition of the middle part, and the use of PDL to illustrate the top-level and detailed design.

D.1 Problem Specification

The Air Traffic Control System (ATCS) displays aircraft tracks obtained from radar sites. It accepts radar data inputs about track location, and operator inputs to establish tracks or change the location of a specified track. It outputs aircraft location to a display. Figure D-1 illustrates the situation, showing the ATCS interaction with the radar, operator, and display.

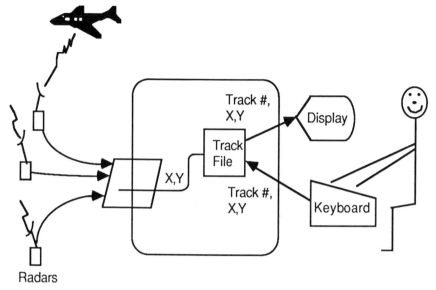

Radars

Figure D-1. ATCS overview.

ATCS periodically extrapolates all aircraft locations and (independently of the radar input) also periodically updates the display. The ATCS level of resolution is the meter, and the system provides for tracking on a two-dimensional grid of 100,000 meters in each direction.

There are three methods of updating an aircraft location in ATCS:

1. Operator initiation or change of a track
2. Radar inputs that correlate with an established track
3. ATCS extrapolation at periodic intervals

The remainder of the specification uses Ada-style names for certain system parameters, such as the frequency of periodic update or number of aircraft tracks. Such parameters are called *adaptation data.* They are to be prominently located and easy to find in the coded solution, and changes to such parameters are to require nothing more than a single change to a literal value and a recompilation. The literal values for the adaptation data will be given at the end of the software requirements.

The operator initiates tracks by providing a location as a set of (x, y) coordinates and a track number of zero. The ATCS assigns track numbers. It may have as many as Maximum_Number_Of_Tracks tracks. After assignment of a track number, the track is recorded in the track file and is said to be established. For simplicity in this case study the ATCS does not immediately inform the operator of the track number. The number is displayed when the ATCS periodically displays the aircraft locations. The operator may change the location of an aircraft by providing the track number (other than zero) and a new set of coordinates. For simplicity in this example, tracks are never dropped.

The radar provides input as a set of coordinates. The data are provided from a number of different radars with varying acquisition rates; hence, the data are presented to ATCS asynchronously.

The ATCS is concerned only with the tracks that have been initiated (i.e., established) by the operator. It attempts to correlate each radar input (x, y) with an established track. If the input coordinates are within Proximity meters of an established track, the input is then said to be successfully correlated with the track. This new input is considered to be the new valid location of the established track, and the track file is updated with the new location. If the radar input does not successfully correlate with any of the established tracks, it is ignored. For simplicity, we are not concerned with "best" correlation. Assume that the first correlation found is correct.

The (x, y) pair and the time of last update are kept in the track file. The (x, y) pairs are updated (extrapolated) by the system on a periodic basis, i.e., at Update_Periodic intervals. For simplicity, assume all aircraft are moving at the same Velocity_Of_Aircraft [i.e., at the same speed and in the same direction (northeast)].

All tracks in the track file are displayed at Display_Periodic intervals. The display consists of the track number and some symbol (the ATCS is not concerned with the details of the display) placed at the coordinates provided by ATCS.

The following items are considered adaptation data:

1. Update_Periodic = 1 second. All the tracks in the track file should be updated every second.

2. Display_Periodic = 5 seconds. All the tracks in the track file should be displayed every 5 seconds.

3. Maximum_Number_Of_Tracks = 200. The software should be sized to handle a maximum of 200 tracks.

4. Proximity = 1000 meters. If the correlation calculation shows a point obtained from the radar data to be within 1000 meters of a data point in the track file, that track is updated with the new data.

5. Velocity_Of_Aircraft = 1000 kilometers per hour to the northeast. All aircraft are assumed to have this same velocity.

6. Speed = 200 meters per second in each of x and y directions. All aircraft are assumed to have this same speed.

We have simplified the aircraft extrapolation calculation by assuming that a velocity of 1000 kilometers per hour to the northeast is about 280 meters per second to the northeast, or 200 meters per second in each of the x and y directions. Therefore the extrapolation consists of adding 200 to each of the x and y coordinates for each second (or fraction of a second) since the last update. The resulting adaptation data is the Speed in the x and y directions.

D.2 Context Schema

The context schema for ACTS is shown in Figure D-2. Radar inputs are received in the form of (x, y) coordinate pairs. These inputs occur asynchronously and must be accepted at any time, and only as little as possible of the incoming data should get lost.

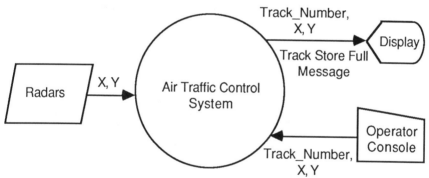

Figure D-2. Context diagram.

Inputs are received from the operator any time a new track is to be added to the system, or whenever the operator wants to update an established track. The operator furnishes a track number of zero for a new track to be established, and the coordinates for the new track. For an established track, the operator provides the track number and the corresponding coordinates for the update.

All the tracks in the track file are displayed periodically on the operator's display device. The output data appears with a track number at the corresponding (x, y) coordinates. If the operator requests a track to be added when the track file is full, a message is displayed to inform the operator that the request was denied.

Our task is to design the real-time control program that will interface with the external devices and perform the functionality given in the problem specification. We will use the design methodology described in Chapters 22 and 23.

D.3   Edges-In Approach

The first step we will take to develop a solution to the problem stated by the ATCS requirement is to identify the processes required to interface with the external devices shown in the context diagram in Figure D-2. Since ATCS interfaces with three external devices, there should be a process in the ATCS for each of these devices. However, part of the ATCS software has already been designed by the company that is building the hardware interfaces to the external devices. This software is the ATCS Executive Services, and hides the details of the hardware interaction from the ATCS application software that we are going to design as part of this case study.

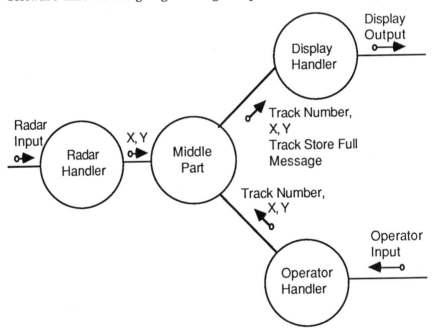

Figure D-3. Processes for edge functions.

Figure D-3 shows the processes for the ATCS edge functions. The large "Middle Part" represents the primary functionality of the system and will be decomposed later.

The three edge processes are virtual machines that operate concurrently. They are described as follows:

1. *Operator Handler.* The Operator Handler obtains a track number and set of coordinates from the operator. If the track number is zero, the coordinates are sent to the Middle Part to initiate a track. Otherwise, the track number and coordinates are sent to the Middle Part to change the location of an aircraft established as an existing track. If the track file is full, the Middle Part prepares a signal to notify the operator that the attempt to initiate a track was not successful. (For simplicity in this problem, the only response to the signal is the output of a message, prepared in the Middle Part.) If the operator has not input any information, this process is blocked and waiting for input.

2. *Display Handler.* The Display Handler periodically obtains the complete set of tracks from the Middle Part and displays the track number and corresponding coordinates of each track.

3. *Radar Handler.* The Radar Handler takes sets of coordinates from the radar and passes them to the Middle Part.

The three device handlers are part of the executive services and are provided as tasks inside an Ada package. The specification is shown in the PDL description below. The radar handler is also in that package, but we don't see it since the radar handler is implemented as a calling task—it puts the x, y coordinates from the radars into a raw data buffer. The executive services include the raw data buffer, as shown below, which the application software will call in order to receive a set of coordinates.

We do not have to be concerned here with the minute details of how to interface with the hardware as we did, for example, in the RTS case study for the processes Receive Host Message, Transmit Host Message, and Digital Thermometer Handler (see Appendix A). We merely have to provide the required interfaces to the device handlers furnished with the executive services.

D.4   Decomposing The Middle Part

The Middle Part is also a virtual machine. It takes sets of coordinates from the Radar Handler and attempts to correlate them with established tracks. If the coordinates correlate successfully, they are used as the new location of the track.

New tracks are established and track coordinates are changed, based on input from the Operator Handler. Periodically, track coordinates are extrapolated. When requested, the track file is provided to the Display Handler.

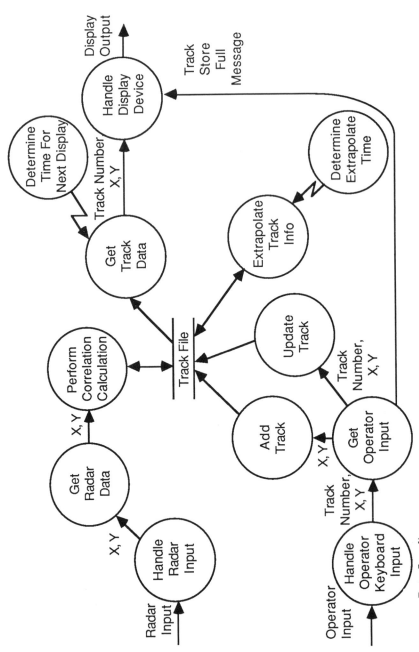

Figure D-4. Data flow diagram.

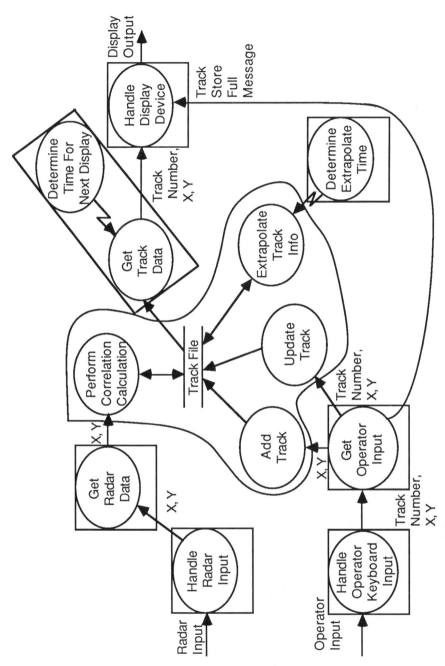

Figure D-5. Process identification.

The Middle Part is quite complicated, and its functionality is illustrated in the DFD shown in Figure D-4. It contains more than a single concurrent function; it must simultaneously do three things:

1. Be prepared to take a track from the Radar Handler.
2. Be prepared to accept a call, asynchronously, from either the operator or display interfaces.
3. Keep track of time until the next extrapolation of tracks.

The decomposition of the Middle Part into a set of cooperating sequential processes is shown in Figure D-5.

Even though the ATCS Executive is providing handlers for the hardware, we will establish a separate process for each of the radar, display, and operator interactions. This includes the transforms Get Radar Data, Get Track Data, and Get Operator Input. We have included the transform Determine Time for Next Display in the process that interacts with the display handler since they represent two highly cohesive functions with a temporal relationship. The choice of these three independent processes is important since the operator and display interfaces provided by the ATCS Executive cause the calling process to block if no interaction is immediately available. If we did not have a separate thread of control for the operator interaction, for example, the entire ATCS application program could be suspended waiting for an operator action. (If we were writing the hardware handlers, we might choose to perform these ATCS functions in the same process as the hardware handlers.)

The four transforms that set values in the track file have been combined into a single process that will protect the track file. This process will be implemented as a monitor and will provide the required mutual exclusion for access to the track file.

Even though the transform Determine Extrapolate Time is cohesive with Extrapolate Track Information, the latter must be part of the monitor, which is independent of time. The former transform is chosen as a separate process since it deals with the periodicity (a temporal condition) for determining when the track file should be extrapolated.

We have now completed the decomposition of the Middle Part, and we have a model of the concurrent elements of our solution. These elements are concurrent virtual machines and illustrate the decomposition of the middle part by the use of *process abstraction*. All the processes are shown in the process structure chart in Figure D-6, and the processes of the Middle Part are described as follows:

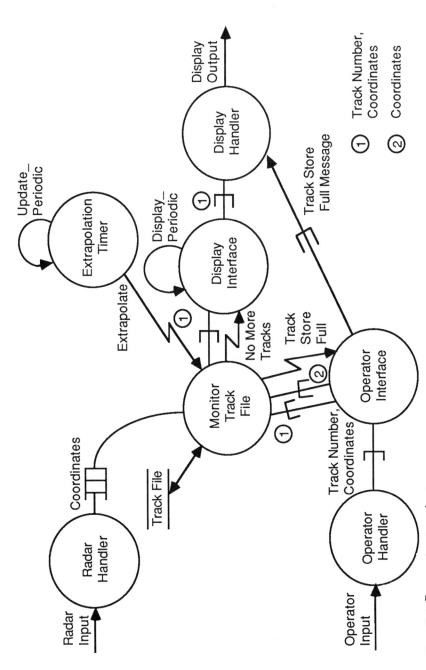

Figure D-6. Process structure chart.

1. *Monitor Track File.* The Monitor accomplishes all the functions connected with the manipulation of the track file (pool). It guarantees mutual exclusion for access to the pool.

2. *Extrapolation Timer.* The Extrapolation Timer process tells the Monitor when it is time to extrapolate all tracks.

3. *Display Interface.* The Display Interface process determines the time for the next display of all the tracks, gets the track information from the Monitor, and sends this information to the Display Handler.

4. *Operator Interface.* The Operator Interface process gets coordinates and corresponding track numbers from the operator device handler. If the track number is zero, coordinates are sent to the Monitor to establish a new track. If the track number is not zero, coordinates are sent to the Monitor to update that track.

The notation shown for the Extrapolation Timer and Display Interface processes indicates processes that have a periodic aspect; the period is indicated near the loop, as in the example, Update_Periodic.

The processes shown in Figure D-6 can be considered nodes in a network of interconnected virtual machines. This structure is "flat" and not hierarchical, as is the case when we use the layered virtual machine concept (see Chapter 12) to decompose the sequential part of a single-thread process. Although we arrived at this design by decomposing the middle part, these machines represent a single layer of concurrent elements; they are not further decomposed into lower layers of concurrent machines. Large processes can be decomposed into a hierarchy of layered virtual machines for the sequential processing within each separate process.

We next consider the interfaces between the processes.

D.5   Process Interfaces

The decomposition of the Middle Part and the device handlers are shown in the process structure chart in Figure D-6. This group of concurrent top-level virtual machines represents the design of our solution as a set of cooperating sequential processes and their interfaces. The interface between Radar Handler and Monitor Track File is pictured as a buffer for the channel data Coordinates obtained by Radar Handler. This allows the handler to operate in synchronization with the natural speed of the radar device and is not dependent on other processing elements in the system. This will provide for a minimum loss of incoming radar data.

The track file must be protected, and will reside entirely within the Monitor Track File process.

When the period expires for the next extrapolation of the track information, a signal is sent from Extrapolation Timer to Monitor Track File. No data is passed between these two processes.

When the period expires for the next display of tracks, the Display Interface process gets a track number and corresponding coordinates from Monitor Track File and passes it to the Display Handler process. This continues until Display Interface receives a signal from Monitor Track File that there are no more tracks to send. The track information is passed as single-element channel data, and no buffering is required.

The Operator Interface process waits to receive a track number and associated coordinates from the Operator Handler. The data is received as single-element channel data. If a track is to be added, the coordinates are sent to Monitor Track File without any buffering. A signal will be returned to Operator Interface if the track store is full. This signal is passed on to the Display Handler as a message. If the operator requests an update of a track, the track number and associated coordinates are sent from Operator Interface to Monitor Track File without any buffering.

D.6 Introducing Intermediary Processes

The only intermediary processes required is for the proper implementation of the buffer between the Radar Handler and Monitor Track File processes. Our first attempt would be to introduce a buffer task, but this would require Monitor Track File to be a caller with respect to the buffer. The monitor should be a pure server, and we thus add a transporter between the buffer and the monitor. The two intermediaries are shown as the tasks Buffer and Transport_Coordinates in the Ada task graph in Figure D-7. This figure represents the complete set of Ada tasks that model the concurrent elements of our design for ATCS. We next describe the caller/called decisions we have made for the interactions of these tasks.

D.7 Caller/Called Decisions

The Buffer task shown in Figure D-7 is a pure server (by convention), and is called by both the Radar_Handler and the Transport_Coordinates tasks.

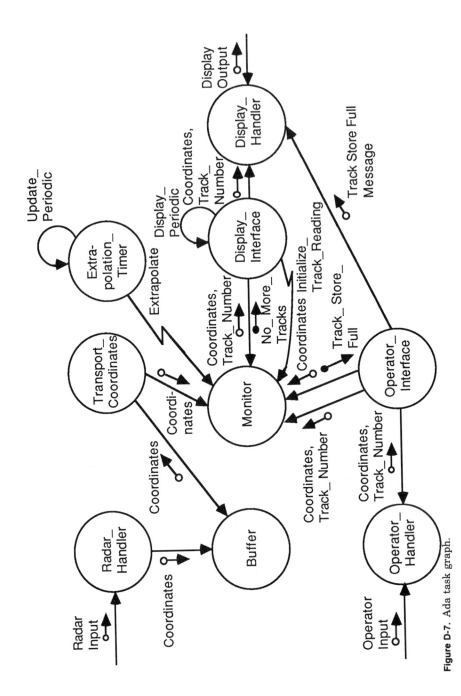

Figure D-7. Ada task graph.

380

The Monitor task is also a pure server (it is a "busy" task with multiple entries) and is called by Transport_Coordinates, Extrapolation_Timer, Display_Interface, and Operator_Interface.

The Display_Handler and Operator_Handler tasks are furnished to us as part of the executive services, and are specified as servers.

This completes the caller/ called decisions we have to make for all the tasks shown in Figure D-7. We note the close relationship between the choice of intermediaries and making proper caller/called decisions.

D.8   Ada Packaging

The packaging of the Ada tasks is shown in Figure D-8. The tasks Radar_Handler, Operator_Handler, and Display_Handler are provided to us with the executive services and are contained in the package External_Devices. The task Buffer is also provided with the executive services and is encapsulated in the package Raw_Data_Buffer.

The tasks Transport_Coordinates, Extrapolation_Timer, and Monitor represent cohesive elements and are encapsulated in the package Track_File_Monitor.

The tasks Display_Interface and Operator_Interface represent independent processing elements that are not cohesive with the other elements in the system. These two tasks are encapsulated in the separate packages Display_Interface and Operator_Interface. When we write the PDL for these tasks we will simplify their names to Interface to avoid having long names that do not support ease of readability. The packages shown in Figure D-8 represent the primary objects of our design for the ATCS.

D.9   Program Design Language

The PDL phase consists of transforming the design described in Figure D-8 into a programming structure using Ada constructs. The top-level design illustrates the overall structure using Ada package specifications and bodies. The details of the algorithms are deferred to the detailed design using the *separate* construct. A description of the top-level design phase is given below, followed by the detailed design.

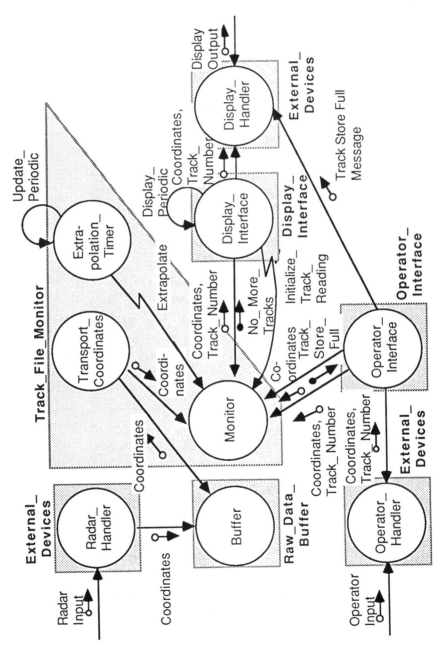

Figure D-8. Ada package graph.

382

```
package Definitions is

   type Coordinates  is range -100_000 .. 100_000;
                                     -- Needed for Proximity
-- Adaptation data

   Update_Periodic        : constant Duration := 1.0;
   Display_Periodic       : constant Duration := 5.0;
   Maximum_Number_Of_Tracks : constant := 200;
   Proximity              : constant Coordinates := 1000;
   Speed                  : constant := 200;

-- Type definitions

   type Track_Count     is range 0 .. Maximum_Number_Of_Tracks;
   subtype Track_Number is Track_Count range 1 .. Track_Count'Last;

end Definitions;
```

Figure D-9. Definitions for ATCS (package specification).

```
----- External_Devices package -----

with Definitions;   use Definitions;
with Raw_Data_Buffer;

package External_Devices is

   procedure Get_Data_From_Operator (X, Y : out Coordinates;
                                     Track_ID : out Track_Number);

   procedure Display_A_Track (X, Y : in Coordinates;
                              Track_ID : in Track_Number);

   procedure Display_Message (Message : in String);

   -- Calls
     -- Raw_Data_Buffer.Enqueue

end External_Devices;
```

Figure D-10. External_Devices (package specification).

```
----- Raw_Data_Buffer package -----

with Definitions;   use Definitions;
package Raw_Data_Buffer is
  procedure Enqueue (X, Y :  in Coordinates);
  procedure Dequeue (X, Y : out Coordinates);
end Raw_Data_Buffer;
```

Figure D-11. Raw_Data_Buffer (package specification).

D.9.1   Top-Level Design

The ATCS top-level design is as follows:

1. *Helper packages.* Helper packages must be prepared in a bottom-up fashion before we start the top-level design of the application packages in a top-down fashion. The following components are used by the application packages:

   a. Definitions. This package contains constants, adaptation parameters, types, and subtypes that are used globally throughout the program. The Ada code is shown in Figure D-9.

   b. External_Devices. This package contains entrance procedures for access to input from the operator, and for sending output to the display device. An entrance procedure for the radar handler is not provided, and we have access to radar data via the buffer task contained in the package Raw_Data_Bufer (described below). The Ada code for External_Devices is shown in Figure D-10.

2. *Communication.* The Buffer task required for the incoming radar data was provided as an executive service package:

   a. Raw_Data_Buffer. The package specification shown in Figure D-11 contains the entrance procedures Enqueue and Dequeue for storing and retrieving radar data, respectively. The task Radar_Handler (in package External_Devices) puts the radar data into the buffer by calling Enqueue. ATCS retrieves the data by calling Dequeue.

3. *Application packages.* The following application packages were prepared for ATCS top-level design:

   a. Track_File_Monitor. The package specification and body are shown in Figure D-12. The specification part contains

```
with Definitions;  use Definitions;
package Track_File_Monitor is

  procedure Add_Track      (X, Y : in Coordinates);
  Track_Store_Full : exception; -- raised by Add_Track

  procedure Initialize_Track_Reading;

  procedure Next_Track  (X, Y      : out Coordinates;
                            Track_ID  : out Track_Number);
  No_More_Tracks : exception; -- raised by Next_Track

  procedure Update_Track (X, Y      : in Coordinates;
                            Track_ID : in Track_Number);

  -- Calls
    -- Raw_Data_Buffer.Dequeue
    -- Track_File_Manager.Add_Track
    -- Track_File_Manager.Initialize_Track_Reading
    -- Track_File_Manager.Next_Track
    -- Track_File_Manager.Update
    -- Track_File_Manager.Correlate
    -- Track_File_Manager.Extrapolate

end Track_File_Monitor;



package body Track_File_Monitor is

----- Monitor  -----

  task Monitor is

    entry Add     (X, Y : in Coordinates);

    entry Initialize_Track;

    entry Next  (X, Y      : out Coordinates;
                    Track_ID  : out Track_Number);
```

Figure D-12. Track_file_Monitor (package specification and body).

```
   entry Update (X, Y      : in Coordinates;
                 Track_ID : in Track_Number);

   entry Correlate (X, Y : in Coordinates);

   entry Extrapolate;

   -- Calls
     -- Track_File_Manager.Initialize_Track_Reading
     -- Track_File_Manager.Next_Track
     -- Track_File_Manager.Add_Track
     -- Track_File_Manager.Update
     -- Track_File_Manager.Correlate
     -- Track_File_Manager.Extrapolate
 end Monitor;

----- Extrapolation_Timer -----

 task Extrapolation_Timer is
   -- Calls
     -- Monitor.Extrapolate

   -- Delays for appropriate extrapolation interval and tells
   -- Monitor that it is time to extrapolate
 end Extrapolation_Timer;




----- Transport_Coordinates -----

 task Transport_Coordinates is
   -- Calls
     -- Raw_Data_Buffer.Dequeue
     -- Monitor.Correlate

   -- Transports a set of coordinates from the
   -- buffer to the track file Monitor
 end Transport_Coordinates;
```

Figure D-12 *(continued)*. Track_file_Monitor (package specification and body).

```
----- task bodies -----

  task body Monitor              is separate;
  task body Extrapolation_Timer  is separate;
  task body Transport_Coordinates is separate;

----- entrance procedures -----

  procedure Add_Track (X, Y : in Coordinates) is
  begin
    Monitor.Add (X, Y);
  end Add_Track;

  procedure Initialize_Track_Reading is
  begin
    Monitor.Initialize_Track;
  end Initialize_Track_Reading;

  procedure Next_Track  (X, Y      : out Coordinates;
                         Track_ID  : out Track_Number) is
  begin
    Monitor.Next (X, Y, Track_ID);
  end Next_Track;

  procedure Update_Track (X, Y      : in Coordinates;
                          Track_ID : in Track_Number) is
  begin
    Monitor.Update (X, Y, Track_ID);
  end Update_Track;

end Track_File_Monitor;
```

Figure D-12 *(continued)*. Track_file_Monitor (package specification and body).

entrance procedures to add a track, initialize the reading of
tracks, obtain the next track for output to the display
device, and to update a track. Exceptions are specified for
attempting to add a track when the track store is full, and
when the last track has been read for display output. The
body part contains task declarations for Monitor which will
guarantee mutual access to the track file; Extrapolation_
Timer which monitors the expiration of time intervals
between extrapolations; and Transport_Coordinates which

```
package Operator_Interface is
  -- Calls
    -- External_Devices.Get_Data_From_Operator
    -- External_Devices.Display_Message
    -- Track_File_Monitor.Add_Track
    -- Track_File_Monitor.Update_Track
end Operator_Interface;


package body Operator_Interface is

  task Interface is
    -- Calls
      -- External_Devices.Get_Data_From_Operator
      -- External_Devices.Display_Message
      -- Track_File_Monitor.Add_Track
      -- Track_File_Monitor.Update_Track
  end Interface;

  task body Interface is separate;

end Operator_Interface;
```

Figure D-13. Operator_Interface (package specification and body).

gets radar data from Buffer and sends this data to Monitor for correlation.

b. Operator_Interface. The package specification given in Figure D-13 only lists the calls made to entrance procedures in other packages; no entrance procedures are required for this package. The package body contains the declaration for the task Interface which gets data from the operator and sends it to the Monitor task.

c. Display_Interface. The package specification given in Figure D-14 lists the calls made to entrance procedures in other packages; no entrance procedures are required for this package. The package body includes the declaration of the Interface task which gets track data from the Monitor task and passes the data to the display handler.

d. Track_File_Manager. The generic package specification shown in Figure D-15 includes the generic type parameters Track_Count and Coordinates, and all the procedures that operate on the track file. The track file is declared in the

```
package Display_Interface is
  -- Calls
    -- Track_File_Monitor.Initialize_Track_Reading
    -- Track_File_Monitor.Next_Track
    -- External_Devices.Display_A_Track
end Display_Interface;


package body Display_Interface is

  task Interface is
    -- Calls
      -- Track_File_Monitor.Initialize_Track_Reading
      -- Track_File_Monitor.Next_Track
      -- External_Devices.Display_A_Track
  end Interface;

  task body Interface is separate;

end Display_Interface;
```

Figure D-14. Display_Interface (package specification and body).

package body and is hidden from the other tasks and sub-programs in the system. This is a generic *helper* package of the type data manager to be used by the Monitor task, and is implemented as a resource, or object manager.

The package Track_File_Manager was not identified as a result of the decomposition into concurrent processes. Rather, it resulted from a realization that a number of functions that were required by the Monitor task could be appropriately grouped together as a package of services. This is an important point; it illustrates that not all top-level design components are identifiable as a result of the analysis of concurrency and the mapping of concurrency from the problem space into the solution space.

D.9.2 Detailed Design

It is useful to introduce the structure graph at this point to provide a road map to the pseudocode to follow. A structure graph of the ATCS is provided as Figure D-16. This graph depicts the packages we have described so far and the interfaces between them. The names and graphic symbols used in the structure graph are isomorphic to the Ada names and constructs used in the PDL.

```
generic
  type Track_Count is range <>;
  type Coordinates is private;
package Track_File_Manager is

  subtype Track_Number is Track_Count range 1 .. Track_Count'Last;

  procedure Add_Track (X, Y : in Coordinates);
  Track_Store_Full : exception; -- raised by Add_Track

  procedure Initialize_Track_Reading;

  procedure Next_Track  (X, Y    : out Coordinates;
                         Track_ID : out Track_Number);
  No_More_Tracks : exception; -- raised by Next_Track

  procedure Update (X, Y    : in Coordinates;
                    Track_ID : in Track_Number);

  procedure Correlate  (X, Y : in Coordinates);

  procedure Extrapolate;

end Track_File_Manager;



with Calendar; use Calendar;
package body Track_File_Manager is

  type Track_Record is
    record
      X, Y   : Coordinates;
      Update : Time;
    end record;

  type Track_File is array (Track_Number) of Track_Record;

  Tracks : Track_File; -- This is the object

  Last_Track  : Track_Count := Track_Count'First;
  Track_Index : Track_Count := Track_Count'First;
```

Figure D-15. Track_File_Manager (package specification and body).

```
procedure Add_Track      (X, Y   : in  Coordinates)              is separate;


procedure Initialize_Track_Reading                              is separate;


procedure Next_Track     (X, Y      : out Coordinates;
                          Track_ID  : out Track_Number)  is separate;

procedure Update         (X, Y      : in Coordinates;
                          Track_ID  : in Track_Number)   is separate;

procedure Correlate      (X, Y      : in Coordinates)           is separate;


procedure Extrapolate                                           is separate;

end Track_File_Manager;
```

Figure D-15 *(continued).* Track_File_Manager (package specification and body).

We will discuss the detailed design of the ATCS in the same order as the presentation of the package specifications and bodies. No additional details can be supplied for the packages External_Devices and Raw_Data_Buffer since these were provided as executive services, and their implementation details are not available. The paragraphs that follow describe the subunits identified during top-level design, and any additional packages determined during detailed design.

1. *Application packages.*

   a. Track_File_Monitor Subunits

      ▪ Monitor. The task body is shown in Figure D-17. The generic package Track_File_Manager is instantiated to declare the track file object, and to make the operations on the track file available to Monitor. Mutually exclusive access to the track file is implemented in Monitor within the select statement.

      ▪ Extrapolation_Timer. The task body shown in Figure D-18 includes the functions to calculate the extrapolation times, to delay for the appropriate amount of time, and to alert the Monitor that it is time to extrapolate. Care must be exercised to avoid drift problems associated with task scheduling and execution of the instructions within the task body.

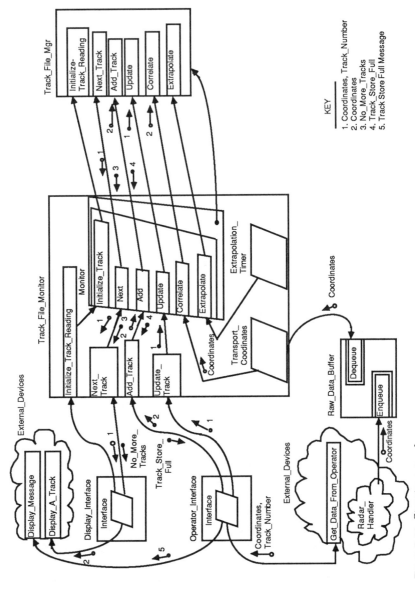

Figure D-16. Structure graph.

KEY
1. Coordinates, Track_Number
2. Coordinates
3. No_More_Tracks
4. Track_Store_Full
5. Track Store Full Message

```
----- Monitor -----

with Track_File_Manager;
separate (Track_File_Monitor)
  task body Monitor is

    package Track_File_Mgr is new Track_File_Manager
                        (Coordinates => Coordinates,
                         Track_Count => Track_Count);
  begin
    loop
      select
        -- when not providing tracks to some other task =>
        accept Initialize_Track do
          Track_File_Mgr.Initialize_Track_Reading;
          -- indicate that Monitor is providing tracks
        end Initialize_Track;
      or
        accept Next (X, Y     : out Coordinates;
                     Track_ID : out Track_Number) do null; --\
          -- use Track_File_Mgr.Next_Track to get next track;
          -- handle the exception Track_File_Mgr.No_More_Tracks;
          -- by indicating that Monitor is no longer providing
          -- tracks, and by raising the local exception
          -- No_More_Tracks
        end Next;
      or
        accept Add (X, Y : in Coordinates) do null; --\
          -- use Track_File_Mgr.Add_Track to add the track;
          -- handle the exception Track_File_Mgr.Track_Store_Full;
          -- by raising the local exception Track_Store_Full
        end Add;
      or
        accept Update (X, Y : in Coordinates;
                       Track_ID : in Track_Number) do null; --\
          -- update with Track_File_Mgr.Update;
        end Update;
      or
        accept Correlate (X, Y : in Coordinates) do null; --\
          -- correlate with Track_File_Mgr.Correlate;
        end Correlate;
      or
```

Figure D-17. Monitor (task body).

```
      accept Extrapolate do
        Track_File_Mgr.Extrapolate;
      end Extrapolate;
    end select;
    -- handle exceptions No_More_Tracks and Track_Store_Full
  end loop;
end Monitor;
```

Figure D-17 *(continued)*. Monitor (task body).

----- Extrapolation_Timer -----

```
with Calendar;  use Calendar;
separate (Track_File_Monitor)
  task body Extrapolation_Timer is
  begin
    -- initialize the next scheduled extrapolation;

    Periodic_Loop:
    loop null; --\

      -- calculate the appropriate delay time until extrapolation as:
      -- (next scheduled extrapolation) - current time;

      -- delay the appropriate time;

      -- alert monitor that it is time to extrapolate;

      -- calculate the next scheduled extrapolation as:
      -- (previous extrapolation time) + Update_Periodic;

    end loop Periodic_Loop;
  end Extrapolation_Timer;
```

Figure D-18. Extrapolation_Timer (task body).

- Transport_Coordinates. This task gets coordinates by calling the buffer within the package Raw_Data_Buffer, and passes the data to Monitor. The pseudocode is shown in Figure D-19.

b. Operator_Interface Subunits

- Interface. This task gets data from the operator and determines whether a new track should be established or

```
----- Transport_Coordinates -----

with Raw_Data_Buffer;
separate (Track_File_Monitor)
  task body Transport_Coordinates is
  begin
    loop null; --\
      -- get the coordinates from the Raw_Data_Buffer;
      -- send the coordinates to Monitor;
    end loop;
  end Transport_Coordinates;
```

Figure D-19. Transport_Coordinates (task body).

an old track should be updated. The required track information is sent to Monitor. If the operator requests that a track be added, this task handles the exception Track_Store_Full which is raised in Monitor. The task body is shown in Figure D-20.

c. Display_Interface Subunits

- Interface. This task monitors the times for the periodic displaying of the track file, gets track data from Monitor, and then passes this data to the Display Handler. It also handles an exception raised in Monitor which indicates that the last track has been sent. Care is taken to avoid the drift problem. The task body is shown in Figure D-21.

d. Track_File_Manager Subunits

- Add_Track. The procedure body is shown in Figure D-22.
- Initialize_Track_Reading. The procedure body is shown in Figure D-23.
- Next_Track. The procedure body is shown in Figure D-24.
- Update. The procedure body is shown in Figure D-25.
- Correlate. The procedure body is shown in Figure D-26. It calculates the distance from each track in the track file to the track coordinates received from the radar. If the distance is within Proximity meters, Monitor is notified to update the track with the new coordinates. The first

```
with Definitions;  use Definitions;
with Track_File_Monitor;
with External_Devices;
separate (Operator_Interface)
  task body Interface is
    X, Y : Coordinates;
    Track_ID : Track_Number;
    Add_Track_Indicator : constant Track_Count := 0;

  begin

    Interface_With_Operator:
    loop
      Handle_Track_Store_Full:
      begin
        External_Devices.Get_Data_From_Operator (X, Y, Track_ID);

        if Track_ID = Add_Track_Indicator then null; --\
          -- call Track_File_Monitor.Add_Track to initiate a track;

          -- Track_File_Monitor.Add_Track may raise Track_Store_Full
          -- exception, transferring control to the exception handler;
        else null; --\
          -- call Track_File_Monitor.Update_Track to update
          -- an established track;
        end if;

      exception
        when Track_File_Monitor.Track_Store_Full => null; --\
          -- provide a message to the operator
      end Handle_Track_Store_Full;
    end loop Interface_With_Operator;
  end Interface;
```

Figure D-20. Interface (task body; parent is Operator_Interface).

track found to satisfy the proximity condition is considered a successful correlation.

- Extrapolate. The procedure body is shown in Figure D-27. All the tracks in the track file are updated with the simplified extrapolation calculation.

2. *Main procedure.* Execution of an Ada program starts with the main procedure. Prior to execution, packages *with*ed by the

```
with Calendar;      use Calendar;
with Definitions;  use Definitions;
with Track_File_Monitor;
with External_Devices;

separate (Display_Interface)
  task body Interface is

    X, Y : Coordinates;
    Track_Index : Track_Number;

    Next_Time : Time := Clock + Display_Periodic;

  begin
        --      Note: The calculation of the delay must provide for
        --            an average delay of Display_Periodic.
        --            It must account for the variable time taken
        --            to execute other processes in order to not allow
        --            the periodic interval to drift away from its
        --            specified value.

    Periodic_Display:
    loop

      -- delay appropriate interval;

      Track_File_Monitor.Initialize_Track_Reading;

      Display_The_Tracks:
      loop null; --\
        -- use Track_File_Monitor.Next_Track
        -- and External_Devices.Display_A_Track
        -- to get and display tracks;
      end loop Display_The_Tracks;

      -- handle the exception Track_File_Monitor.No_More_Tracks

    end loop Periodic_Display;
  end Interface;
```

Figure D-21. Interface (task body; parent is Display_Interface).

main procedure must be elaborated. The chain of elaboration
causes the execution of all parts of the program. The main

```
----- Add_Track -----

separate (Track_File_Manager)
  procedure Add_Track (X, Y : in Coordinates) is
  begin
    if Last_Track = Track_Count'Last then
      raise Track_Store_Full;
    end if;

    -- add the track

  end Add_Track;
```

Figure D-22. Add_Track (procedure body).

```
----- Initialize_Track_Reading -----

separate (Track_File_Manager)
  procedure Initialize_Track_Reading is
  begin
    Track_Index := Track_Count'First;
  end Initialize_Track_Reading;
```

Figure D-23. Initialize_Track_Reading (procedure body).

```
----- Next -----

separate (Track_File_Manager)
  procedure Next_Track  (X, Y     : out Coordinates;
                         Track_ID : out Track_Number) is
  begin
    if Track_Index = Last_Track then
      raise No_More_Tracks;
    end if;

    -- provide next track

  end Next_Track;
```

Figure D-24. Next_Track (procedure body).

procedure for ATCS is shown in Figure D-28. The packages
Operator_Interface and Display_Interface are imported to start
the chain of elaboration. The executable part of the main procedure is simply a null statement.

```
----- Update -----

with Calendar; use Calendar;
separate (Track_File_Manager)
  procedure Update (X, Y        : in Coordinates;
                    Track_Number : in Track_Count) is
  begin null; --\
    -- update the indicated track, based on Track_Number, with the
    -- input X, Y, and the current time;
  end Update;
```

Figure D-25. Update (procedure body).

```
separate (Track_File_Manager)
  procedure Correlate   (X, Y : in Coordinates) is

    -- Attempts to correlate the input X,Y with a track in the
    -- track file.  If the coordinates correlate, they are used
    -- to update the location of the track. The time of Last
    -- update is set to current time.

    Distance : Coordinates;

  begin

    Correlation_Loop:
    for Track_Index in Tracks'Range loop

      -- calculate the Distance from the track to the input
      -- X and Y;

      if Distance <= Proximity then null; --\
        -- update the track with the input X, Y, and the
        -- current time;
        -- exit Correlation_Loop;
      end if;

    end loop Correlation_Loop;
  end Correlate;
```

Figure D-26. Correlate (procedure body).

We have now reached a point in the design where both the interfaces and the internal logic of the processes are well defined. All
that remains is the filling in of final data structures and completion

----- Extrapolate -----

```
with Calendar;           use Calendar;
separate (Track_File_Manager)
  procedure Extrapolate;

    -- Extrapolates all tracks to current Time.
    -- All aircraft travel the same speed
    -- and in northeast direction.

    Time_Of_This_Update : Time := Clock;
    Delta_Time      : Duration;
    Delta_Distance : Coordinates;

  begin

    -- update all tracks
    for Track_Index in Tracks'Range loop null; --\

      -- calculate time since last update;
      -- calculate distance traveled in time since last update;
      -- add the distance to each of the X and Y coordinates for
      -- the track;
      -- update the time that the track was last updated;

    end loop;

  end Extrapolate;
```

Figure D-27. Extrapolate (procedure body).

```
with Operator_Interface;
with Display_Interface;

procedure ATCS is
begin
  null;
end ATCS;
```

Figure D-28. ATCS main procedure.

of coding details to implement the algorithms defined in pseudocode. The next incremental step is to change any abstract entry and procedure calls to actual calls and to complete the details of the algorithms in the procedures and task bodies. This is not included in this case study.

D.10 Exercises

The following exercises are suggested for this case study:

1. Complete the details of the data structures and algorithms and create a compilable program.

2. Write a simulator for the radar device, and device handlers for the radar, display, and keyboard. Execute the program using simulated input from the radar and actual input from your keyboard. Direct the display output to your CRT and/or hard copy device.

3. Include the transform Get Track Data shown in Figure D-5 with the other transforms that make up the process Monitor Track File, as shown in Figure D-6. Discuss the effect this has on the various design steps (e.g., caller/called decisions, packaging, etc.).

4. Eliminate the process Transport_Coordinates. What does this do to the caller/called style of Monitor_Track_File? Is this a major change?

5. Eliminate the process Extrapolation_Timer. Is this a major change? Discuss the implementation of periodicity in Ada.

6. Depending upon a specific compiler implementation, a rapid input of tracks could prevent extrapolation, display, and track update. Use guards in the select statement of Monitor_Track_File to prevent this. Discuss the general issue of using guards to implement a desired order and precedence of operations.

7. Provide for a separate copy of the entire track file in the process Display_Interface, to provide for better overlap of the display function with other processing. (This is especially important when there is a separate display processor.) Have the Track_File_Monitor provide a copy of the complete track file (only for actual tracks) when requested.

Case Study 5:
Robot Controller

We are here applying our real-time design methodology to the solution of a general purpose robot control system. This problem has been adapted from the example used by Gomaa [GOM84] in his presentation of Design Approach for Real-Time Systems (DARTS). This problem is particularly attractive as an inherently concurrent system. It is sufficiently complex to illustrate the complete methodology, and we can make reasonable problem simplifications to limit the size of our presentation.

E.1 Problem Specification

The functions of our robot system are to control several axes of motion of the robot, and to interface with a control panel and with I/O sensors. The problem is specified in terms of the control panel functions and the required states of the system. The external interfaces are described for the control panel, the robot, and the sensors. The required processing of inputs, outputs, and stored program commands completes the problem specification.

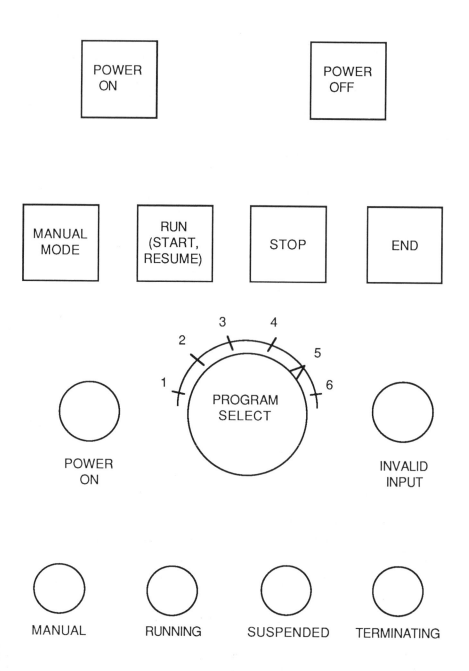

Figure E-1. Control panel layout.

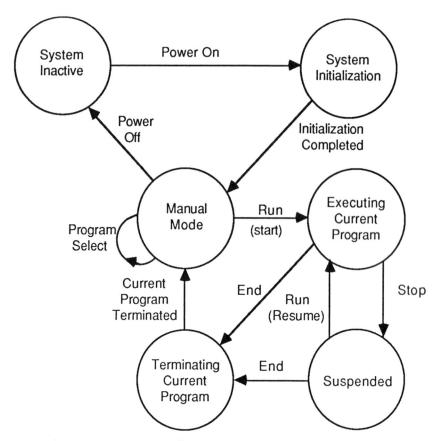

Figure E-2. State-transistion diagram.

E.1.1 Control Panel Functions

The system is controlled by an operator using a set of push buttons and a program selector dial on a control panel, as shown in Figure E-1. The small circles in this figure illustrate lights that indicate the state of the system. The system state-transition diagram is shown in Figure E-2. The system functions associated with the control panel are the following:

1. *Power on.* The operator pushes the ON button to power up the system.

2. *Power off.* The operator pushes the OFF button to turn the system off.

3. *Manual mode.* When the MANUAL button is pushed, the system is waiting until the operator either hits the RUN button for

executing a selected program, or the OFF button to power the system off.

4. *Program select.* The operator can select a particular program to be executed by turning the PROGRAM SELECT switch to the appropriate program identification number. (We can assume that a number of programs are already stored in memory, and can be executed via a proper program identification number.)

5. *Run (Start).* The system transitions to a running state and starts to execute the program selected by the operator.

6. *Stop.* When the STOP button is pushed, the system is suspended and waiting for another panel input of either RUN to resume execution, or END to terminate execution of the current program.

7. *Run (Resume).* Execution will continue with the current program when the RUN button is pushed and the system is in a suspended state.

8. *End.* The current program will terminate from either a running state or a suspended state when the END button is pushed.

E.1.2 External Interfaces

The system must provide the following interfaces to external devices:

1. *Control Panel*

   a. *Input.* Control panel inputs are accepted as commands. The Run (Start) command also needs a program identification number indicated by the program select switch. The format for the commands is a string of ASCII characters (assume the length of the string is one). The program identification number is a single ASCII character.

   b. *Output.* Control panel outputs are created and sent to the control panel to reflect the current state of the system. The format for the outputs is an ASCII string (assume a length of 1).

2. *Robot Axes*

   a. *Input.* Inputs are read from the robot buffer to determine the current position of an axis. Assume a single-digit axis number, and two-digit values for an (x, y, z) triplet.

    b. *Output.* Outputs are created and sent to the robot as axis commands. The format of these commands is ASCII strings. Assume a length of 16 characters for each command.

3. *Sensors*

    a. *Input.* Inputs are received from the sensors as they report critical values. Assume these values are two digit integer numbers.

    b. *Output.* Outputs are created and sent to the sensors for critical values. Assume a single sensor and a critical pressure of x PSI, where x is a two digit integer value.

E.1.3 Processing

The robot control system will perform the following processing functions:

1. *Control panel inputs.* Control panel inputs will be accepted and validated. Invalid commands will not be further processed, and an error signal will be returned to the control panel (this will register on the panel as a light indicating an input error). Valid panel input will be processed, based on the current system state, to determine if a new program should be executed, or if the current program should continue execution. A request to end execution of the current program could also be processed.

2. *Control panel outputs.* Appropriate outputs will be created and sent to the control panel to indicate the current state of the system, and to report invalid input.

3. *Program interpretation.* When a request for the execution of a new set of program commands is accepted, the system will first fetch the program from memory using the program identifier. The system will then interpret the various commands of the pre-stored program. The commands include arithmetic statements, logical statements, I/O commands to the sensors, and motion commands to the robot.

4. *Motion commands.* The system performs mathematical transformations on the data and converts the data to the required format for axis data (axis block). The axis block is sent to an axis controller that interfaces with the robot. The system must be prepared to stop sending axis blocks to the controller when a stop command is received, and to resume the sending when a run command is received (while in the suspended state). The axis controller generates an acknowledgement when it has

completed the processing of an axis block. This acknowledgement is a signal to continue the interpretation of the program statements.

5. *Sensor commands.* Processing is performed to send the required output to the sensors, and to read sensor input. Assume that we read the input after polling a status register to detect a change that indicates that a new value is available.

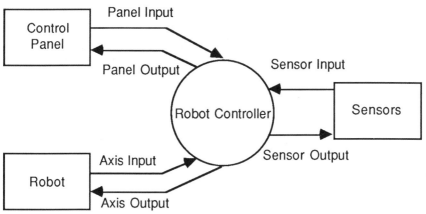

Figure E-3. Context diagram.

E.2 Context Schema

The context schema of the robot controller is illustrated by the context diagram shown in Figure E-3. The single transformation represents the entire system we are going to design and implement. The context diagram also shows the external interfaces between our system and the environment, and the sources and destinations of data flows that enter and leave the system. Inputs are received from the control panel and are used to transition the system to the appropriate state. Outputs are returned to the panel as signals that turn on lights to remind the operator of the current status of the system, and to indicate invalid input. Inputs indicating the current position of the various axes are received from the robot, and outputs are sent to the robot as commands for the proper positioning of the axes. The system sends outputs to the sensors in the form of critical measures such as maximum pressure allowed on an element to be manipulated, or extreme position points for any of the axes or the robot hand. Inputs are received from the sensors periodically, or when any of the critical measures have been reached.

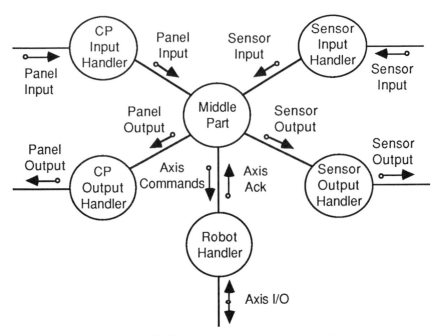

Figure E-4. Preliminary concurrent process graph.

E.3 Edges-In Approach

The Edges-In approach is employed by first determining the processes required to interface with the external devices. Figure E-4 represents a process graph that shows five processes interfacing with the external devices. We have used the first rule of the process selection rules (see Section 9.1) and assigned a process to each external device. The remaining functionality of the robot controller is contained in the "Middle Part" and will be decomposed later. It is possible that during this decomposition some functionality may be shifted from the middle part to the edge processes, and some of these processes may then not be pure device handlers. The five preliminary edge processes are:

1. *CP Input Handler.* This process will interface with the control panel and accept the inputs received via interrupts. The inputs will consist of commands, or a command and a program identification number.

2. *CP Output Handler.* The control panel output handler will be sending signals that reflect the current state of the system, or invalid input commands, to the panel. These signals will be interpreted by the panel and transformed to the appropriate panel lights.

3. *Sensor Input Handler.* This process will scan the sensors periodically to determine if a critical value has been reached.

4. *Sensor Output Handler.* This process is scheduled on demand whenever new sensor output is required.

5. *Robot Handler.* This process interacts with the robot to control the axes. Our preliminary choice is to assign a single process to this function rather than a separate process to axis input and output. The input and output to the axes are closely related and should be handled by a single process.

E.4 Decomposing The Middle Part

To decompose the middle part, we use data flow diagrams (DFDs) and a set of heuristics (Process Selection Rules, Section 9.1) to determine a suitable set of processes. The DFD for the robot controller is shown in Figure E-5 and represents a functional restatement of the problem specification (including the edge functions).

We use our heuristics to combine the transforms of the middle part into processes, as shown in Figure E-6. This figure depicts all the robot controller processes, including the three for the external devices.

The transforms Validate Panel Input and Interpret Panel Input have been combined into the process CP Processor based on temporal cohesion. We want to make sure that the panel input is interpreted immediately after it has been validated. This may not be the case if the transform Interpret Panel Input was located in another process.

The transforms Interpret Program Statement, Process Motion Command, and Process I/O Command have been combined into the process Program Interpreter based on functional cohesion.

The transforms Output Axis Data and Receive Axis Ack have been combined into the process Axis Manager based on temporal cohesion. A new axis block will not be sent to the transform Control Axis until an acknowledgement for the current axis block has been received. Our system would not gain any efficiency by having Receive Axis Ack as a separate process, because Output Axis Data would have to wait for the acknowledgement in either case before it could send the next axis block.

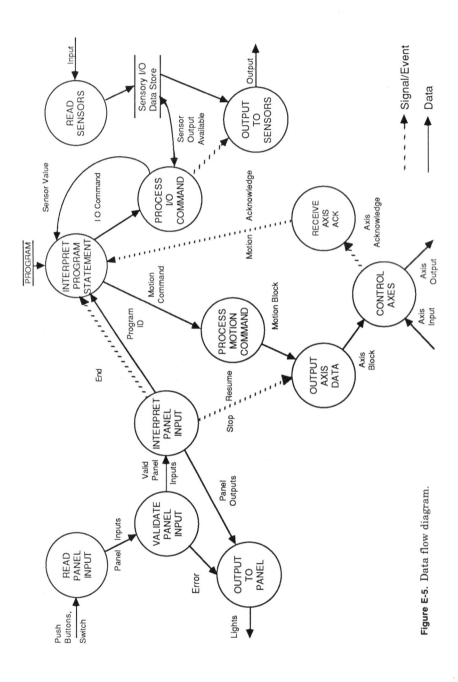

Figure E-5. Data flow diagram.

410

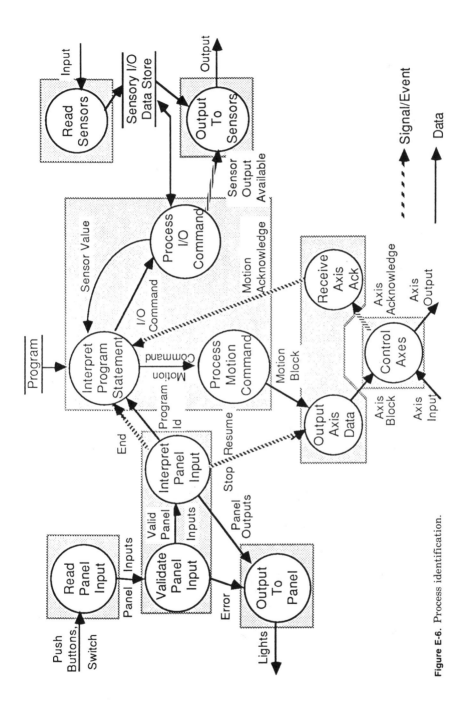

Figure E-6. Process identification.

411

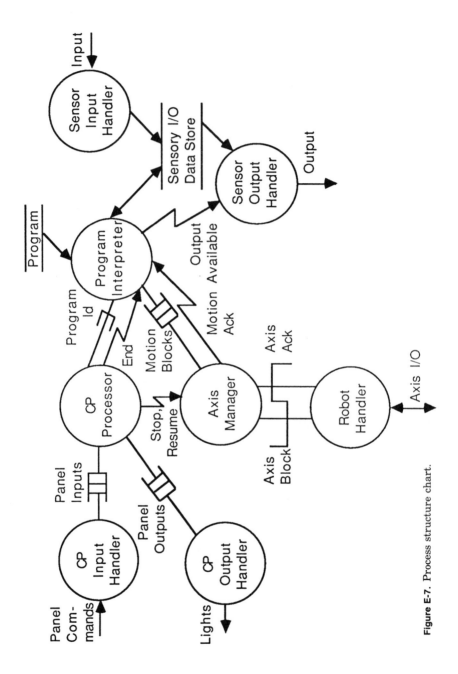

Figure E-7. Process structure chart.

412

E.5   Process Interfaces

The processes identified in Figure E-6 are pictured in the process structure chart shown in Figure E-7, and it includes all the interfaces between the processes. A loose coupling is required for the channel data that is passed between CP Input Handler and CP Processor. The same coupling is required for the channel data passed between CP Processor and CP Output Handler. For a Run (Start) command, CP Processor will pass the program identification number to Program Interpreter. This will occur infrequently, and there is no need to place a buffer between these two processes. When CP Processor encounters an End command, it will send an End signal to Program Interpreter, indicating that the current program should be terminated.

Motion blocks are generated by Program Interpreter and consumed by Axis Manager. Some of these blocks will imply short axis moves, whereas others will imply long moves. The buffer between these two processes will smooth out the differences in the processing time of the various blocks. When Program Interpreter encounters an I/O sensor command, it is required to wait until the current axis motion is completed before it can execute the I/O command. It will wait for an acknowledgement from Axis Manager indicating that all axis blocks associated with a motion have been completed.

When CP Processor receives a Stop or Run (Resume) command from the input panel, it sends these commands as signals to Axis Manager. When Axis Manager receives a motion block from Program Interpreter, it checks to see if a Stop signal has been received. If so, it waits for a Resume signal from CP Processor. If it has not received a Stop signal, or if it receives a Resume signal, Axis Manager sends an axis block to Robot Handler and waits for an acknowledgement that the block has been processed.

The Sensory I/O Data Store pool contains the current values of the sensor data. When Program Interpreter executes an I/O sensor command, it updates the sensory data in the pool and signals Sensor Output Handler that new output is available. Sensor Input Handler periodically scans the sensors and updates the pool when changes are detected.

E.6   Introducing Intermediary Processes

The next step in our methodology is to translate the processes shown in Figure E-7 into Ada application tasks, and to introduce intermediary Ada tasks to implement the required coupling between some of the producer/consumer pairs. The queues between CP Input

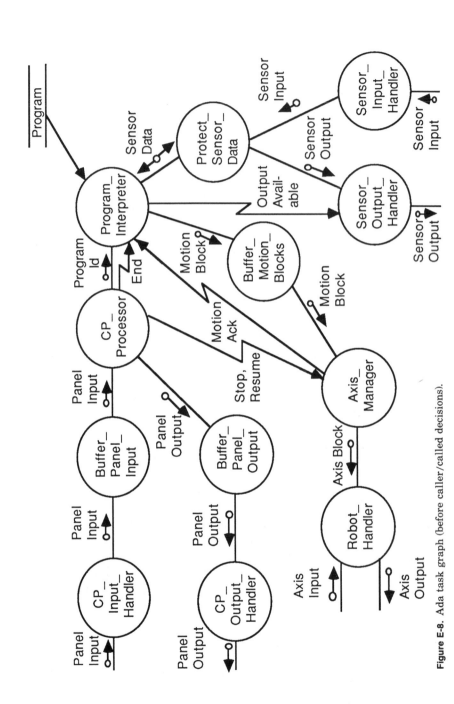

Figure E-8. Ada task graph (before caller/called decisions).

414

Handler and CP Processor for panel inputs, between Program Interpreter and Axis Manager for motion blocks, and between CP Processor and CP Output Handler for panel outputs, are implemented with buffer tasks. The intermediaries (Ada tasks) as shown in Figure E-8 are:

1. Buffer_Panel_Input
2. Buffer_Panel_Output
3. Buffer_Motion_Blocks

The passing of the program identification number between CP Processor and Program Interpreter [as a result of a Run (Start) command], will be implemented using the Ada rendezvous with the identification number as a parameter. The End command will be sent as a signal via a parameterless entry call. The latter will also be the mechanism for sending the signals Stop and Resume from CP Processor to Axis Manager. The Resume signal occurs as a result of a Run (Resume) command. A signal will also be sent via a parameterless entry call by Program Interpreter to inform Sensor Output Handler that new sensor data is ready for output.

The tight coupling between Axis Manager and Robot Handler will be implemented with an entry call from Axis Manager to Robot Handler. The completion of the rendezvous will constitute an implicit acknowledgement, provided that all the processing of the axis block is performed inside the rendezvous.

The process structure illustrated in Figure E-7 shows three processes accessing the pool Sensory I/O Data Store. This pool must be protected to prevent an erroneous program. This protection is provided with the task Protect_Sensor_Data. The pool will be declared inside the task body, and can only be accessed via entry calls.

The complete set of Ada tasks that represents the concurrency model of our solution, is shown in Figure E-8. We can now make the necessary caller/called decision to complete the Ada task interfaces.

E.7 Caller/Called Decisions

Any task that interfaces with interrupt driven devices needs to have a task entry associated with the interrupt, and is thus called with respect to the device. This is the case for CP_Input_Handler, CP_Output_Handler, and Robot_Handler. Sensor_Input_Handler will be polling the sensor for input, and will not be called. Sensor_Output_Handler will be placing output in the sensor hardware buffer, and will have an interrupt entry.

The three buffer tasks are by convention always called. Similarly, the monitor task (Protect_Sensor_Data) protecting the pool is also a pure server.

The task CP_Processor determines the type of command received from the operator and where the command should be sent. Since CP_Processor knows *why* the command is received, it is logical to have it be a caller with respect to Program_Interpreter.

Axis_Manager fetches motion blocks from Buffer_Motion_Blocks and creates axis blocks. It is an algorithmically complex task, and we make it a caller with respect to Robot_Handler.

This completes the caller/called decisions for this set of tasks, and the resulting task interfaces are shown in Figure E-9. We can now proceed with the packaging of the Ada tasks.

E.8 Ada Packaging

The tasks shown in Figure E-9 have been encapsulated in Ada packages as shown in Figure E-10. Packaging decisions have been made based on functionality and minimization of coupling as we described in Chapters 13 and 22. The package Control_Panel contains the two tasks that interface with the control panel, CP_Input_Handler and CP_Output_Handler. The package CP_Processing contains the task CP_Processor and the two buffer tasks for control panel input and output. The package Motion includes the task Program_Interpreter and the buffer task for motion blocks. The package Sensors includes the two tasks that interface with the sensors, and the monitor task that protects the sensor pool. The package Axis contains the task Axis Manager that creates the axis blocks, and the task Robot_Handler that controls the axes. We have now determined the structure of our real-time system and can next start to implement this design using an Ada PDL.

E.9 Program Design Language (PDL)

The PDL phase consists of transforming the design described in Figure E-10 into a programming structure using Ada constructs. The top-level design illustrates the overall structure using Ada package specifications and bodies. The details of of the algorithms are deferred to the detailed design using the *separate* construct. A description of the top-level design phase is given below, followed by the detailed design.

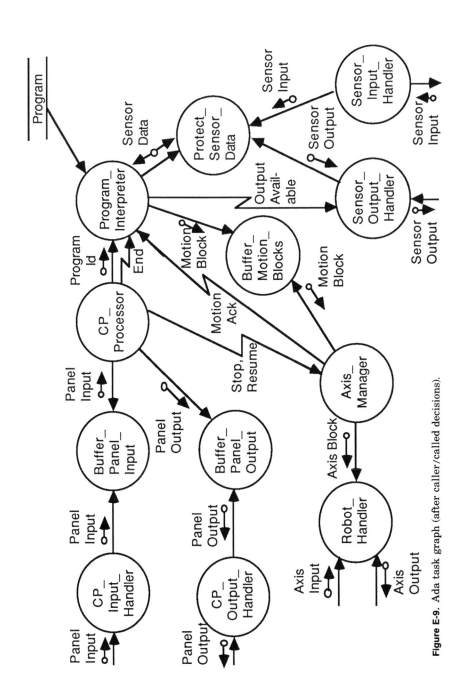

Figure E-9. Ada task graph (after caller/called decisions).

417

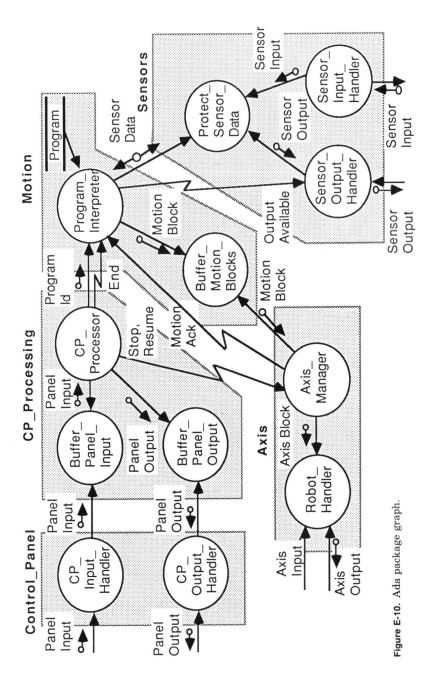

Figure E-10. Ada package graph.

418

```
----------- Global Definitions -----------

package Definitions is
  Max_CP_Chars       : constant := 2;   -- max length of CP command
  Max_CP_Input       : constant := 10;  -- max input to be buffered
  Max_CP_Output      : constant := 10;  -- max output to be buffered
  Max_Commands       : constant := 36;  -- max commands in a program
  Command_Length     : constant := 16;  -- length of program command
  Max_Motion_Chars   : constant := 24;  -- max length of Motion block
  Max_Axis_Chars     : constant := 12;  -- max length of Axis block
  Max_Motion_Blocks  : constant := 10;  -- max motion blocks to buffer
  Max_Sensory_Data   : constant := 8;   -- max sensory data to buffer
  Sensor_Data_Length : constant := 26;  -- max length of sensory data
  Sensor_Scan_Period : constant Duration := 3.0;
                                  -- scan sensors every 3 seconds

  subtype CP_Index        is Positive range 1 .. Max_CP_Chars;
  subtype Motion_Index    is Positive range 1 .. Max_Motion_Chars;
  subtype Axis_Index      is Positive range 1 .. Max_Axis_Chars;
  subtype CP_Input        is String (CP_Index);
  subtype CP_Output       is Integer range 1 .. 9;
  subtype Motion_Command  is String (1 .. Command_Length);
  subtype Axis_Command    is String (1 .. Command_Length);
  subtype Motion_Block    is String (Motion_Index);
  subtype Axis_Block      is String (Axis_Index);
  subtype Sensory_Data    is String (1 .. Sensor_Data_Length);
  subtype Program_Command is String (1 .. Command_Length);
  subtype Program_Id      is Character;
  subtype Command_Index   is Positive range 1 .. Max_Commands;

  type Command_Type is
    record
      Index   : Positive;
      Command : Program_Command;
    end record;

  type CP_Command    is (Run_Start, Stop, End_Program, Run_Resume);
  type CP_Input_Code is ('S', 'H', 'E', 'R');
                      -- S: Start;  H: Stop;  E: End;  R: Run;
```

Figure E-11. Definitions (package specification).

```
type CP_Output_Code is (R_On_M_Off, T_On_M_On, S_Off_R_On,
                        R_Off_S_On, Invalid_On);

        -- R_On_M_Off : Running on, Manual off
        -- T_On_M_On  : Terminating on, Manual on
        -- S_Off_R_On : Suspended off, Running on
        -- R_Off_S_On : Running off, Suspended on
        -- Invalid_On : Invalid on
    for CP_Output_Code use (1, 2, 3, 4, 9);

end Definitions;
```

Figure E-11 *(continued).* Definitions (package specification).

```
--------- Hardware Dependent Constants ---------

package Robot_HDP is

    CP_In_Int_Address        : constant := 16#00A0#; -- interrupt loc
    CP_In_Buff_Address       : constant := 16#00A4#; -- h/w buffer loc

    CP_Out_Int_Address       : constant := 16#00B0#;
    CP_Out_Buff_Address      : constant := 16#00B4#;

    Axis_In_Int_Address      : constant := 16#00C0#;
    Axis_In_Buff_Address     : constant := 16#00C4#;

    Axis_Out_Int_Address     : constant := 16#00D0#;
    Axis_Out_Buff_Address    : constant := 16#00D4#;

    Sensor_In_Int_Address    : constant := 16#00E0#;
    Sensor_In_Buff_Address   : constant := 16#00E4#;

    Sensor_Out_Int_Address   : constant := 16#00E8#;
    Sensor_Out_Buff_Address  : constant := 16#00F0#;
end Robot_HDP;
```

Figure E-12. Robot_HPD (package specification).

E.9.1 Top-Level Design

The robot controller top-level design is as follows:

1. *Helper packages.* Helper packages must be prepared in a bottom-up fashion before we start the top-level design of the

```
generic
  Size : in Natural := 20;
  type Item is private;

package Buffer_Overwrite is
  procedure Enqueue (I : in Item);
  procedure Dequeue (I : out Item);
  pragma Inline (Enqueue, Dequeue);
end Buffer_Overwrite;

package body Buffer_Overwrite is
  task Buffer is
    entry Enqueue (I : in Item);
    entry Dequeue (I : out Item);
  end Buffer;

  task body Buffer is separate;

  procedure Enqueue (I : in Item) is
  begin
    Buffer.Enqueue (I);
  end Enqueue;

  procedure Dequeue (I : out Item) is
  begin
    Buffer.Dequeue (I);
  end Dequeue;

end Buffer_Overwrite;
```

Figure E-13. Buffer_Overwrite (package specification and body).

application packages in a top-down fashion. The following components are used by the application packages:

a. Definitions. This package contains constants, adaptation parameters, types, and subtypes that are used globally throughout the program. The Ada code is shown in Figure E-11.

b. Robot_HDP. This package contains hardware dependencies for the devices that our tasks need to interface with. Absolute addresses (fictitious) are listed for interrupts and buffers for the control panel input and output, the robot axes, and the sensors. The Ada code is shown in Figure E-12.

```
package Control_Panel is

  -- Calls
    -- CP_Processing.Take_CP_Input
    -- CP_Processing.Provide_CP_Output

end Control_Panel;


with Robot_HDP;  use Robot_HDP;
package body Control_Panel is

  task CP_Input_Handler is
    entry CP_In_Interrupt;
    for CP_In_Interrupt use at CP_In_Int_Address;
    -- Calls
      -- CP_Processing.Take_CP_Input
  end CP_Input_Handler;

  task CP_Output_Handler is
    entry CP_Out_Interrupt;
    for CP_Out_Interrupt use at CP_Out_Int_Address;
    -- Calls
      -- CP_Processing.Provide_CP_Output
  end CP_Output_Handler;

  task body CP_Input_Handler  is separate;
  task body CP_Output_Handler is separate;

end Control_Panel;
```

Figure E-14. Control_Panel (package specification and body).

2. *Communication.* Only a single communication package was used in this solution:

   a. Buffer_Overwrite. The generic package specification shown in Figure E-13 contains generic parameters for the size of the buffer, and the type of elements to be stored. This particular buffer will be implemented to overwrite the oldest elements, rather than to lose input when the buffer is full.

3. *Application packages.* The following application packages were prepared for the robot controller top-level design:

```
with Definitions;  use Definitions;

package CP_Processing is

  procedure Take_CP_Input (T : in CP_Input);
  procedure Provide_CP_Output (CP_Out : out CP_Output_Code);

  -- Calls
    -- Motion.Start_Program
    -- Motion.End_Event
    -- Axis.Stop
    -- Axis.Resume

end CP_Processing;


with Buffer_Overwrite;
package body CP_Processing is

    task CP_Processor is
    -- Calls
      -- Buffer_Panel_Input.Dequeue
      -- Validate_Panel_Input
      -- Send_Input_Command
      -- Send_Panel_Output
    end CP_Processor;

-- Instantiate buffer task for CP input

    package Buffer_Panel_Input is new Buffer_Overwrite
        (Size    => Max_CP_Input,
         Item    => CP_Input);


  -- Instantiate buffer task for CP output

    package Buffer_Panel_Output is new Buffer_Overwrite
        (Size    => Max_CP_Output,
         Item    => CP_Output_Code);
```

Figure E-15. CP_Processing (package specification and body).

```
package CP_Manager is

   procedure Validate_Panel_Input (Panel_Input : in      CP_Input;
                                   Valid       : out     Boolean;
                                   Command     : in out  CP_Command;
                                   Program_No  : out     Program_Id);

   procedure Send_Input_Command  (Command : in out CP_Command;
                                  Id      : in     Program_Id);

   procedure Send_Panel_Output   (Command : in out CP_Command;
                                  Valid   : in     Boolean);
end CP_Manager;

package body CP_Manager is separate;
task body CP_Processor  is separate;

procedure Take_CP_Input (T : in CP_Input) is
begin
   Buffer_Panel_Input.Enqueue (T);
end Take_CP_Input;

procedure Provide_CP_Output (CP_Out : out CP_Output_Code) is
begin
   Buffer_Panel_Output.Dequeue (CP_Out);
end Provide_CP_Output;

end CP_Processing;
```

Figure E-15 *(continued).* CP_Processing (package specification and body).

a. Control_Panel. The package specification and body are shown in Figure E-14. The specification part only contains comments for calls made to program units in another package. Entrance procedures are not required here, since no calls are made from other packages. The body part contains the specification of the two tasks that interface with the control panel. The interrupt entries are associated with hardware addresses via the importation of Robot_HDP. The details of the task implementations are deferred with the *separate* statement.

b. CP_Processing. The package specification and body are shown in Figure E-15. The specification part contains the declaration of entrance procedures for access to the panel

```
package Axis is
  procedure Stop;
  procedure Resume;
  -- Calls
    -- Motion.Motion_Ack
    -- Motion.Dequeue_Motion_Block
end Axis;

with Definitions;  use Definitions;
with Robot_HDP;    use Robot_HDP;
package body Axis is

  procedure Prepare_Axis_Block (M : in Motion_Block;
                                A : out Axis_Block) is separate;
  task Robot_Handler is
    entry Take_Block (B : in Axis_Block);

    entry Axis_In_Interrupt;
    for Axis_In_Interrupt use at Axis_In_Int_Address;

    entry Axis_Out_Interrupt;
    for Axis_Out_Interrupt use at Axis_Out_Int_Address;
  end Robot_Handler;

  task Axis_Manager is
    entry Stop;
    entry Resume;
    -- Calls
      -- Motion.Motion_Ack
      -- Motion.Dequeue_Motion_Block
  end Axis_Manager;

  task body Robot_Handler is separate;
  task body Axis_Manager  is separate;

  procedure Stop is
  begin
    Axis_Manager.Stop;
  end Stop;

  procedure Resume is
  begin
    Axis_Manager.Resume;
  end Resume;

end Axis;
```

Figure E-16. Axis (package specification and body).

```
with Definitions;   use Definitions;
package Motion is
  procedure Start_Program (Id : in Program_Id);
  procedure End_Event;
  procedure Motion_Ack;
  procedure Dequeue_Motion_Block (M : out Motion_Block);
  -- Calls
    -- Sensors.Update_Data
    -- Sensors.Output_Available
    -- Sensors.Provide_Sensor_Data
end Motion;


with Buffer_Overwrite;
package body Motion is

-- Instantiate buffer task for motion blocks

    package Buffer_Motion_Blocks is new Buffer_Overwrite
         (Size    => Max_Motion_Blocks,
          Item    => Motion_Block);

  package Program_Commands is
    function End_Of_Program return Boolean;
    function Motion_Command (C : Command_Index) return Boolean;
    function Sensor_Input_Command (I : Command_Index) return Boolean;
    procedure Process_Motion_Command (I : in Command_Index;
                                      M : out Motion_Block);
    procedure Process_Sensor_Output  (I : in Command_Index;
                                      S : out Sensory_Data);
    procedure Process_Sensor_Input   (I : in Command_Index;
                                      S : out Sensory_Data);
  end Program_Commands;

  package body Program_Commands is separate;

  task Program_Interpreter is
    entry Start_Program (Id : in Program_Id);
    entry End_Event;
    entry Motion_Ack;
```

Figure E-17. Motion (package specification and body).

```
-- Calls
    -- Buffer_Motion_Blocks.Enqueue
    -- Sensors.Update_Data
    -- Sensors.Output_Available
    -- Sensors.Provide_Sensor_Data
    -- Motion_Command (function)
    -- Process_Motion_Command
    -- Process_Sensor_Output
    -- Process_Sensor_Input
end Program_Interpreter;

task body Program_Interpreter is separate;

procedure Start_Program (Id : in Program_Id) is
begin
    Program_Interpreter.Start_Program (Id);
end Start_Program;

procedure End_Event is
begin
    Program_Interpreter.End_Event;
end End_Event;

procedure Motion_Ack is
begin
    Program_Interpreter.Motion_Ack;
end Motion_Ack;

procedure Dequeue_Motion_Block (M : out Motion_Block) is
begin
    Buffer_Motion_Blocks.Dequeue (M);
end Dequeue_Motion_Block;

end Motion;
```

Figure E-17 *(continued)*. Motion (package specification and body).

input and output buffers. The body part contains the task declaration for CP_Processor which validates and transfers panel input and prepares panel output. Generic packages are instantiated for buffer tasks of panel input and output. The nested package CP_Manager is an object that will be used by the task CP_Processor. The implementations of CP_Processor and CP_Manager have been deferred.

```
with Definitions;  use Definitions;
package Sensors is

  procedure Update_Data (D : in out Sensory_Data);
  procedure Output_Available;
  procedure Provide_Sensor_Data (S : out Sensory_Data);
end Sensors;

with Robot_HDP;  use Robot_HDP;
package body Sensors is

  task Protect_Sensor_Data is
    entry Update_Data (D : in out Sensory_Data);
    entry Take_Input (D : in Sensory_Data);
    entry Provide_Output (D : out Sensory_Data);
  end Protect_Sensor_Data;

  task Sensor_Output_Handler is
    entry Output_Available;
    entry Sensor_Output;
    for Sensor_Output use at Sensor_Out_Int_Address;

    -- Calls
      -- Protect_Sensor_Data.Provide_Output
    -- H/W interface
      -- Places output in the sensor H/W buffer
  end Sensor_Output_Handler;

  task Sensor_Input_Handler is
    -- Calls
      -- Protect_Sensor_Data.Take_Input
    -- H/W interface
      -- Polls sensors for new input data
  end Sensor_Input_Handler;

  task body Protect_Sensor_Data   is separate;
  task body Sensor_Output_Handler is separate;
  task body Sensor_Input_Handler  is separate;

  procedure Update_Data (D : in out Sensory_Data) is
  begin
    Protect_Sensor_Data.Update_Data (D);
  end Update_Data;
```

Figure E-18. Sensors (package specification and body).

```
procedure Output_Available is
begin
  Sensor_Output_Handler.Output_Available;
end Output_Available;

procedure Provide_Sensor_Data (S : out Sensory_Data) is
begin
  Protect_Sensor_Data.Provide_Output (S);
end Provide_Sensor_Data;

end Sensors;
```

Figure E-18 *(continued).* Sensors (package specification and body).

```
with Control_Panel;
procedure Robot_Controller is
begin
  null;
end Robot_Controller;
```

Figure E-19. Robot_Controller (package specification and body).

c. Axis. The package specification shown in Figure E-16 contains parameterless entrance procedures for the signals Stop and Resume. The package body contains the declarations for the procedure Prepare_Axis_Block, and the tasks Robot_Handler and Axis_Manager. The implementations of these three program units are deferred by using the *separate* construct.

d. Motion. The package specification and body are shown in Figure E-17. Entrance procedures in the specification part include Start_Program and Dequeue_Motion_Block, and End_Event and Motion_Ack for the signals End (of current program) and Motion Block Acknowledgement. The package body includes an instantiation of the generic buffer package for buffering of motion blocks, a declaration of the virtual machine Program_Commands, and a declaration of the task Program_Interpreter. The implementations of the application machine and the task are deferred.

e. Sensors. The package specification and body for Sensors is shown in Figure E-18. The specification includes entrance procedures for access to the sensor pool. The package body contains declarations for the task that protects the sensor pool, and the tasks that interface with the sensors. The task implementations are deferred.

4. *Main procedure.* Ada requires a main program to start the elaboration process of packages and their objects, subprograms, and tasks. This main procedure is called Robot_Controller and is shown in Figure E-19. This procedure simply imports the package Control_Panel and has a *null* body. This is sufficient to start the elaboration of the other packages (which contain their own *with* clauses) and the activation of tasks encapsulated within these packages. Code to be used during the testing phase could be placed in this driver: declarations of simulation tasks and subprograms, test data, and so on.

This completes the top-level design phase. The remaining part of the design process is to supply the Ada subunits that contain the details of the robot controller implementation.

E.9.2 Detailed Design

The detailed design consists of supplying all the subunits that were deferred during the top-level design, and having the Ada compiler check interfaces and proper importation of required entities. These entities should be imported by having the subunits *with* the necessary packages and subprograms, if possible. This will reduce the amount of recompilation required if the imported library units are changed.

The interfaces between the various subprograms and tasks in the application packages are depicted in the Ada structure graph in Figure E-20.

The paragraphs that follow describe the subunits for the communication package and application packages specified during the top-level design phase.

1. *Communication packages*

    a. Buffer_Overwrite. The implementation of this subunit is shown in Figure E-21 as complete code, with comments to explain the details of the algorithm.

2. *Application packages*

    a. Control_Panel subunits

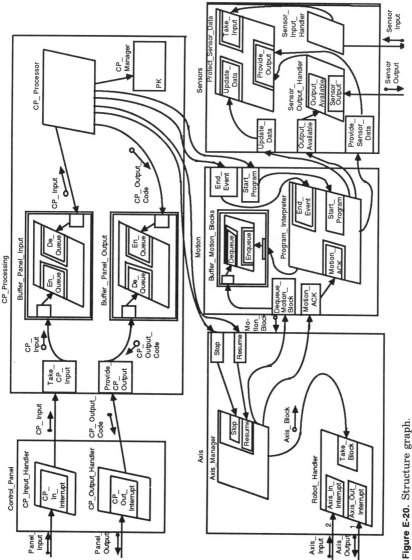

Figure E-20. Structure graph.

431

```ada
separate (Buffer_Overwrite)

task body Buffer is
  subtype Index_Type is Positive range 1 .. Size;
  subtype Count_Type is Natural  range 0 .. Size;

  Buf : array (Index_Type) of Item;
  Insert : Index_Type := 1;
  Remove : Index_Type := 1;
  Count  : Count_Type := 0;
begin
  loop
    select
      accept Enqueue (I : in Item) do
        Buf (Insert) := I;
      end Enqueue;
      Insert := (Insert mod Buf'Last) + 1;

      if (Insert = Remove) then
        Remove := (Remove mod Buf'Last) + 1;
      else
        Count  := Count + 1;
      end if;
        -- If (Insert = Remove), the buffer is full.
        -- We will put the new element on
        -- top of the oldest.  We advance the Remove
        -- pointer to prevent the element just inserted
        -- from being removed next.  We do not
        -- increment Count.
    or
      when Count > 0 =>
        accept Dequeue (I : out Item) do
          I := Buf (Remove);
        end Dequeue;
        Remove := (Remove mod Buf'Last) + 1;
        Count  := Count - 1;
    or
      terminate;
    end select;
  end loop;
end Buffer;
```

Figure E-21. Buffer (task body).

```
with Definitions;  use Definitions;
with CP_Processing;

separate (Control_Panel)

task body CP_Input_Handler is
  Input : CP_Input;
  Buffer : Character;
  for Buffer use at CP_In_Buff_Address;

begin
  loop
    for I in CP_Input'Range loop
      accept CP_In_Interrupt;
      Input (I) := Buffer;
    end loop;

    CP_Processing.Take_CP_Input (Input);  -- save input in buffer
  end loop;
end CP_Input_Handler;
```

Figure E-22. CP_Input_Handler (task body).

```
with Definitions;  use Definitions;
with CP_Processing;
separate (Control_Panel)

task body CP_Output_Handler is
  Output_Buffer : CP_Output_Code;
  for Output_Buffer use at CP_Out_Buff_Address;

begin
  loop
    CP_Processing.Provide_CP_Output (Output_Buffer);

    accept CP_Out_Interrupt; -- wait here until CP is ready for
                             -- next output
  end loop;
end CP_Output_Handler;
```

Figure E-23. CP_Output_Handler (task body).

```
separate (CP_Processing)

task body CP_Processor is
  use CP_Manager;
  Panel_Input : CP_Input;
  Valid       : Boolean;
  Command     : CP_Command;
  Program_No  : Program_Id;
begin
  loop
    Buffer_Panel_Input.Dequeue (Panel_Input);
    Validate_Panel_Input (Panel_Input, Valid, Command, Program_No);

    if Valid then
      Send_Input_Command (Command, Program_No);
    end if;

    Send_Panel_Output (Command, Valid);
  end loop;
end CP_Processor;
```

Figure E-24. CP_Processor (task body).

    i. Cp_Input_Handler. Shown in Figure E-22.

    ii. CP_Output_Handler. Shown in Figure E-23.

  b. CP_Processing subunits

    i. CP_Processor. Shown in Figure E-24. The structure of the program within this task is shown in Figure E-25.

    ii. CP_Manager. Shown in Figure E-26. The composition of the data manager is illustrated in Figure E-27, and the code for the procedures in Figures E-28 through E-32. Figure E-27 represents a graphical description of a state machine.

  c. Axis subunits

    i. Axis_Manager. Shown in Figure E-33.

    ii. Robot_Handler. Shown in Figure E-34.

    iii. Prepare_Axis_Block. Shown in Figure E-35.

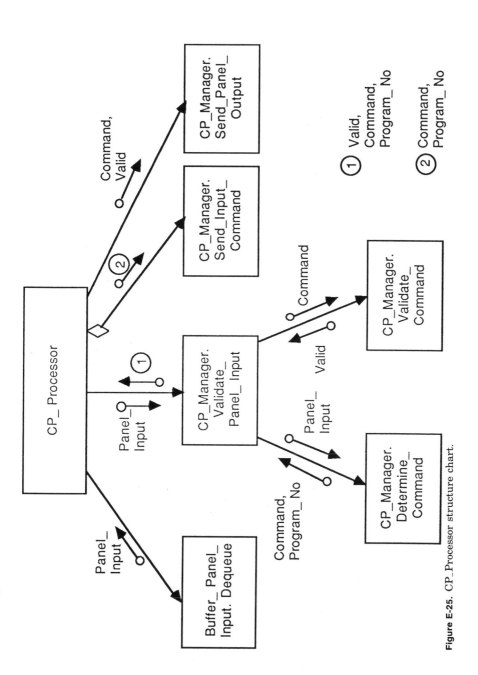

Figure E-25. CP_Processor structure chart.

435

```
separate (CP_Processing)
package body CP_Manager is

   type State_Type  is (Manual, Running, Suspended);
   State_Variable : State_Type := Manual;

   procedure Determine_Command (Panel_Input : in      CP_Input;
                                Command     : in out CP_Command;
                                Program_No  : out     Program_Id)
                                             is separate;


   procedure Validate_Command  (Command : in out CP_Command;
                                Valid   : out     Boolean)
                                             is separate;


   procedure Validate_Panel_Input (Panel_Input : in      CP_Input;
                                   Valid       : out     Boolean;
                                   Command     : in out CP_Command;
                                   Program_No  : out     Program_Id)
                                                is separate;


   procedure Send_Input_Command  (Command : in out CP_Command;
                                  Id      : in      Program_Id)
                                               is separate;


   procedure Send_Panel_Output  (Command : in out CP_Command;
                                 Valid   : in      Boolean)
                                              is separate;

end CP_Manager;
```

Figure E-26. CP_Manager (package body).

d.   Motion subunits

    i.   Program_Commands. Shown in Figure E-36.

    ii.   Program_Interpreter. Shown in Figure E-37.

e.   Sensors subunits

    i.   Sensor_Input_Handler. Shown in Figure E-38.

    ii.   Sensor_Output_Handler. Shown in Figure E-39.

    iii.   Protect_Sensor_Data. Shown in Figure E-40.

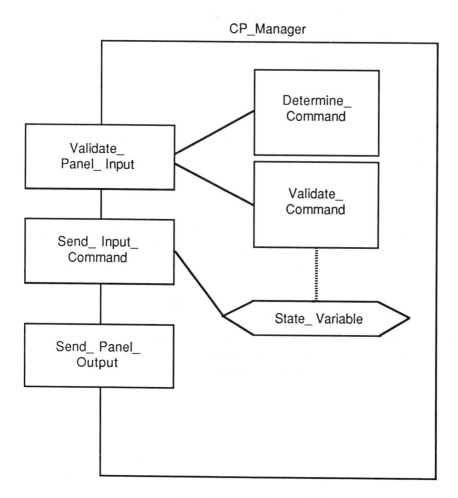

Figure E-27. CP_Manager object.

The detailed design phase is now completed, and any remaining code (for example, for the procedure Prepare_Axis_Block) and test drivers and simulators) are supplied during the code and unit test phase.

E.10 Exercises

The following exercises are suggested for this case study:

1. For the interface shown in Figure E-7 as a buffer between the producer/consumer pair CP Input Handler and CP Processor,

```
separate (CP_Processing.CP_Manager)

procedure Validate_Panel_Input (Panel_Input : in      CP_Input;
                                Valid       : out     Boolean;
                                Command     : in out  CP_Command;
                                Program_No  : out     Program_Id) is

begin
  Determine_Command (Panel_Input, Command, Program_No);
  Validate_Command  (Command, Valid);
end Validate_Panel_Input;
```

Figure E-28. Validate_Panel_Input (procedure body).

replace the buffer with a single-item relay. Redesign the system, and discuss the effect on the various design steps.

2. Implement the following change in the problem specification: If the program interpreter detects a sensor value that exceeds a critical value, it immediately sends a signal to the robot handler to halt the current motion command.

3. Locate coordinate transformation programs that are written in Fortran, C, or Pascal, and interface to them from your Ada program using the pragma Interface.

```
separate (CP_Processing.CP_Manager)
procedure Determine_Command (Panel_Input : in     CP_Input;
                             Command     : in out CP_Command;
                             Program_No  : out    Program_Id) is

begin
  Program_No := ' ';  -- initialize with blank

  case Panel_Input (1) is
    when 'S' =>
      Command    := Run_Start;
      Program_No := Panel_Input (2);

    when 'H' =>
      Command := Stop;

    when 'E' =>
      Command := End_Program;

    when 'R' =>
      Command := Run_Resume;

    when others =>
      null;

  end case;

end Determine_Command;
```

Figure E-29. Determine_Command (procedure body).

```
separate (CP_Processing.CP_Manager)

procedure Validate_Command   (Command : in out CP_Command;
                              Valid   : out     Boolean) is
begin
  case Command is

    when Run_Start =>
      Valid := (State_Variable = Manual);

    when Stop =>
      Valid := (State_Variable = Running);

    when End_Program =>
      Valid := ((State_Variable = Running) or
               (State_Variable = Suspended));

    when Run_Resume =>
      Valid := (State_Variable = Suspended);

  end case;

end Validate_Command;
```

Figure E-30. Validate_Command (procedure body).

```
with Motion;
with Axis;
separate (CP_Processing.CP_Manager)

procedure Send_Input_Command  (Command : in out CP_Command;
                               Id      : in      Program_Id) is
begin
  case Command is
    when Run_Start =>
      Motion.Start_Program (Id);
      State_Variable := Running;

    when Stop =>
      Axis.Stop;
      State_Variable := Suspended;

    when End_Program =>
      Motion.End_Event;
      State_Variable := Manual;

    when Run_Resume =>
      Axis.Resume;
      State_Variable := Running;
  end case;

end Send_Input_Command;
```

Figure E-31. Send_Input_Command (procedure body).

```
separate (CP_Processing.CP_Manager)

procedure Send_Panel_Output    (Command : in out CP_Command;
                                Valid   : in      Boolean) is

  Output_Code : CP_Output_Code := Invalid_On;

begin
  if Valid then
    case Command is
      when Run_Start =>
       Output_Code := R_On_M_off;

      when Stop =>
        Output_Code := R_Off_S_On;

      when End_Program =>
        Output_Code := T_On_M_On;

      when Run_Resume =>
        Output_Code := S_Off_R_On;

    end case;
  end if;

  Buffer_Panel_Output.Enqueue (Output_Code);
end Send_Panel_Output;
```

Figure E-32. Send_Panel_Output (procedure body).

```
with Motion;
separate (Axis)

task body Axis_Manager is
  Stop_Flag    : Boolean := False;
  Axis_Motion : Motion_Block;
  Axis_Output : Axis_Block;
begin
  loop
    select
      accept Stop;
      Stop_Flag := True;
    else
      if Stop_Flag then
        accept Resume;
        Stop_Flag := False;
      end if;

      Motion.Dequeue_Motion_Block (Axis_Motion);
      Prepare_Axis_Block (Axis_Motion, Axis_Output);

      Robot_Handler.Take_Block (Axis_Output);
      -- Task waits here for block completion
      Motion.Motion_Ack;
    end select;
  end loop;
end Axis_Manager;
```

Figure E-33. Axis_Manager (task body).

```
separate (Axis)

task body Robot_Handler is
  Local_Axis : Axis_Block;
begin
  loop
    accept Take_Block (B : in Axis_Block) do
      Local_Axis := B;

      accept Axis_Out_Interrupt;
        -- send axis output

      accept Axis_In_Interrupt;
        -- process axis input
    end Take_Block;
  end loop;
end Robot_Handler;
```

Figure E-34. Robot_Handler (task body).

```
separate (Axis)

procedure Prepare_Axis_Block (M : in Motion_Block;
                              A : out Axis_Block) is
begin
  -- while not end of motion block loop
    -- determine axis
    -- determine motion for this axis
    -- prepare output for this axis
  -- end loop
  null;   --\
end Prepare_Axis_Block;
```

Figure E-35. Prepare_Axis_Block (task body).

```
separate (Motion)
package body Program_Commands is
  function End_Of_Program return Boolean is separate;
  function Motion_Command (C : Command_Index) return Boolean
                                               is separate;
  function Sensor_Input_Command (I : Command_Index) return Boolean
                                               is separate;
  procedure Process_Motion_Command (I : in Command_Index;
                                    M : out Motion_Block)
                                               is separate;
  procedure Process_Sensor_Output  (I : in Command_Index;
                                    S : out Sensory_Data)
                                               is separate;
  procedure Process_Sensor_Input   (I : in Command_Index;
                                    S : out Sensory_Data)
                                               is separate;
end Program_Commands;
```

Figure E-36. Program_Commands (task body).

```
with Sensors;
separate (Motion)

task body Program_Interpreter is
  use Program_Commands;
  Program_No   : Program_Id;
  Sensor_Data  : Sensory_Data;
  Motion       : Motion_Block;
  Index        : Command_Index := 1;
begin
  loop
    accept Start_Program (Id : in Program_Id) do
      Program_No := Id;
    end Start_Program;

    -- Fetch program using Program_No

    Interpreting_Loop:
    while not End_Of_Program loop
      select
        accept End_Event;
        exit Interpreting_Loop;
      else
        if Program_Commands.Motion_Command (Index) then
          Process_Motion_Command (Index, Motion);
          Buffer_Motion_Blocks.Enqueue (Motion);
          Index := Index + 1;
        else
          accept Motion_ACK;
          while not Program_Commands.Motion_Command (Index) loop
            if Sensor_Input_Command (Index) then
              Sensors.Provide_Sensor_Data (Sensor_Data);
              Process_Sensor_Input (Index, Sensor_Data);
            else
              Process_Sensor_Output (Index, Sensor_Data);
              Sensors.Update_Data (Sensor_Data);
              Sensors.Output_Available;
            end if;
            Index := Index + 1;
          end loop;
        end if;
      end select;
```

Figure E-37. Program_Interpreter (task body).

```
      select   -- interpreting suspended until an End event or
               -- completion of a set of axis blocks
        accept End_Event;
        exit Interpreting_Loop;  -- end of current program
      or
        accept Motion_ACK;
      or
        terminate;
      end select;
    end loop Interpreting_Loop;
  end loop;
end Program_Interpreter;
```

Figure E-37 *(continued)*. Program_Interpreter (task body).

```
separate (Sensors)

task body Sensor_Input_Handler is

  type Status_Register is array (0 .. 15) of Boolean;
  Sensor_Register : Status_Register;
  for Sensor_Register use at 16#0040#;
  New_Sensor_Data : Boolean renames Sensor_Register (3);
                          -- we want to access bit 3
  Sensor_Input : Sensory_Data;
  for Sensor_Input use at Sensor_In_Buff_Address;

  Sensor_Value : Sensory_Data;
begin
  loop
    while not New_Sensor_Data loop
      delay Sensor_Scan_Period; -- not busy wait
    end loop;

    Sensor_Value := Sensor_Input;

    Protect_Sensor_Data.Take_Input (Sensor_Value);
  end loop;
end Sensor_Input_Handler;
```

Figure E-38. Sensor_Input_Handler (task body).

```
separate (Sensors)
task body Sensor_Output_Handler is
  Sensor_Buffer : Character;
  for Sensor_Buffer use at Sensor_Out_Buff_Address;

  Sensor_Output_Data : Sensory_Data;
begin
  loop
    accept Output_Available;
    Protect_Sensor_Data.Provide_Output (Sensor_Output_Data);

    for I in Sensor_Output_Data'Range loop
      Sensor_Buffer := Sensor_Output_Data (I);
      accept Sensor_Output;
    end loop;

  end loop;
end Sensor_Output_Handler;
```

Figure E-39. Sensor_Output_Handler (task body).

```
separate (Sensors)
task body Protect_Sensor_Data is

begin
  loop
    select
      accept Update_Data (D : in out Sensory_Data) do
        -- update the data in the sensor pool from a command
        null; --\
      end Update_Data;
    or
      accept Provide_Output (D : out Sensory_Data) do
        -- furnish data from the sensor pool
        null; --\
      end Provide_Output;
    or
      accept Take_Input (D : in Sensory_Data) do
        -- accept data from the sensors
        null; --\
      end Take_Input;
    or
      terminate;
    end select;
  end loop;
end Protect_Sensor_Data;
```

Figure E-40. Protect_Sensor_Data (task body).

References

ABB83   Abbott, R. J.: Program Design by Informal English Description, *Comm. ACM*, vol. 26, no. 11, November 1983.

ALL81   Allworth, S. T.: *Introduction to Real-Time Software Design*, Springer-Verlag, New York, 1981.

AND83   Andrews, G. R., and Schneider, F. B.: Concepts and Notations for Concurrent Programming, *Computing Surveys*, vol. 15, no. 1, March 1983.

AUS85   Ausnit, C. N., et al.: *Ada in Practice*, Springer-Verlag, New York, 1985.

BAR84   Barnes, J. G. P.: *Programming in Ada*, 2nd ed., Addison-Wesley, Reading, Mass., 1984.

BEN82   Ben-Ari, M.: *Principles of Concurrent Programming*, Prentice-Hall International, Englewood Cliffs, N.J., 1982.

BIR85   Birrell, N. D. and Ould, M. A.: *A Practical Handbook for Software Development*, Cambridge University Press, Cambridge, England, 1985.

BOO83   Booch, G.: *Software Engineering with Ada*, Benjamin/Cummings, Menlo Park, Calif., 1983.

BOO86   Booch, G.: Object-Oriented Development, *IEEE Transactions on Software Engineering*, vol. SE-12, no. 2, February 1986.

BOO87   Booch, G.: *Software Components with Ada*, Benjamin/ Cummings, Menlo Park, Calif., 1987.

BRI73   Brinch Hansen, P.: Concurrent Programming Concepts, *Computing Surveys*, vol. 5, no. 4, December 1973.

BRI78   Brinch Hansen, P.: Distributed Processes: A Concurrent Programming Concept, *Comm. ACM*, vol. 21, no. 11, November 1978.

BUH84   Buhr, R. J. A.: *System Design with Ada*, Prentice-Hall, Englewood Cliffs, N.J., 1984.

BUR85   Burns, A.: *Concurrent Programming in Ada*, Cambridge University Press, Cambridge, England, 1985.

BUR87   Burger, T. M., and Nielsen, K. W.: An Assessment of the Overhead Associated with Tasking Facilities and Paradigms in Ada, *Ada Letters*, vol. VII, no. 1, January/February 1987.

CON87   Conn, R.: *The Ada Software Repository and the Defense Data Network*, Zoetrope, New York, 1987.

DEM78   DeMarco, T.: *Structured Analysis and System Specification*, Yourdon, New York, 1978.

DIJ68   Dijkstra, E. W.: The Structure of the "THE"—Multiprogramming System, *Comm. ACM*, vol. 11, no. 5, May 1968. DIJ68a Dijkstra, E. W.: Co-operating Sequential Processes, in *Programming Languages*, F. Genuys (ed.), Academic Press, New York, 1968.

DIJ71   Dijkstra, E. W.: Hierarchical Ordering of Sequential Processes, *Acta Informatica*, vol. 1, 1971, pp. 115–138.

DIJ72   Dijkstra, E. W.: Notes on Structured Programming, in *Structured Programming*, O.-J. Dahl et al., Academic Press, London, England, 1972.

DOD83   Reference Manual for the Ada Programming Language, ANSI/MIL-STD 1815A, U.S. Department of Defense, 17 February 1983.

DOD85   Military Standard, Defense System Software Development, DOD-STD-2167, U.S. Department of Defense, 4 June, 1985.

DOL78   Doll, D. R.: *Data Communications*, John Wiley & Sons, New York, 1978.

EVB85   An Object Oriented Design Handbook for Ada Software, EVB Software Engineering, Inc., January 9, 1985.

FOR85   Ford, G., and Wiener, R.: *Modula-2: A Software Development Approach*, John Wiley & Sons, New York, 1985.

GEH84   Gehani, N.: *Ada Concurrent Programming*, Prentice-Hall, Englewood Cliffs, N .J., 1984.

GOM84   Gomaa, H.: A Software Design Method for Real-Time Systems, *Comm. ACM*, vol. 27, no. 9, September 1984.

GRO86   Groover, M. P., et al.: *Industrial Robotics: Technology, Programming, and Applications*, McGraw-Hill, New York, 1986.

HAB80   Habermann, A. N., and Nassi, I. R.: *Efficient Implementation of Ada Tasks*, Carnegi-Mellon University, Pittsburgh, Penn., January 1980.

HAM85   Hammons, C., and Dobbs, P.: Coupling, Cohesion, and Package Unity in Ada, *Ada Letters*, vol. IV, no. 6, May/June 1985.

HIL82   Hilfinger, D. N.: Implementation Strategies for Ada Tasking Idioms, Proceedings of the AdaTEC Conference on Ada, October 6–8, 1982.

HOA74   Hoare, C. A. R.: Monitors: An Operating System Structuring Concept, *Comm. ACM*, vol. 17, no. 10, October 1974.

HOA78   Hoare, C. A. R.: Communicating Sequential Processes, *Comm. ACM*, vol. 21, no. 8, August 1978.

HOA85   Hoare, C. A. R.: *Communicating Sequential Processes*, Prentice-Hall International, London, England, 1985.

ICH79   Ichbiah, J. D., et al.: Rationale for the Design of the Ada Programming Language, *SIGPLAN Notices*, vol. 14, no. 6, part B, June 1979.

INT85   *Byron Program Development Language and Document Generator*, Version 1.3 for IBM CMS, Intermetrics, Inc., Cambridge, Mass., October 21, 1985.

KLE81   Kleine, H., and Callender, E. D.: Software Design and Documentation Language, Software Development Team Communication, September 1981.

KNU69   Knuth, D. E.: *The Art of Computer Programming, Volume 1: Fundamental Algorithms*, Addison-Wesley Publishing Company, Reading, Mass., 1969.

LEV80   Levy, H. M., and Eckhouse, R. H.: *Computer Programming and Architecture: The VAX-11*, Digital Press, Bedford, Mass., 1980.

LIS86   Liskov, B., and Guttag, J.: *Abstraction and Specification in Program Development*, The MIT Press, Cambridge, Mass., 1986.

MAC80   MacLaren, L.: Evolving Toward Ada in Real Time Systems, *SIGPLAN Notices*, vol. 15, no. 11, November 1980.

MAR85   Martin, J., and McClure, C.: *Diagramming Techniques for Analysts and Programmers,* Prentice-Hall, Englewood Cliffs, N.J., 1985.

MEL86   Mellor, S. J., and Ward, P. T.: *Structured Development for Real-Time Systems, Volume 3: Implementation Modeling Techniques*, Yourdon, New York, 1986.

MYE78   Myers, G. J.: *Composite/Structured Design*, Van Nostrand Reinhold, New York, 1978.

NIE86   Nielsen, K. W.: Task Coupling and Cohesion in Ada, *Ada Letters*, vol. VI, no. 4, July/August 1986.

PAG80   Page-Jones, M.: *The Practical Guide to Structured Systems Design*, Yourdon, New York, 1980.

PAR72   Parnas, D. L.: On the Criteria To Be Used in Decomposing Systems Into Modulues, *Comm. ACM*, vol. 15, no. 12, December 1972.

PYL85   Pyle, I. C.: *The Ada Programming Language*, 2d ed., Prentice-Hall International, London, England, 1985.

SHU84   Shumate, K. C.: *Understanding Ada*, Harper & Row, New York, 1984.

SHU88   Shumate, K. C.: *Understanding Concurrency in Ada*, McGraw-Hill, New York, 1988.

SIM79   Simpson, H. R., and Jackson, K.: Process Synchronisation in MASCOT, *Computer Journal*, vol. 22, no. 4, 1979.

STO82   Stotts, P. D.: A Comparative Survey of Concurrent Programming Languages, *SIGPLAN Notices*, vol. 17, no. 9, September 1982.

TAK86   Takagi, H.: *Analysis of Polling Systems*, The MIT Press, Cambridge, Mass., 1986.

WAR85a Ward, P. T., and Mellor, S. J.: *Structured Development for Real-Time Systems, Volume 1: Introduction and Tools,* Yourdon, New York, 1985.

WAR85b Ward, P. T., and Mellor, S. J.: *Structured Development for Real-Time Systems, Volume 2: Essential Modeling Techniques,* Yourdon, New York, 1985.

WEG84   Wegner, P.: Capital-Intensive Software Technology, *IEEE Software,* vol. 1, no. 3, July 1984.

WEL81   Welsh, J., and Lister, A.: A Comparative Study of Task Communication in Ada, *Software—Practice and Experience,* vol. 11, 1981.

WIR71   Wirth, N.: Program Development by Stepwise Refinement, *Comm. ACM,* vol. 14, no. 4, April 1971.

YOU79   Yourdon, E., and Constantine, L. L.: *Structured Design,* Prentice-Hall, Englewood Cliffs, N.J., 1979.

YOU82   Young, S. J.: *Real Time Languages: Design and Development,* Ellis Horwood Limited, Chichester, England, 1982.

Index

abstraction 17, 35, 46, 219
  data 33, 35, 132, 207
  functional 36, 39, 44,
    130–132, 207, 340
  layers of 44, 219
  levels of 44, 66, 320, 340,
    348
  procedural (see functional
    abstraction)
  process 32, 34, 42–43, 46–48,
    208, 376
  programming 30, 46
abstract
  specifications 33, 35, 38
  data type (see type manager)
ACP diagram 202
active program units 95
activity 146
actors 35

Ada 94
  as program design language
    229–244
  package graph 61, 233, 254,
    286, 382, 418
  structure graph 69, 301, 392,
    431
  task graph 59, 118, 159, 221,
    284, 380, 414, 417
Ada Software Repository 156,
    263–264
adaptation data 95, 100, 158,
    260, 287, 369, 384, 421
ADT 104
  closed 105, 109
  open 104, 108
agent process 93
Air Traffic Control System
    (ATCS) 368–401